God's Book of Works

God's Book of Works

The Nature and Theology of Nature

Glasgow Gifford Lectures

R. J. Berry

Illustrations by John Busby

T & T CLARK
A Continuum imprint
LONDON • NEW YORK

T&T CLARK LTD
A Continuum imprint

The Tower Building 370 Lexington Avenue
11 York Road New York 10017–6503
London SE1 7NX USA
UK

www.continuumbooks.com

First published 2003

ISBN 0 567 08876 6 HB
ISBN 0 567 08915 0 PB

British Library Cataloguing-in-Publication Data
A catalogue record for this book is available from the British Library

Typeset by Fakenham Photosetting Ltd, Fakenham
Printed and bound in Great Britain by Bookcraft, Midsomer Norton

From the verso of the fly-leaf of Charles Darwin's *The Origin of Species* (all editions, beginning with the original of 1859):

Let no man out of a weak conceit of sobriety, or an ill-applied moderation, think or maintain, that a man can search too far or be too well studied in the book of God's words, or in the book of God's works; divinity or philosophy; but rather let men endeavour an endless progress or proficience in both.

Bacon: *Advancement of Learning*

Contents

Preface

An invitation to be a Gifford Lecturer is a great honour. Principal Knox of St Andrews put it on a par with receiving a Nobel Prize, as 'one of the two highest honours which a scholar could receive'. I have never had delusions or aspirations about rowing in the Nobel League, so it is an especial privilege to join the Gifford one – but a daunting challenge to follow in the footsteps of such scientists as Niels Bohr (Edinburgh, 1949–50), Sidney Brenner (Glasgow, 1979–80), Hans Driesch (Aberdeen, 1906–8), John Eccles (Edinburgh, 1977–9), Arthur Eddington (Edinburgh, 1926–7), Charles Sherrington (Edinburgh, 1937–8), Bill Thorpe (St Andrews, 1969–71) and J. Z. Young (Aberdeen, 1975–7), never mind my PhD examiner C. H. Waddington (Edinburgh, 1971–3) as well as a galaxy of theologians and philosophers. It is small encouragement to know that many of my predecessors drew only small audiences despite Lord Gifford's expressed intention that the lectures should be 'public and popular' and published in inexpensive format so that they would have a wide circulation. Bohr rapidly became known as 'boring Bohr', while it is said A. N. Whitehead (Edinburgh, 1927–8) began with an audience and ended with a Chairman.

What do I have to offer? Formally, I am a Professor of Genetics. My sort of genetics is concerned with the factors that affect and change the inherited constitution of natural populations of animals, rather than the fashionable molecular variety; I am a naturalist rather than a genetic engineer or a gene manipulator in the narrow sense. Perhaps I ought to call myself an evolutionary biologist, following more closely in the steps of Charles Darwin and Julian Huxley than Jim Watson and Frances Crick. But wherever my professional expertise fits within the spectrum of biology, I am indubitably a natural scientist and hence specifically qualified by Lord Gifford, who wished 'the lecturers to treat their subject as a strictly natural science, the greatest of all possible sciences, indeed in one sense the only science, that of Infinite Being, without reference to or reliance upon any supposed special exceptional or so-called miraculous revelation'. Ernst Mayr (1982:81), of Harvard, one of the architects of the neo-Darwinian synthesis and an atheist, believes that 'virtually all biologists are religious in the deeper sense of this word, even though it may be a religion without revelation, as it was called by Julian Huxley'. He surmises that 'the unknown and maybe unknowable instils in us a sense of humility and awe'.

Besides being a natural scientist, I am a Christian. Although I am prepared to believe in religion without revelation, it seems to me highly unlikely that any God worth believing in would not seek to reveal himself (or herself – I do not want to pick quarrels over imponderables) in some effective way. This does not, of course, disqualify me as a Gifford Lecturer, even though the only negative stipulation made by Lord Gifford about his endowment was that 'the lecturers appointed shall be subjected to no test of any kind, and shall not be required to take any oath, or to emit or subscribe any declaration of belief ... provided that they be able, reverent men, true thinkers, sincere lovers of and earnest inquirers after truth'. To me Gifford is describing science as it should be: rigorous, rational, consistent and fearless. I have no hesitation in submitting my own beliefs to any objective or subjective test anyone can devise. I hope this attitude will be evident in this book. Where science and faith meet, they must be congruent; if they are not, both the science and the religion ought to be examined. Religion cannot drive the content of science, nor can science properly determine the nature of religion.

But this is to anticipate some of my argument. I have four specific aims in this book:

1. to explore religious faith(s) in the light of biological science;
2. to test whether scientific understanding is a sufficient description of the human condition;
3. to investigate the credibility of religious belief in the twenty-first century;
4. to seek a robust basis for behaviour in a crowded and ill-treated world.

Reviewing the Gifford Lectures a hundred years after their foundation, Neil Spurway wrote:

> the late twentieth-century intellectual climate is a substantially more fertile one for Natural Theology than that prevailing when the Gifford Lectureships were founded. Many of the themes are of like kind to those discussed in Lord Gifford's day, yet the strength of several arguments has substantially increased ... however, the most widely-influential change has been in attitudes to the environment. Perhaps the paradigm shift had begun in Gifford's time, but its developments have been immense and its ramifications enormous. Until the concept of evolution took hold, the processes of civilisation had increasingly detached humankind from its environment physically, intellectually and spiritually. Darwin's was the first of the intellectual critiques which shook that detachment. Following him

came the psychoanalysts (both Freud and Jung), the animal behaviourists
and now the socio-biologists. In parallel with their ideas, the largely
twentieth-century developments of anthropology, physiology, biochem-
istry and pathology have displayed *Homo sapiens*, with ever more persuasive
force, as just one of the most complex (and, in some respects one of the
more vulnerable) species of animals. Recently, and perhaps most directly
of all, the protagonists of Planet Earth and the Green Movement have
dealt the *coup de grâce* to any remaining illusions of the detachment ...
There is undoubtedly scope for a future series on the Natural Theology of
the Ecology Movement. (Spurway, 1993:24)

The lectures I gave in Glasgow in 1997–8 could be regarded as a
contribution to such a natural theology, although I am perhaps
more concerned with a theology of nature than natural theology in
its traditional sense. Natural theology as traditionally understood
(and expounded by Thomas Aquinas) is the extent to which we can
know about God by reason, based on our understanding of the
created world without the aid of revelation; the theology of nature
'starts from a religious tradition and is based on religious experience
and historical revelation' (Barbour, 1998:100). Ian Barbour has
identified four possible relationships between religion and science:
conflict, independence, dialogue and integration (Barbour, 2000).
He regards natural theology as one of the components of dialogue
(the others are 'methodological parallels' and 'nature-centred spirituality') but identifies most current interest and potential as being
concentrated on integration through a theology of nature, which in
turn leads to a concern for both creation and social justice. My
conviction is that both natural theology and a theology of nature
converge as we get closer to their determinants – in other words, the
creator (Gunton, 1993).

My title, *God's Book of Works*, is intended to link God (assuming
[s]he exists) with the living world of genetic variety, never mind with
the synthetic dreams of theoreticians of producing a 'Theory of
Everything'. The first three chapters set the science–faith debate in
its historical context and describe the scientific enterprise as it
actually occurs (i.e. as practised by scientists and not as interpreted
by philosophers). Chapter 4 is a slight digression from the main
theme, to unpack the nature of life, which too often confuses ethical
debate in biology. The next five chapters (5–9) set out in detail the
background to our current situation, particularly the shift from
regarding the world as a divine given to treating it as nothing but
a commodity, and the environmental, religious, philosophical
and political consequences of this. The last three chapters are an
attempt to bring positive solutions from these debates into a

synthesis, incorporating a reading of God's Book of Works as well as his Book of Words. I have tried to make the text accessible to people of all backgrounds. There is a danger in this, because specialists may find grounds to carp about topics within their particular expertise. I believe the risk is worth taking. The subject of this book is too important for theologians, philosophers, scientists, etc., on their own.

I first wrote on the topics expounded here in a booklet, *Ecology and Ethics*, published in 1972, part of an effort to help people understand the moral issues surfacing at the United Nations Conference on the Human Environment held in Stockholm that year, the first major international gathering on the subject. I was conscious of a lack of helpful literature, but I did not realise I was something of a pioneer until reading in Michael Northcott's magnificent *The Environment and Christian Ethics* (1996: 147) that 'In 1972 John B. Cobb wrote a path-breaking book on Christianity and the ecological crisis entitled, *Is It Too Late?* The book is significant not just because it establishes a new eco-theological paradigm which has been highly influential . . .'[1]

My own ideas and knowledge developed both from my scientific work in ecological and conservation genetics, and from interacting with ethicists and theologians, especially in chairing working parties for the General Synod of the Church of England which led to *Our Responsibility for the Living Environment* (1986), *Personal Origins* (1985) and *Christians and the Environment* (1991), and for the Economic Summit Nations (the G7), in producing a Code of Environmental Practice (1990). My Gifford Lectures (and this book) are an expansion and updating of my 1992 London Lectures in Contemporary Christianity, delivered at the Institute for Contemporary Christianity in London under the title 'Greens, Gaia and God', and it is proper for me to acknowledge those who invited and stimulated me in preparing and delivering my London Lecture series.

Many people have helped and influenced my thinking. I want to acknowledge my debt to Nick Clark-Lowes, who taught me chemistry and divinity at school, and must have sown in me the realisation that science and faith are not irreconcilable;[2] to Charles Raven (Edinburgh Gifford Lecturer, 1950–2), who introduced me to science as a human activity dependent on observation and reason, rather than an impersonal quantification of the world about us, and to a history of modern times shaped by biologists as distinct from the apostolic succession of Copernicus, Galileo, Newton, Descartes and Rutherford which recurs in popular writing; to John Barrett and Bernard Kettlewell, who opened my eyes to the wonders of the living world and the excitement of studying it in depth; to Oliver

Barclay and Donald MacKay (Glasgow Gifford Lecturer, 1986), who made me read and think about the implications of a God who is creator, redeemer and sustainer of the whole cosmos; to Eric Ashby, who taught me more about the practicalities of environmental care than I could ever have learned from books, and inculcated in me a healthy scepticism about many of the books written about the environment; and to John Stott, who has written many books which *are* worth reading, and who has inspired many thousands with his own love for Jesus Christ and who took the lead in inviting me to give the 1992 London Lectures. I am indebted also to those who have commented on parts of this manuscript and whose scholarship far outweighs mine, particularly Neil Spurway, Gifford scholar supreme. I have tried to incorporate all their criticisms but as always the ultimate responsibility rests with the author. I am grateful to Jim Lovelock for sending me Jaroslav Havel's speech given in Philadelphia on Independence Day 1994; I acknowledge with thanks permission from Sir Peter Maxwell Davies to reproduce some of his *Notes from a Cold Climate*, to Jim Perrin for the extract from *Spirits of Place*, to Mr R. P. Rendall for Robert Rendall's *Orkney Crofter*, and to Mrs Winifred Boyd and Mrs Valerie MacKay for allowing me to quote from published work by their late husbands. John Busby has drawn the pictures which preface each chapter and which help to leaven the tedium of unremitting text; I am in his debt.

My thanks are also due to Principal Sir William Fraser of Glasgow University for his invitation to be a Gifford Lecturer, his successor, Sir Graeme Davies, and to the Glasgow Gifford Committee, particularly the Chairman, Professor Neil Spurway, and the Secretary, Mrs Eileen Reynolds. Their hospitality and practical help made my visits to Glasgow times of pleasure rather than trial.

NOTES

1   Northcott is not wholly accurate in describing Cobb's book as theologically 'pathbreaking'. Joseph Sittler was raising significant theological issues during the 1960s, culminating in a much quoted paper in 1970 (Sittler, 1970; Bouma-Prediger and Bakken, 2000). In Britain two previous trailblazing studies on ecotheology were published three years before Cobb's 1972 volume: Hugh Montefiore's *The Question Mark* and a major Church of England report, *Man in His Living Environment*.
2   I attended the same school as Charles Darwin (Shrewsbury School), entering it 130 years after the young Darwin. I was clearly luckier than him. He wrote in his *Autobiography* (Darwin, 1887:8): 'Nothing could have been worse for my mind than Dr Butler's School [Samuel Butler, grandfather of

the novelist and critic of natural selection – an earlier Samuel Butler, was Headmaster], as it was strictly classical, nothing else being taught, except a little ancient geography and history. The school as a means of education to me was simply a blank ... When I left the school I was, for my age, neither high nor low in it; and I believe that I was considered by all my masters and by my father as a very ordinary boy, rather below the common standard in intellect. To my deep mortification my father once said to me, "You care for nothing but shooting, dogs, and rat-catching, and you will be a disgrace to yourself and all your family."'

1
Design and Deity

It may be *lèse-majesté* even to ask the question, but was Lord Gifford behind the times when in 1885 he endowed lectures for 'Promoting, Advancing, Teaching, and Diffusing the Study of Natural Theology in the widest sense of that term'? Put another way, was not natural theology already a historical curiosity by 1885, and any attempt to 'advance' it akin to flogging a dead horse? In notorious words by Richard Dawkins (1986:6): 'Although atheism might have been logically tenable before Darwin [who published his *The Origin of Species* in 1859], Darwin made it possible to be an intellectually fulfilled atheist.' Did Darwin kill God – or at least remove any traces of him from the natural world? Certainly there have been Gifford Lecturers who have had no doubts whatsoever that natural theology is a mirage, a valueless pursuit (most notoriously Karl Barth, Aberdeen, 1937–8; q.v. James Barr in his 1990–1 Edinburgh lectures published as *Biblical Faith and Natural Theology* [1993]). I am not qualified to comment on nor particularly interested in theological or philosophical disputes about the meaning of texts; the underlying (and to me much more important) question is the credibility of belief in any divine input to, or control of, the natural order. It is all very well to ask what we can learn about God without appealing to special revelation (an abstinence which is the subject matter of natural theology), but such an endeavour is meaningless if Dawkins is right and there is no God or at least if (s)he does not interact with the world in any discernible way.

Two centuries before Gifford, John Ray (1627–1705) was able to write about *The Wisdom of God Manifested in the Works of Creation* (1691) without contradiction and with acclaim; his book was reprinted more than twenty times before 1846 (Berry, 2001). At the beginning of the nineteenth century, Archdeacon William Paley rewrote without acknowledgement almost the whole of Ray's *Wisdom* in his *Natural Theology* (1802), which was read with approval by Charles Darwin at Cambridge (and reread in 1843, at a time when he was already preparing a detailed synopsis of the ideas he went on to develop in *The Origin of Species* [1859]).[1]

Although the books of Ray and Paley have much in common, they were poles apart. Ray worshipped God for his marvellous works in nature; Paley saw nature as the proof of God's handiwork. Ray believed in a personal creator-God, distinct from the world but active in it; Paley's God was much more restricted, a great watchmaker who lived mainly above the bright blue sky. Were the changes from Ray to Paley and thence to Darwin inevitable coffin-nails for natural theology?

Extinctions, Fossils and Floods

The decades between Ray and Paley saw tensions beginning to appear over the understanding of creation. Although the traditional story that God created the Earth and its creatures around 6000 years ago had problems (e.g. Thomas Burnet calculated in his *Sacred Theory of the Earth* [1684], that eight times the volume of water in the present oceans would be needed to cover all the terrestrial areas of the Earth as implied by Noah's flood; he suggested that this water must have come from hitherto unsuspected undersea caverns), the real difficulties came from growing evidence that the surface of the Earth has not always been the same. nt lava. At about the same time, it was realised that many – indeed, most – geological strata, sometimes thousands of metres thick, are sedimentary, deposited from water. This was extremely disturbing: it must have taken an immense amount of time for such thicOne of the first pointers was the reinterpretation of certain land forms in central France as extinct volcanoes; this led on to the identification of basalt, a widely distributed rock, as nothing but anciek strata to be laid down, implying that the Earth might be much older than previously thought. Even worse was the finding that neither the volcanic nor the sedimentary rocks have remained unchanged after being laid down. They have been eroded by water cutting valleys through them, and in many cases sedimentary layers have been folded and occasionally turned over completely at some time after their formation.

All of this stimulated interest in the age of the Earth. Isaac Newton (1642–1727) calculated that the Earth must have cooled for at least 50,000 years until it was sufficiently cold to allow life to exist, but he felt that something must be wrong with his sums because this was so much longer than the Church's teaching that creation took place less than 6,000 years before his time (Young, 1982).

In *Les Epoches de la Nature* (1779), the Comte de Buffon (1739–88), Director of the Royal Botanic Garden in Paris, reported on some experiments he had performed, involving heat loss from a group of spheres of various sizes. He suggested that 74,832 years were required for the Earth to cool from white heat to its present condition. (He privately estimated that the earth was at least half a million years old, but did not publish this figure, because an earlier book of his had been censored.) In an attempt to harmonise his results with Scripture, Buffon suggested that there had been seven epochs of earth history, more or less matching the days of creation in Genesis.

Another problem for the eighteenth-century understanding of the Genesis story was the ever-increasing knowledge of fossils. Fossils were, of course, well known, but many believed them to be nothing more than an accident of nature (*lusus naturae*) rather than the remains of once living creatures. The last capable naturalist to advocate an inorganic origin seems to have been Johan Beringer of the University of Würzburg. Beringer loved to collect and sketch fossils, but was convinced that they were simply curious shapes produced by nature. His *Lithographiae Wirceburgeinsis* (1726) contained drawings and descriptions of all manner of objects dug from local quarries, including many genuine fossils, but also images of birds sitting on their nests, entirely imaginary animals, and Hebrew letters. Such extremely odd discoveries confirmed Beringer in his belief that fossils were not buried organisms – until one day he discovered a rock with his own likeness and name on it. Hoaxers had baked and carved fossils and planted them in Beringer's favourite collecting spots. Beringer spent the rest of his life attempting to recall all copies of his book.

However, the common assumption was that fossils represented creatures drowned in Noah's flood. In very early Christian times Tertullian (160–225) wrote of fossils in mountains as demonstrating a time when the globe was overrun by water, although it is not clear whether or not he was talking about Noah's time. Both Chrysostom and Augustine thought of the flood as being responsible for fossils, and Martin Luther was even more certain. Notwithstanding, there were two problems about the 'flood theory'.

First, unknown and – as the knowledge of living animals and plants increased apace – presumably extinct organisms were found as fossils. John Ray thought that fossils were probably derived from dead animals and plants, but was confused by the fact that many fossils were not identical with living forms, although clearly very similar. His problem was an unwillingness to accept the possibility of extinction, on the grounds that God would be unlikely to permit any of his creatures to disappear, having described creation as 'very good'. This was a misconception: the discovery of extinct organisms conflicted not so much with the Bible as with the 'principle of plenitude', which held that 'no potentiality of being can remain unfulfilled, [so] the extent and abundance of the creation must be as great as the possibility of existence' (Lovejoy, 1936:50–2), in other words that God in the breadth of his mind must surely have created any creature that was possible; and conversely that God in his benevolence could not possibly permit any of his own creatures to become extinct. Plenitude was usually linked with the idea of a *scala naturae*, with no 'gaps' between similar forms. It also commonly involved an assumption of increasing perfection, more 'soul', more consciousness, more ability to reason, a greater advance towards God. Extinctions were a problem for interpretation rather than a true conflict with Scripture.

The second problem arose from information collected by an English surveyor, William Smith (1769–1839), and a French zoologist, Baron Cuvier (1769–1832), which indicated that particular rock strata have distinctive fossils. Smith was involved in canal-building and attempting to trace coal seams for mining (Winchester, 2001). He realised that geological strata could be characterised by the fossils in them. Such strata can sometimes be followed for hundreds of miles even when the rock formation changes. Smith developed these principles between 1791 and 1799, although his 'stratigraphic map' of England and Wales was not published until 1815. During the same period French naturalists were actively collecting fossils in the limestone quarries around Paris, and Cuvier worked out the exact stratigraphy of these fossils (mainly mammals) in detail. The conclusion – unpalatable as it was at the time – was that there is a time sequence involved in the laying down of fossil-bearing strata, with the lowest strata being the oldest. Later it became possible to correlate strata, not only across England or western Europe, but between different parts of the world, if allowance was made for the same kinds of regional differences which exist today in living faunas and floras.

The Achilles Heel of Natural Theology

At the end of the eighteenth century most geologists regarded the change between successive strata as the result of recurring catastrophes, later forms being replacements specially made by the creator. The Edinburgh geologist, James Hutton (1726–97) believed the Earth to be almost infinitely old, but he was an honest observer and wrote in his *Theory of the Earth* (1788): 'Let us, therefore open the book of Nature, and read in her records.' A major stumbling block was the hangover from Plato's ideas about the impossibility of change; this prevented the fossil record being interpreted as a sequence of continuing changes, as seems obvious to us today.

Notwithstanding, the idea of evolution was in the air during the second half of the eighteenth century. Maupertuis, Buffon and Diderot (Frenchmen), and Rodig, Herder, Goethe and Kant (Germans) have all been claimed as evolutionists, albeit without general support from historians of science. They all postulated new origins (rather than a change in an existing type) or a simple 'unfolding' of innate potential. Nevertheless, they are significant as being the immediate predecessors of Lamarck, who was the first to make a real break with the old, Plato-dominated world view.

Jean-Baptiste Lamarck (1744–1829) was a protégé of Buffon, and from 1788 until his death worked in the Natural History Museum in Paris. His key work was an evolutionary *Philosophie zoologique* (1809), wherein he sought to explain two phenomena: (1) the gradual increase in 'perfection' from the simplest animals to humankind, seen particularly in terms of complexity; and (2) the amazing diversity of organisms.

Lamarck claimed that a species may, over a long period of time, become 'transformed' into a new species. Such evolutionary change removes the problem about extinctions, but in solving one difficulty, Lamarck produced a greater one. 'Transformism' – that is evolution – introduces a time factor. Ernst Mayr (1982:349) has described this as the 'Achilles heel of natural theology': although a creator could be presumed to design a perfect organism for an unchanging world, the perfection would disappear if the environment changed. Adaptation to changes of climate, to the physical structure of the earth's surface, and to predators and competitors is possible only if organisms can adjust to their circumstances; in other words, if they evolve.

The idea that change could take place over time was the important contribution of Lamarck. Scientifically his ideas had little credence outside his native France although they were adopted by intellectual radicals in Britain as a justification for attacking the social status quo (Desmond, 1989). As an evolutionist, he prepared the way for Darwin in pointing to evidence that evolutionary change must have occurred, but it is not true to claim that the two men's approaches or contributions were similar. Fifty years after Lamarck, Darwin wrote that the *Philosophie zoologique* was 'veritable rubbish ... I got not a fact or idea from it'. But increasingly, the date of creation was being pushed back in time.

All these discussions about the age of the Earth happened in the so-called Enlightenment decades between Ray and Paley, a dull period occupied by dull people, as Charles Raven (1954) unfairly described it. By the time of Paley, the devotion and commitment of the Puritans had faded into rationalism and debates between deists and latitudinarians. God, whose wisdom had aroused Ray's love and adoration, had become the distant First Cause, the Master-mathematician and Artificer of the universe (Porter, 2000). And despite the unfolding vistas of science and technology, the natural theologians of the time were like Renaissance scholastics, looking back rather than around them, at traditional arguments rather than current opportunities.

In 1829 when the future Lord Gifford was nine years of age, the Reverend Francis Egerton, eighth Earl of Bridgewater, died and in expiation for a mis-spent life charged his executors, the Archbishop of Canterbury, the Bishop of London and the President of the Royal Society of London, to pay eight scientists one thousand pounds each to examine 'the Power, Wisdom, and Goodness of God, as manifested in the Creation; illustrating such work by all reasonable arguments'. Their books were published between 1833 and 1837, repeating with prolix but best-selling tedium the theses of John Ray as mangled by Archdeacon Paley. But knowledge of the world had moved on; the Scottish anatomist Robert Knox, client of Burke and Hare, called them the Bilgewater Treatises. The static world of earlier times was being swallowed up by technological progress and industrial revolution; at the same time as Messrs Chalmers, Kidd, Whewell, Bell, Roget, Buckland, Kirby and Prout were labouring over their Bridgewater Treatises, Charles Darwin was sailing round the world on HMS *Beagle* (1831–6), and the outline of his evolutionary theory was in place by early summer 1837 (Sulloway, 1982). Natural theology in the traditional sense was dying. It was helped on its way by the Edinburgh publisher Robert Chambers's *Vestiges of the Natural History of Creation* (1844), which was effectively a tract against Paley's version of deism (Secord, 2000). Chambers wrote that when there is a choice between special creation and the operation of general laws instituted by the creator, 'I would say that the latter is greatly preferable as it implies a far grander view of the divine power and dignity than the other'. Since there was nothing in the inorganic world 'which may not be accounted for by the agency of the ordinary forces of nature', why not consider 'the possibility of plants and animals having likewise been produced in a natural way'. In other words, he sought to replace natural theology by verifiable natural law(s). William Whewell, one of the Bridgewater authors, had argued similarly, but in less accessible prose. Darwin quoted from Whewell opposite the title page of *The Origin*: 'But with regard to the material world, we can at least go so far as this – we can perceive that events are brought about not by insulated interpositions of Divine power, exerted in each particular case, but by the establishment of general laws.'

Chambers was condemned from all sides. Adam Sedgwick, Professor of Geology at Cambridge and geological mentor of Charles Darwin, had seen the Bridgewater Treatises as an opportunity to demonstrate the 'ennoblement' of empirical discovery by morality. He lambasted the *Vestiges* in an eighty-five page diatribe in the *Edinburgh Review*. He wrote to his colleague Charles Lyell:

> If the book be true, the labours of sober induction are in vain; religion is a lie; human law is a mass of folly, and a base injustice; morality is moonshine; our labours for the black people of Africa were works of madmen; and man and woman are only better beasts.

In his review, he identified himself with the old stable order: 'The world cannot bear to be turned upside down; and we are ready to wage an internecine war with any violation of our modest and social manners ... It is our maxim that things must keep their proper places if they are to work together for any good ...'

The *Vestiges* was an immediate best-seller. In its first ten years it sold more copies than did *The Origin* fifteen years later. But it was full of errors. For Darwin, 'the prose was perfect, but the geology strikes me as bad & his zoology far worse'. Notwithstanding it stirred debate in Britain; Darwin welcomed it on the grounds that 'it has done excellent service in calling in this country attention to the subject and in removing prejudices'.

A Blind Watchmaker

The Origin was a crushing blow to the credibility of a divine watchmaker. In his Bampton Lectures published in 1885, Frederick Temple, Bishop of Exeter, pronounced obsequies on the old order. He wrote:

> [God] did not make the things, we may say; no, but He made them make themselves. And surely this adds rather than withdraws force from the great argument. It seems in itself something more majestic, something more befitting Him to Whom a thousand years are as one day and one day as a thousand years, thus to impress His Will once for all on creation, and

provide for all its countless variety by this one original impress, than by special acts of creation to be perpetually modifying what He had previously made. It has often been objected to Paley's argument that it represents the Almighty rather as an artificer than a creator, a workman dealing with somewhat intractable materials and showing marvellous skill in overcoming difficulties rather than a beneficent Being making all things in accordance with the purpose of His love. But this objection disappears when we put the argument into the shape which the doctrine of Evolution demands and look on the Almighty as creating the original elements of matter, determining their number and the properties, creating the law of gravitation whereby as seems probable the worlds have been formed, creating the various laws of chemical and physical action by which inorganic substances have been combined, creating above all the laws of life, the mysterious law which plainly contains such wonderful possibilities within itself, and thus providing for the ultimate development of all the many wonders of nature. (Temple, 1885:115–16)

Four years later, Aubrey Moore declared in *Lux Mundi*, a collection of theological essays, that Darwin had done the work of a friend under the guise of a foe: he had made it impossible to accept the image of an absentee landlord who interfered on rare occasions. Darwin had made belief about God all or nothing: either God was an active participant, immanent in the world, or completely absent.[2]

The compatibility of evolution and Christian doctrine was gradually acknowledged 'among more educated Christians' between 1860 and 1885; after 1876 acceptance of evolution was 'both permissible and respectable' (Chadwick, 1970:23-8). Reviewing the controversies about evolution sparked by Darwin, James Moore wrote:

> Darwin's burial in Westminster Abbey in 1882 and Frederick Temple's 1884 Bampton Lectures, *The Relations Between Religion and Science*, were amongst the events which highlighted the progressive accommodation, and Temple's consecration in 1896 as Archbishop of Canterbury may be taken to mark the final acceptance of the doctrine of evolution among the divines, clergy and leading laity of the established church. (Moore, 1979:10)

This brings us back to Adam Gifford's endowment 'for the teaching and diffusion of sound views' about natural theology, a wish made and formally sealed in the year that Temple's lectures were published, and dressed in language not unlike that of the Earl of Bridgewater's will fifty years previously. Gifford lived through the years of debate sparked by Chambers and then Darwin. Was Gifford harking back to Ray and Paley? Did he see his lecturers continuing the Bridgewater initiative? Did Gifford – lawyer and hence traditional conservative that he was – want to stem the evolutionary tide? He was certainly not what we would call a fundamentalist. His brother wrote of him: 'The Bible he knew well and studied much, though he did not hold the doctrine of a verbal inspiration. He ever sought and found in it the highest and purest thoughts this world contains. The Gospel of John was more in harmony with his mind than the Pauline writings' (cited by Jaki, 1995:126). He explored other ideas widely: the pantheism of Spinoza, the non-materialism of Bishop Berkeley, the mysticism of Ralph Waldo Emerson, the eclecticism of Hinduism (q.v. Spurway, 1993:4–9).

Was Gifford unhappy with the way that the Christian faith had been narrowed by Paley and his ilk? Charles Gillispie has written that

> during the decades between the birth of modern geology and the publi-
> cation of *On the Origin of Species*, the difficulty as reflected in the scientific
> literature appears to be one of religion (in a crude sense) in science
> rather than of religion *versus* science. The most embarrassing obstacles
> faced by the new sciences were cast up by the curious providential materi-
> alism of the scientists themselves and of those who relied upon them to
> show that the materials of a material universe exhibit the sort of necessity
> which results from control instead of the sort which springs from self-
> sufficiency. (Gillispie, 1951:ix)

Was this a difficulty sensed by Gifford and those among whom he moved? It would not be surprising if he felt an instinctive desire to re-establish the certainties of John Ray – and what better way to do this than to encourage the study of natural theology? The problem for us today is that there can be no turning the clock back to John Ray; and as Paley's divine watchmaker is no longer credible, neither is Frederick Temple's accommodation of it. Even though many Gifford Lecturers have paid little more than lip service to natural theology, it is proper to ask whether it is a valid study and how it relates to a theology of nature. Can we learn anything about God from nature?

Whither Natural Theology?

I have no competence to trace the intellectual fate of natural theology from its heyday with Newton, Ray and the Boyle lecturers, up to the present. Certainly there are continuing themes in Tillich's existential ontology and the process theology developed from the ideas of A. N. Whitehead (Olding, 1991), together with notions of panentheism, particularly as expounded by Jürgen Moltmann (see, for example, his Gifford Lectures, published as *God in Creation*, 1985). We shall return to some of these, but for the moment I am more concerned with science rather than theology. Alister Hardy (1975) called the future of natural theology 'the biology of God'. John Polkinghorne has explored this theme in depth (particularly in *Science and Creation* [1988:2-16]; and in his Edinburgh Gifford Lectures, published as *Science and Christian Belief* [1994: 41–6]). He wants a 'revised and revived form of natural theology which seeks to offer insight rather than proof and which appeals to the given fabric of the universe (which science assumes) and not to occurrences within its evolving history (which it is science's role to seek to explain)'. Polkinghorne adduces hope for this in the Anthropic Principle (i.e. that the physical properties of the universe contain too many 'coincidences' in their inter-relations for them to have arisen by chance) and what he refers to as the 'rational transparency' of the universe (i.e. the accessibility of our mind to order within the cosmos). For him, scientific progress 'involves the "unreasonable effectiveness of mathematics" (Eugene Wigner's description), that is the way that the search for beautiful equations has time after time been the key to advances in fundamental physics (Einstein discovered general relativity precisely through such a quest for mathematical beauty)'.

Polkinghorne believes that natural theology is essential to theological enquiry. He quotes Tom Torrance (1985:40):

> If we reject a deistic disjunction between God and the world ... natural theology cannot be pursued in its traditional abstractive form as a prior conceptual scheme on its own, but must be brought within the body of positive theology ... intrinsic to the knowledge of God, it will function as a necessary infra-structure of theological science.

Polkinghorne judges that:

> natural theology is currently undergoing a revival, not so much at the hands of the theologians (whose nerve, with some honourable exceptions, has not yet returned) but at the hands of the scientists. There has grown up a widespread feeling, especially among those who study fundamental physics, that there is more to the world than meets the eye. Science seems to throw up questions which point beyond itself and transcend its power to answer. They arise from recognising the potentiality inherent in the structure of the world, its interlocking tightly-knit character, and, indeed, its very intelligibility which makes it open to our inquiry. Thus a physicist such as Paul Davies, who is notably unsympathetic to conventional

religion, can nevertheless write, 'It may be bizarre but in my opinion science offers a surer road to God than religion' (Davies, 1983:ix). We are concerned not only with a revived natural theology but also with a *revised* natural theology. It points to law and circumstance (the assumed *data* of science and so not open to scientific inquiry) rather than to particular occurrences (such as the coming-to-be of life or of the eye). These latter questions are legitimate subjects for scientific investigation and the attempt to capture them for theology is just the error of the God of the Gaps.[3] On the other hand, the formal matters of law and circumstance are part of the founding faith of science which it has to assume as the basis of its inquiry. They bring us back to the themes of cosmology and design, pursued at a deeper level than the scientific, in a search for the fullest possible understanding of the world.[4] The insights thus obtained must find their integration within the totality of theological thinking. (Polkinghorne, 1988:15–16)

Torrance, Polkinghorne and those who argue with them are concerned to establish that science is not a complete explanation for everything; in crude terms, that science has not disproved religion. They are implicitly reclaiming their territory from the fading triumphalism of scientific humanism – Bertrand Russell, Julian Huxley, J. B. S. Haldane and J. S. Bernal from a previous generation; Peter Singer, Peter Atkins, Will Provine and Richard Dawkins in more recent times. The dogmatic certainties of logical positivism are gone. We now have to recognise that science has limits intrinsic to itself; there are certain questions outside the province and competence of scientific enquiry.

This was clearly expounded by Peter Medawar in his last book (apart from his autobiography), *The Limits of Science* (1984). He was happy to accept that there are no discernible limits to the power of science to answer questions that science can answer, mainly those where questions can be tested by one means or another; in other words where we can suggest and investigate the cause(s) of some phenomenon. But Medawar believed that there are questions beyond elucidation by science; he distanced himself from Kant, for whom it was unconditionally true of any hypothesis that it might be true. Medawar strongly dissented from this: for him there was a class of so-called 'ultimate questions' which are simply outside scientific logic, in the same way as it is impossible to deduce 'from the axioms and postulates of Euclid a theorem having to do with how to bake a cake' (Medawar, 1984:67).

Medawar believed a limit upon science was 'made very likely by the existence of questions that science cannot answer and that no conceivable advance of science would empower it to answer. There are the questions that children ask – the "ultimate questions" of Karl Popper'.[5]

> I have in mind such questions as:
> • How did everything begin?
> • What are we all here for?
> • What is the point of living?'
> Doctrinaire positivism[6] – now something of a period piece – dismissed all such questions as non-questions or pseudo-questions as only simpletons ask and only charlatans of one kind or another profess to be able to answer. This peremptory dismissal leaves one empty and dissatisfied because the questions make sense to those who ask them, and the answers to those who try to give them; but whatever else may be in dispute, it would be universally agreed that it is not to science that we should look for answers. (Medawar, 1984:66)[7]

The idea that science has limits is more commonly used as an accusation by non-scientists than an acknowledgement of a problem by scientists, but we shall find it repeatedly recurs in the writings of scientists. J. B. S. Haldane speculated about a wide-ranging mind 'behind nature' which incorporated his own 'very finite and imperfect mind' (p. 24); many other scientists have felt there is 'something more' when they have faced the awesomeness of nature (Chapter 10).

Conflicts between Science and Religion

In practice it is not worth fighting over the demarcation line between science and religion, because the position of such a line (and, for that matter, its existence) depends on definitions. The relationship between science and religion is more profitably approached as a multidimensional question than as one of competing regimes, and I will develop my approach to the nature of natural theology in this way (in contrast to Gould [1999], who regarded science and religion as separate 'domains', intrinsically incapable of mutual hostility). However, the science–religion interface has often led to intense conflict and for that reason needs examination. I am not claiming that conflicts do not arise between scientific and religious interpretations, but I want to assert strongly that they tend to be improperly dramatised, often for irrelevant reasons.

The problems that Galilei Galileo had with Pope Urban VIII (and vice versa) are a classical, albeit usually oversimplified, example of how not to approach scientific problems when they impinge on religion (reviewed by Brooke and Cantor in their Glasgow Gifford Lectures [1998:106–38]). In his book *De Revolutionibus Orbium Coelestium*, the Polish astronomer Nicholas Copernicus put forward the idea that the Earth and the other planets moved round the Sun, rather than the Earth being the static centre of the system. The reason for this was dissatisfaction with the Ptolemaic system, not experimental evidence. There was no great debate at the time, although some decades later the Reformer Melanchthon objected on the grounds that 'the sun, which is like a bridegroom coming forth ... rises at one end of the heavens and makes its circuit to the other' (Psalm 19:4–6) and 'You [God] established the earth' (Psalm 119.90). John Calvin rejected a moving Earth, but on the basis of common sense, not of Scripture. Then in 1610, Galileo reported observations made with his newly invented telescope, which could be taken as showing that the Earth was indeed in motion. He was condemned on the grounds that Joshua had commanded the Sun to stand still (Joshua 10.12) (implying that it normally moves), and it was made abundantly clear that the intervention of a layman in matters of theological principle was unwelcome. In 1616 the Congregation of the Index concluded that to teach the Copernican doctrine that the Sun was at the centre of the universe 'expressly contradicts the doctrine of Holy Scripture in many passages'.

Galileo was called to Rome and reminded that Copernican teaching was officially unsanctioned, and that might have been the end of the story. In 1632, however, he published his *Dialogue Concerning the Two Principal Systems of the World*, in which one of the disputants was pictured as a buffoonish and dim champion of orthodoxy – clearly a caricature of the pope himself, Urban VIII. Galileo was summoned before the Inquisition and forced to recant. (Rumour has it that on rising from his knees, he said 'But it [the Earth] does move'.)

There can be very few people nowadays who still hold to the idea of a stationary Earth at the heart of the solar system, and examination of the verses used against Galileo shows that they are concerned with the immutability of God, not details of astronomy. As Galileo himself wrote in his *Letter to the Grand Duchess Christina* (1615), the Bible 'teaches us how to go to heaven, not how the heavens go'. Kidner (1967:31) comments that 'it was Galileo's telescope, not his church, that conclusively refuted the interpretation of Psalm 96:10 ['The world is fixed immovably.'] as a proof-text against the earth's rotation.'

The Vatican revoked its anti-Copernican edict in 1757 and removed Galileo's *Dialogue* from the Index in 1831, but it was not until 1992 that Galileo was formally declared to have been right all along. This conclusion, however, was tempered by the observation that both Galileo and his persecutors acted 'in good faith', and that the Inquisition, faced with the creation account in Genesis on the one hand and Galileo's claims on the other, had no choice but to believe the former.

These events have been revisited so many times over the past three and a half centuries that there is almost certainly nothing sensible to add. The tragedy is that similar confusions keep recurring: the Darwinian debate was a near rerun of the Galileo one, and historical parallels regularly reappear in disputes about the nature of life, the moral legitimacy of new reproductive technologies, the status and proper treatment of the environment, and so on. The Editor of *Nature* commented on the Vatican's reappraisal of Galileo: 'With the passage of so much time, many will say that this old tale, however heroic, has no present significance. But this would be mistaken. The Galileo business remains a present problem because it provides a perpetual licence for prejudice in the evaluation of discovery' (*Nature*, 360:2, 5 November 1992).

And this is the crux: how do we relate to the world around us – what we call the natural world, however much it has been modified, 'improved' and defiled by our actions? Accepting that the world is 'real' and not merely a figment of our imagination, how do we learn about its properties and structure? How can we deal with our preconceptions? Is nature merely a neutral substrate from which we have emerged and which is available for us to use within limits defined only by the interests of ourselves and our immediate neighbours/ friends/family? Or are there restrictions due to the characteristics of 'nature' itself, and wider responsibilities we may have towards its inhabitants, both human and non-human? Is it meaningful to attempt a natural theology and, if so, what should be its content and extent? Or is God-language nothing more than a hangover from pre-scientific times when the unknown could be most easily explained by invoking divine or devilish agents?[8]

I would like to think that these questions would have been the ones that Adam Gifford had in mind when he endowed his lectureships. If they are, it would be wrong to accuse him of looking back to an older, more certain world. Whether or not Gifford would have approved, these are the questions I want to examine in this book, not primarily to understand the past, but because of the need to live sensibly in the present. We may be able to learn from the past to avoid repeating mistakes, but surely the vital element is to avoid 'prejudice in the evaluation of discovery'. Put positively, we need a framework for examining and coping with an ever-changing world.

This is where science (in its widest sense) meets everyday life, and where life meets God (assuming of course, that there is a God).

NOTES

1   Darwin wrote his first extended account of his theory of natural selection during a visit to his in-laws (the Wedgwoods, at Maer in Staffordshire) and his parents (in Shrewsbury) in summer 1843, although an earlier draft may have been written in 1839 (De Beer, 1958:28–9). The 1843 'Essay', as it has come to be called, forms the basis of the note to the Linnean Society (1 July 1858) which was the first public airing of Darwin's ideas.

2   Moore's statement that Darwinism did the work of a friend in the guise of a foe is often repeated. The whole passage is relevant to the theme of this book and is worth quoting in full: 'The break up of the mediaeval system of thought and life resulted in an atomism, which, if it had been more perfectly consistent with itself, would have been fatal alike to knowledge and society ... Its theory of knowledge was a crude empiricism; its theology unrelieved deism. God was "throned in magnificent inactivity in a remote corner of the universe," and a machinery of "secondary causes" had practically taken His place. It was even doubted, in the deistic age, whether God's delegation of His power was not so absolute as to make it impossible for Him to "interfere" with the laws of nature. The question of miracles became the burning question of the day, and the very existence of God was staked on His power to interrupt or override the laws of the universe. Meanwhile His immanence in nature, the "higher pantheism," which is a truth essential to true religion, as it is to true philosophy, fell into the background.

Slowly but surely that theory of the world has been undermined. The one absolutely impossible conception of God, in the present day, is that which represents Him as an occasional Visitor. Science had pushed the deist's God farther and farther away, and at the moment when it seemed as if He would be thrust out altogether, Darwinism appeared, and, under the disguise of a foe, did the work of a friend. It has conferred upon philosophy and religion an inestimable benefit, by showing us that we must choose between two alternatives. Either God is everywhere present in nature, or He is nowhere. He cannot be here and not there. He cannot delegate His power to demigods called "secondary causes." In nature everything must be His work or nothing. We must frankly return to the Christian view of direct Divine agency, the immanence of Divine power in nature from end to end, the belief in a God in Whom not only we, but all things have their being, or we must banish Him altogether. It seems as if, in the providence of God, the mission of modern science was to bring home to our unmetaphysical ways of thinking the great truth of the Divine immanence in creation, which is not less essential to the Christian idea of God than to a philosophical view of nature. And it comes to us almost like a new truth, which we cannot at once fit in with the old' (Moore, 1889:99–100).

3   A term which can be traced back at least to Henry Drummond (1894:426): 'There are reverent minds who ceaselessly scan the fields of nature and the books of science in search of gaps – gaps which they fill up with God. As if God lived in gaps'. However, the idea was popularised by Charles Coulson (1955): when science has unanswered questions, we should beware of inserting God into the gaps of our knowledge, in the belief that we have thereby found a space for God. As science answers more and more of the questions within its own territory and the gaps close, God is pushed into irrelevancy. Religious apologists have repeatedly trumpeted a place for God in the causal nexus of the physical world (in Heisenberg's Uncertainty Principle, in quantum leaps, in genetic plasticity, etc.), but have convinced few people beyond themselves.

4   In his Gifford Lectures, Polkinghorne (1994:44) states his belief that 'if natural theology is truly to flourish again it will ... benefit greatly from a more serious involvement by scientists with a biological background'. As a scientist 'with a biological background', I hope this book will be part of such a 'serious involvement'.

5   Popper (1978:342) noted: 'science does not make assertions about ultimate questions – about the riddles of existence, or about man's task in this world'.

6   According to Medawar this was defined by Popper as 'The world is all surface.'

7   Medawar claimed to be an unbeliever in supernatural religion, but Medawar's widow records in her autobiography that her husband's motive in writing *The Limits of Science* was to stress 'that science should not be expected to provide solutions to problems such as the purpose of life or the evidence of God for which it was unfitted' (Jean Medawar, 1990:220).

8   Don Cupitt (1984:59) expressed this well: 'Mechanistic science was allowed to explain the structure and workings of physical nature without restriction. But who had designed this beautiful world-machine and set it going in the first place? Only Scripture could answer that question. So science dealt with the every day tick-tock of the cosmic clockwork, and religion dealt with the ultimates: first beginnings and last ends, God and the soul. This demarcation of the provinces of scientific and theological explanations had the authority not only of Galileo but also of Sir Francis Bacon behind it.

It was a happy compromise while it lasted. Science actively promoted the cause of religion by showing the beautiful workmanship of the world. No mechanical theory seemed able to account for the origin of life and the adaptation of organisms to their ways of life. Only the wise and good Creator could have originally made ducks' feet and bills to be just the shape they would need for their survival. It was a good God who had thought of putting the mountains in the right places to precipitate rain from the clouds and give us fresh water to drink. Such is the old Argument from Design, and if it seems quaint to us now, it once seemed cogent and did a good job by shifting people's eyes away from seeing God at work in the freakish and fearful to admiring his wisdom and workmanship in the ordinary course of things. Religion became less nervous and superstitious, more calm and rational. Belief in witchcraft and evil spirits, omens and portents, and little particular judgments and providences gradually faded. People ceased to think that God was sending occult messages to them all the time. Faith became milder and cooler. The typical believer was a man like Gilbert White of Selbourne, the most sensible sort of saint that any religion has ever produced.

But there was a fatal flaw in the synthesis. Religious ideas were being used to plug the gaps in scientific theory. Science could not yet explain how animals and plants had originated and had become so wonderfully adapted to their environment – so everything to do with human inwardness and personal and social behaviour remained the province of the preacher and moralist.'

2
The Nature and Practice of Science

Science is about how things happen, about causes. Scientists want to know what causes particular phenomena, and how (or if) these fit into a wider context, whose extent will vary according to the science and scientist concerned. Philosophers of science try to dig more deeply than this, but the practising scientist is concerned not with abstractions, but with how a particular event emerges from a previously existing (and in principle recognisable) set of circumstances.

The methodology of investigating causation varies enormously. It may involve nothing more than repeating observations, with the repetition ranging from something extremely simple (such as breathing out or in) to something extremely sophisticated (like some experiments in particle physics); it may involve a wholly controlled experiment in a laboratory, or depending upon a 'natural' experiment (such as a drought, a volcanic eruption, an eclipse); it may use a model or simulation to compare 'real' events with ones postulated from certain premises; it may depend on events in the past (such as the characteristics of the expanding universe) or the future (such as the forecast of a disease epidemic or its course); it may dispose of wrong ideas (like phlogiston or swallows hibernating in mud) or depend on new ones (such as the hierarchy of subatomic particles or the population biology of jumping genes). But in all cases the problem is, why does such and such an event or thing happen? What causes it?

Cause is superficially an extremely simple concept: if I stick a pin in someone, it causes pain; if I put a kettle of water on a hot plate, the water warms up; if I pull the legs off a flea, it cannot jump. The problem is that Scientists are often too simple-minded: the common assumption is that we know *the* cause of something once we know *a* cause for it. For example, we know that we get AIDS if we are infected by HIV. But we immediately have to amplify that statement. Some people apparently never get the disease despite being infected. Do their bodies reject the virus or neutralise it in some way? And why do we become infected? What are the preconditions? How many viral particles are needed before I am infected? Is it possible to be infected by ingesting or inhaling the virus? Would I be more at risk if (say) I had a duodenal ulcer and was bleeding into my gut? Or if my immunological responses were reduced by stress, deprivation or drugs? And so on. Whilst it is true that AIDS is a clearly defined disease, it is inadequate to claim that *the* cause of AIDS is HIV infection. To know about AIDS means knowing about human motivations, situations and susceptibilities as well as the pathogenenicity of viruses.

Unfortunately, we tend in practice to be disingenuous about causation. As a theologian and apologist, Lesslie Newbigin (1986:25) has protested forcefully about our naivety: we think that 'to have discovered the cause of something is to have explained it. There is no need to invoke purpose or design as an explanation.'[1] Consequently we separate facts from values.

Yet as long ago as the fourth century BC Aristotle in the *Metaphysics* pointed out that there were differences between material, efficient, final and formal causes (roughly the matter, cause of change, purpose and essential nature of a thing). We rarely separate all four causes in this way, but we commonly distinguish ultimate from proximate causes. In the AIDS example, the proximate cause of the disease would be virus presence and replication in the body; the ultimate cause would usually be transfusion with infected blood or sexual intercourse with an infected person. It is legitimate to concentrate on a particular cause for the purpose of analysis or experiment; this is part of the normal practice of science and can be described as operational reductionism. On the other hand it is unhelpful as well as positively confusing to insist that the cause in question is the only relevant one; such an assumption should be distinguished as doctrinaire or ontological reductionism (Ayala, 1974).

Many scientists are either implicit or explicit ontological reductionists. Lewis Wolpert may be regarded as falling into the first group, because of his insistence that scientists have no responsibility for the consequences of their research. He quotes Tolstoy's assertion that science does not tell us how to live: that it has nothing to contribute on moral issues. His attitude is that 'it is the politicians, lawyers, philosophers and finally all citizens who have to decide what sort of society we will live in' (Wolpert, 1992:172). In other words, there are well-defined boundaries around science, particularly if it is defined narrowly in terms of an experimental methodology. Explicit reductionists are those like Peter Atkins and Richard Dawkins who deny all possibility of anything other than material or efficient causes. In her Gifford Lectures (Edinburgh, 1989–90, published as

Science as Salvation [1992]), Mary Midgley upbraids scientists for answering 'how' questions and pretending these are the same as 'why' questions. This is precisely the approach of Atkins and Dawkins and their ilk; their approach is to assert that 'why' questions have no meaning. It is doubtful whether this denial is helpful even within their respective specialities of physical chemistry and evolutionary biology, but it is certainly constricting. For example, Richard Dawkins wrote in *The Blind Watchmaker* (1986:10): 'The body is a complex thing with many constituent parts, and to understand its behaviour you must apply the laws of physics to its parts, not to the whole. The behaviour of the whole will then emerge as a consequence of interaction of the parts.' In contrast, Steven Jones, writing like Dawkins from the standpoint of a professional evolutionary biologist, takes a different attitude:

> It is the essence of all scientific theories that they cannot resolve everything ... Genetics has almost nothing to say about what makes us more than just machines driven by biology, about what makes us human. These questions may be interesting, but scientists are no more qualified to comment on them than is anyone else. In its early days, human genetics suffered greatly from its high opinion of itself. It failed to understand its own limits. Knowledge has brought humility to genetics as to other sciences; but the new awareness which genetics brings will also raise social and ethical problems which have as yet scarcely been addressed. (Jones, 1993: xi)

Doctrinaire reductionism has problems explaining emergent properties, that is, new properties or functions that arise through the interaction of simpler traits; proceeding down from higher to lower levels of organisation or structure will inevitably miss them. Emergent properties are normally the result of increasing complexity (e.g. social behaviour will almost certainly be preceded by the gathering together of organisms of the same species in some ordered way). Dawkins regards complexity as nothing but a simple straightforward statistical concept (Dawkins, 1983:404). But emergent properties need not involve complexity in the normally understood meaning of the word. For example, water is composed of only two constituents, hydrogen and oxygen, but it is impossible to predict the properties of a liquid which freezes at 0°C but has its maximum density at 4°C simply from knowing the properties of hydrogen and oxygen.

Donald MacKay (Glasgow Gifford Lecturer, 1986) coined the term 'nothing-buttery' to describe excessive and, to him, illegitimate reductionism. He illustrated his point with someone receiving a message in Morse Code. To the uninitiated or even a physicist analysing the periodicity and spectrum of the light, the flashes would be 'nothing but' flashes of light; but someone who could decode the message might be informed about a ship in distress or told about impending danger to himself. Such a message would be undetectable to an ardent reductionist.

The converse of the same point was made forcibly by J. B. S. Haldane in an essay, 'When I Am Dead'. He raises questions which we will have to return to later:

> If my mental processes are determined wholly by the motion of atoms in my brain, I have no reason to suppose that my beliefs are true. They may be sound chemically, but that does not make them sound logically ... In order to escape from this necessity of sawing away the branch on which I am sitting, so to speak, I am compelled to believe that mind is not wholly conditioned by matter. But as regards my own very finite and imperfect mind, I can see by studying the effects on it of drugs, alcohol, disease and so on, that its limitations are largely at least due to my body. Without my body, it may perish altogether, but it seems to me quite as probable that it will lose its limitations and be merged into an infinite mind or something analogous to a mind which I have reason to suspect exists behind nature. How this might be accomplished I have no idea. (Haldane, 1927:209)

MacKay has examined this problem in terms of 'complementarity', albeit building on neo-Thomist thought and the works of Austin Farrer (Edinburgh Gifford Lecturer, 1956–7) and Michael Polanyi (Aberdeen Gifford Lecturer, 1951–2). They bring us back again to Aristotle and causation. Farrer suggested that God's action in the universe can usefully be described in terms of 'double agency'. He argued that it is impossible to conceive of God's ways of acting simply in terms of our own, and therefore the 'causal joint' between God's action and ours must remain hidden.[2] Consequently each event in the universe must have a double description and therefore can be spoken of in terms of the providential action of God while at the same time having a full natural explanation:

> God's agency must actually be such as to work omnipotently on, in and through creaturely agencies, without either forcing them or competing with them ... He does not impose an order against the grain of things, but makes them follow their own beat and work out the world by being themselves ... He makes the multitude of created forces make the world in the process of making or being themselves. (Farrer, 1966:76, 90)

This sounds very like Frederick Temple, almost a century earlier (p. 9).

Michael Polanyi attacked the problem from another angle, that of a many-layered world with different 'levels' of explanation. He argued that all machines (including life itself) operate by principles *made possible* and *limited* by physical and chemical laws, but not *determined* by them. This means that all machines, whether they are physical or biological, restrict nature through 'boundary conditions'. Without transgressing the laws of physics or chemistry, machines can be controlled by another set of laws which enable them to harness the lower (physico-chemical) laws by a principle different from those laws, and for a purpose outside those laws. In other words, the basic laws do not fully describe the machine because they have boundary conditions imposed on them (Polanyi, 1969:232).

Boundary conditions limit processes at different levels. Polanyi regarded the functioning of a whole organism and of the chemistry of the genes which formed its blueprint, as being on different levels in this sense. He points out that the rules applying to different levels are different, and hence are subject to different understandings.

God, Providence and Complementarity

Donald MacKay has done more than anyone else to bring together and apply these insights in ways relevant and useful for natural law and natural theology, most successfully by formulating a model for divine providence in a scientifically tractable deterministic world. To understand the conclusions in later chapters, it is necessary to digress and describe his model.

MacKay built upon the well-known contradiction that light and electrons can behave – or be described – as either particles or waves.[3] The Danish physicist Niels Bohr (Edinburgh Gifford Lecturer, 1949–50) suggested that such apparently different properties could be usefully described as *complementary*: 'The phenomena transcend the scope of classical physical explanation, [but] the account of all evidence must be expressed in classical terms ... evidence obtained within a single picture must be regarded as *complementary* in the sense that only the totality of the phenomena exhausts the possible information about the objects' (Bohr, 1958:39). He believed that this could provide a model for other situations analysable by alternative conceptual systems. For example,

> In biological research, references to features of wholeness and purposeful reactions or organisms are used together with the increasingly detailed information on structure and regulatory processes ... It must be realised

that the attitudes termed mechanistic and finalistic are not contradictory points of view, but rather exhibit a complementary relationship which is connected with our position as observers of nature. (Bohr, 1958:92)

Other scientists have seized upon complementarity as a valuable concept. Robert Oppenheimer applied it to mechanistic versus organic analyses of life-processes, and to behavioural versus introspective descriptions of personality; Charles Coulson to problems of mind versus brain, free will versus determinism, theology versus mechanism; William Pollard to human freedom versus divine providence (Barbour, 1966:292). MacKay went further and extended the notion to dynamic processes. It is difficult to improve on MacKay's own explanation:

An imaginative artist brings into being a world of his own invention. He does it normally by laying down patches of paint on canvas, in a certain spatial order (or disorder!). The *order* which he gives the paint determines the *form* of the world he invents. Imagine now an artist able to bring his world into being, not by laying down paint on canvas, but by producing an extremely rapid succession of sparks of light on the screen of a television tube. (This is in fact the way in which a normal television picture is held in being.) The world he invents is now not static but dynamic, able to change and evolve at his will. Both its form and its laws of change (if any) depend on the way in which he orders the sparks of light in space and time. With one sequence he produces a calm landscape with quietly rolling clouds; with another, we are looking at a vigorous cricket match on a village green. The scene is steady and unchanging just for as long as he wills it so; but if he were to cease his activity, his invented world would not become chaotic; it would simply cease to be ...

Suppose that we are watching a cricket match 'brought into being' and 'held' in being' by such an artist. We see the ball hit the wicket and the stumps go flying. The 'cause' of the motion of the stumps, in the ordinary sense, is the impact of the ball. Indeed, for any happening in and of the invented scene, we would normally look for – and expect to find – the 'cause' in some other happenings in and of that scene. Given a sufficiently long and self-consistent sample, we might in fact imagine ourselves developing a complete predictive *science* of the cricket world displayed before us, abstracting 'laws of motion' sufficient to explain satisfactorily (in a scientific sense) every happening we witness – so long as the artist keeps to the same regular principle in maintaining the cricket scene in being.

Suppose, however, that someone suggests that our scientific explanation of these happenings is 'not the only one,' and that all our experience of them owes its existence to the continuing stability of the will of the artist who shapes and 'holds in being' the whole going concern. However odd this may sound at first, it is obvious that in fact he is not advancing a *rival* explanation to the one we have discovered in our 'science' of the cricket field; he has no need to cast doubt on ours in order to make room for his own, since the two are not explanations *in the same sense.* They are answers to different questions, and both may, in fact be entirely valid.

The parallel I think is clear as far as it goes. The God in whom the Bible invites belief is no 'cosmic mechanic'. Rather is he the Cosmic Artist, the creative Upholder, without whose continual activity there would be not even chaos, but just nothing. What we call physical laws are expressions of the regularity that we find in the pattern of created events that we study as the physical world. Physically, they express the nature of the entities 'held in being' in the pattern. Theologically, they express the stability of the great Artist's creative will. Explanations in terms of scientific laws and in terms of divine activity are thus not rival answers to the same question; yet they are not talking about different things. They are (or at any rate purport to be) complementary accounts of different aspects of the same happening, which in its full nature cannot be adequately described by either alone. (MacKay, 1960)

An enormous benefit of MacKay's model is that it allows a traditional and robust understanding of God's providence. It also permits a God who is outside time as well as space. This is difficult for us to comprehend. To picture God outside time is not to imagine him as static or uninvolved but as seeing creation – its complete span of space and time – as a whole. The purpose-making, the planning, the unfolding of the drama with all its interconnected parts, combine to make up that whole.

We may find it just about possible to conceive God within time and even of God outside time, but thinking of God as both together is really difficult. John Polkinghorne (1989:ch. 7) talks of God 'being' (God outside time) and God 'becoming' (God within time) as the two opposite poles of the model; in contrast MacKay (1988:193) distinguishes between two persons in one Godhead: God-in-eternity and God-in-time; God transcendent and God immanent.

The two interpretations are fundamentally different. MacKay believes that God's sovereignty is unaffected by the discoveries of modern science. No hidden gap is needed, for God is able to write into the history of the universe whatever he chooses. This is backed up by what MacKay called 'logical indeterminacy', the idea that no human agent can give an absolute prediction of the future without changing the conditions on which the prediction was made. This means that the future cannot be determined, even in a totally deterministic world.

Polkinghorne's approach is to refer to the 'inherent openness' of complex dynamical systems. For him the future is contained within an envelope of possibilities so that the actual pathway followed could be selected by input of confirmation by the mind. The difficulty with this is that

> to attribute the information input to an act of the mind, it needs to be preceded by a mental decision on the desired outcome. But if the mind is embodied, this decision would already have a physical correlate and so the information input cannot be the point of choice. Freedom must lie elsewhere. Alternatively, if the information input is not seen to be the result of a previous state of mind, then we get back to a 'liberty of indifference' – and what causes this information input, chance? All such attempts to explain the freedom of a non-dualistic mind through the openness of physical process are likely to meet this problem. (Doye *et al.* 1995:127)

This leads on to wider questions of determinism and consciousness which are beyond my current theme: my immediate aim is to examine the complementarity model as it applies to God's work in general. I believe MacKay's complementarity approach is the most satisfactory one available.

Criteria for Complementarity

Richard Dawkins regards complementarity as the most viable approach to science–faith issues. He calls it the 'no-contest' model, on the grounds that its adherents regard science and religion as about different things, albeit 'equally true, but in their different ways' (Dawkins, 1992). He prefers it to the two other common models, which he describes as 'inevitable conflict' and 'total independence'. He labels the latter as respectively 'know-all' (defined as religion being good for you, although its truth does not matter) and 'know-nothing' (i.e. that a main function of religion is to explain what we call science). However, he seeks to deflate the 'no-contest' model by claiming that its adherents assume that:

> the biblical account of the origin of the universe (the origin of life, the diversity of species, the origin of man) – all those things [which] are now known to be untrue ... they regard it as naive in the extreme, almost bad taste, to ask of a biblical story, is it true? (Dawkins, 1992)

Now it is true that many people reject many parts of the Bible, but it is unnecessary and illogical to claim that this is an inevitable component of the 'no-contest' approach to science and religion.

Indeed a 'no-contester' is more accurately one who holds definite beliefs which do not lead to a contest, like a physicist who firmly believes that light is incontestably particulate but indubitably wave-like. Moreover, Dawkins cannot even claim the intellectual high ground. Max Perutz, who received a Nobel Prize in 1962 with Jim Watson and Francis Crick for the elucidation of the structure of DNA, has specifically dissociated himself from Dawkins's attacks on theology:

> Science teaches us the laws of nature, but religion commands us how to live ... Dr Dawkins does a disservice to the public perception of scientists by picturing them as the demolition squad of religious beliefs. Isaac Newton and the other founders of modern science pursued their studies of nature in order to discover the nature of God ... (letter to the *Independent*, 23 March 1992)

Colin Russell (1989) has criticised the complementarity model as commonly used in science and religion on the grounds that it ignores the links and stimuli between science and theology. He acknowledges that complementarity is a much better way of approaching the relationship between the two than assuming either total independence or inevitable conflict but suggests a better model would be symbiosis. However, there seems no reason why positive feedback between science and theology should not be allowed to fertilise the complementarity picture, whilst acknowledging that there are dangers in confusing explanations and concepts by extrapolating from one level to another.

To label two explanations as 'complementary' does not thereby remove all problems from the science–religion interface, nor reinstate natural theology as a valid discipline. How do we distinguish between two explanations which are genuinely complementary, or two which are in truth wholly incompatible? MacKay recognised the difficulty:

> Whenever a new concept swims into philosophical ken there is a danger that it will be overworked by the Athenians on the one hand and abused by the Laodiceans on the other ... Complementarity is no universal panacea, and it is a relationship that can be predicated of two descriptions only with careful safeguards against admitting nonsense. Indeed the difficult task is not to establish the possibility that two statements are logically complementary, but to find a rigorous way of detecting when they are not ... A good deal of consecrated hard work is needed on the part of the Christian to develop a more coherent and more biblical picture of the relationship between the two ... (cited by Jeeves, 1968:70)

The conditions under which two or more descriptions may legitimately be called logically complementary are (Barbour, 1974:77–8):

1. that they purport to have a common reference;
2. that each is in principle exhaustive (in the sense that none of the entities or events comprising the common reference need be left unaccounted for); yet
3. they make different assertions because
4. the logical preconditions of definition and/or the use (that is the context in which they are set) of concepts or relationships in each are mutually exclusive, so that the significant aspects referred to in one are necessarily omitted from the other.

MacKay pointed out that nothing in the idea of logical complementarity excludes the possibility of a higher mode of representation which could synthesise two or more complementary descriptions; nor is it necessary that one description should be inferable from the other.

The obvious but important point is that before religious and scientific statements are debated as rivals, it is essential that we should establish that they are not in fact complements. It is equally necessary to realise and to recognise that proof of complementarity does not establish that either account is true. The value of complementarity in natural theology is in transforming negative debates (about where God is not) into positive ones (about how God can be envisaged in particular situations). John Polkinghorne argues that complementarity models can be particularly important when we seek to explain what it means to be human. It is relevant to record that MacKay was a computer scientist who had a professional concern for brain mechanism and frequently discussed the question of how the I-story (the internal account of personal experience) relates to the O-story (the external account given by an observer) (e.g. in his Gifford Lectures, published under the title *Behind the Eye* [1991]).

For science, the value of a theory (or in Kuhnian language, a paradigm) is enormously enhanced if it opens new ways of explanation or experiment, or renders old problems redundant. This is exactly what MacKay's approach offers for understanding divine action. Virtually all theologians who have ventured into this arena have assumed that scientific determinism and human free will must limit God's freedom and foreknowledge. They argue that God necessarily restricts his freedom and ability to act by entering into a partnership with his creation and creatures, especially humankind. They are then forced to assume that God will not intervene to break scientific laws, because this would be inconsistent with his own character (although he may 'work miracles' on occasion, albeit somewhat arbitrarily; the problem is often expressed as 'why did God not prevent the holocaust?')

MacKay stands in contrast to the conventional approach (well exemplified by the writings of John Polkinghorne and Arthur Peacocke, two of the most informed modern scholars) by affirming the unqualified compatibility between God's unrestricted sovereignty and full human responsibility. He condemns the idea of God as a machine-tender on the grounds that although it can

> be stretched *ad hoc* to fit the biblical data it purports to embody, the *expectations* it evokes are radically out of key with much of what the Bible has to say about God's activity. Instead of finding a ready place within its framework, concepts such as creation or miracle appear as disconcerting 'difficulties', felt by non-Christians at least to be vaguely incoherent with the rest of the picture they are offered. Worst of all, the whole facet of biblical teaching that deals with God as immanent in the events of nature is made to seem quite intelligible.

MacKay forces us to look hard at the relationship of God to creation. When we do this, it is clear that the Bible as a whole represents God in far too intimate and active a relationship to daily events to be represented in simple mechanical terms. He does not come in only at the beginning of time merely to 'wind up the works' or 'light the touch paper' for the Big Bang; rather, he continually 'upholds all things by the word of his power' (Hebrews 1.3); 'In him [i.e., Christ] all things hold together' (Colossians 1.17). This is an idea radically different from that of tending or interfering with a machine. It affects not only physically inexplicable happenings (if any), but the whole concern the Bible has with the constant activity of God. God is the primary agent in feeding the ravens and clothing the lilies (Luke 12.22–28); it is he who is active in the 'natural' processes of rainfall and of growth; and even the wicked depend on him for their existence (Matthew 5.45) and serve his purposes (Acts 2.23). 'The whole multi-patterned drama of our universe is declared to be continually 'held in being' and governed by him' (MacKay, 1960).

Can we make sense of this unfamiliar idea of 'holding in being'? Obviously it describes a mystery that we need not expect to understand fully, but unless we can make something of it we cannot come to grips with its relation to our scientific and everyday ways of thinking about the world.

To dispute, for example, as some of our forebears did, whether something 'came about by natural causes *or* required an act of God' is simply not to take seriously the depth and range of the doctrine the Bible asks us to consider. To invoke 'blind chance' as if it were an *alternative* to the action of God in creating us, as Jacques Monod did in his book *Chance and Necessity* (1972), misunderstands the Christian doctrine of creation and providence. What in science we term 'chance events' are recognised in biblical theism as no more and no less dependent upon the sovereign creative power of God than the most law-abiding and predictable of happenings (Proverbs 16.33 ['The lots may be cast into the lap, but the issue depends wholly on the Lord']). We may dislike this doctrine; but it is theologically inept to pretend that science as such has any quarrel with it. The trouble (to quote J. B. Phillips) is that our ideas of God are too often far too small.

> The question whether physical laws are deterministic or indeterministic in the scientific sense is irrelevant to the Bible's claim that they indicate the continuance of God's maintaining 'programme'. Thus whereas some have argued that only an indeterministic physics leaves room for God to act in our world, and others, like Monod, see the element of randomness as *eliminating* the possibility of divine control, biblical theism accepts neither of these mutually cancelling arguments. For the Christian, the events we classify scientifically as 'chance' are as much divinely given as any others; and natural law is primarily an expression of God's faithfulness in giving a succession of experience that is coherent and predictable. 'While the earth remains, seed-time and harvest, cold and heat, summer and winter, day and night shall not cease' (Genesis 8:22). Thus the common expression that God can 'use' natural means to achieve his ends, while undoubtedly true in its intended sense, implies quite the wrong relationship of God to natural law. It is more correct to say that God sometimes achieves his ends in '*natural*' ways (i.e. in ways that do not upset precedent from a scientific point of view). God is not like a man, using his laws as tools that would exist independently of him; it is he who brings into being and holds in being the activities, whether scientifically 'lawful' or otherwise, that we may recognise to be serving his ends. (MacKay, 1960)

The Two Books of God

It is not illogical or unreasonable to envisage a God who interacts with the world known to us through science; on this basis and if we are honest, we have to admit that the God revealed to us in the Bible is intellectually credible. One way of expressing this is the idea that God wrote two books, one of words (the Bible) and one of works (creation), a suggestion which goes back to Pelagius (early fifth century), although more generally credited to Francis Bacon (1561–1626).

Peter Harrison (1998) has pointed out that the 'Two Books' was a common metaphor in the Middle Ages, but that the Book of Works was used almost wholly in pre-Reformation times to contribute allegories for the Book of Words. He quotes Hugh of St Victor (d. 1142): 'For the whole sensible world is like a kind of book written by the finger of God – that is, created by divine power – and each particular creature is somewhat like a figure, not invented by human decision but instituted by the divine will to manifest the invisible things of God's wisdom', and Vincent of Beauvais (1190–1264) who spoke of 'the book of creatures given to us for reading'. The Two Books for such medieval scholars were not complementary accounts of God's work; study of the natural world for them was primarily an aid to knowing the God of the Bible, 'to know the world is not merely to come to know God, it is to become *like* God: it is to restore a likeness which had been lost' (Harrison, 1998:57). Harrison argues powerfully that the study of nature for its own sake was

> not simply the result of stripping away unwanted and extraneous symbolic elements ... but due to the efforts of Protestant reformers [who] insisted that the book of scripture be interpreted only in its literal historical sense ... In this way the study of the natural world was liberated from the specifically religious concern of biblical interpretation and the sphere of nature was opened up to new ordering principles. (Harrison 1998:4)

I have called this book *God's Book of Works* in the modern (or at least, post-Reformation) sense. By this I mean it is impossible to *prove* that God wrote a 'Book of Works', but equally impossible to disprove it (except by denying the existence of God, or by assuming that he has no effective interaction with the natural world). 'Words without works lack credibility; works without words lack clarity. Jesus' works made his words visible; his words made his works intelligible' (Stott, 1992:345). As I believe that God exists and that he acts in history and human life, I want to affirm that the natural world is 'God's world' in that he created and sustains it, and (as we shall see, p. 245) has redeemed it.

Now if God did indeed write Books of both Words and Works, it follows that they cannot conflict with each other. The problem for us is that they are written in different languages and mixing the languages of 'philosophy' (science) and divinity is an excellent recipe for confusion.

The Two Books notion can be regarded as an early understanding of complementarity; it can also be regarded as an expression of the unity of true knowledge. Three and a half centuries before Francis

Bacon, his namesake Roger Bacon (1214–94) argued for a proper study of nature in a way that anticipated modern science, averring that 'of the three ways of acquiring knowledge – authority, reasoning and experience – only the last is effective'. He believed that all certain knowledge is experimental, but he distinguished two kinds of experiment: that made on external nature, the source of certainty in natural science; and experimental acquaintance with the work of the Holy Spirit within the soul, which culminates in the vision of God. Seven hundred years later, the arch-naturalist – and for some the arch-heretic – Charles Darwin quoted Francis Bacon (presumably with approval) on the verso of the fly-leaf of *The Origin of Species*:

> To conclude, therefore, let no man out of a weak conceit of sobriety ... think or maintain that a man can search too far or be too well studied in the book of God's word or in the book of God's works; divinity or philosophy; but rather let men endeavour an endless progress or proficence in both.

Without ducking the changes in interpretation chronicled by Peter Harrison, there is a sense in which all endeavours in natural theology from those of the early Christian Fathers to modern scientists' and theologians' are attempts to read the Two Books together. The hazards attending this exercise surface repeatedly – persecution and imprisonment for Roger Bacon, the harrowing of Galileo, the agonising of Calvin and Newton, the simple faith of John Ray, the rationalities of Archdeacon Paley, the Bridgewater enterprise, the evolutionary debates, the nihilism and reductionism of Jacques Monod and Richard Dawkins, the frantic denials of the 'creationists', the ingenuity of modern scientists like Ian Barbour, John Polkinghorne, Arthur Peacocke and Robert Russell. One of the few certain lessons from the history of science is that complex problems rarely have simple solutions. Often answers have to be sought by combining data from different disciplines and methodologies. Therein lies complementarity, and therein lies the task laid down by Adam Gifford.

NOTES

1   David Wilkinson (1993:98) has pointed out that a kiss can be defined as 'the mutual approach of two pairs of lips, the reciprocal transmission of carbon dioxide and microbes, and the juxtaposition of two orbicular muscles in a state of contraction' – but that his wife had another and non-scientific but more vivid description of the same event.

2   Polkinghorne (1994:82) has castigated this as 'theological double-speak'.
3   A problem not resolved by Sir Lawrence Bragg when he is alleged to have decreed that one interpretation might be held on Mondays, Wednesdays and Fridays, and the other on Tuesday, Thursdays and Saturdays (see Russell, 1985:208).

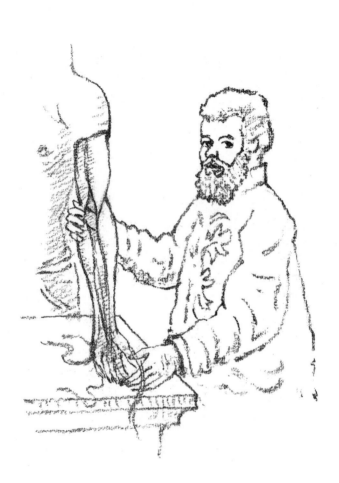

3
1543 and All That

1543 is not a date on the tip of one's tongue in the same way as 55 BC or AD 1066, but it is arguably more pivotal. It is the year that many science historians see as modern science beginning. Two books were published in 1543: Nicholas Copernicus's *De Revolutionibus Orbium Coelestium* was an epilogue and eventual coffin-nail for Greek cosmology, appearing in the year of the author's death; Andreas Vesalius's *De Fabrica Humani Corporis* was a model of observation and accuracy produced when Vesalius was 28 years old and actively working as a public dissector – a treatise on human anatomy omitting for the first time since the Talmudic era the mythical Bone of Luz (supposedly the seed from which the resurrection body grows) and Adam's 'missing rib' (from which Eve had been made). They represent two incompatible worlds. As C. S. Lewis has pointed out, an upward look in the pre-Copernican universe meant an *inward* look to a harmonious and animated world, in which all celestial movement derived from hypothetical spheres, whose own motion came from a *primum mobile* to share in the perfection of God; whereas in the post-Copernican universe, an observer looked *outward* to the night sky and might like Pascal be terrified at the silence of infinite space (quoted by Brooke, 1991:85). Copernicus demonstrated that traditional ways of understanding the cosmos were not the only or necessarily the best ways; Vesalius destroyed the myths enshrined in biological and medical texts on the authority of Galen and other ancient authorities, and laid the ground for modern scientific rigour.

Attitudes and methodology did not of course change overnight sometime during 1543. Copernicus was neither an innovator nor a luddite; Vesalius was an artist in the tradition of Leonardo da Vinci who made few discoveries and held fast to the Aristotelian framework of physiological explanation. Nevertheless, 1543 is a convenient watershed between old and new. It is also a useful reference when setting out a history of modern science, because it diverts attention from the great men (and the few great women) of science to the nature of science itself. We need to get away from the tendency to portray science as an apostolic succession of Copernicus, Kepler,

Galileo, Newton and Einstein, with Boyle and Hooke and a few others wedged into the series, '[which] is only possible on the assumption that the important contributions are those which led up to the dominant mechanism and determinism of the late nineteenth century, and the astonishing achievements of zoologists and botanists in the sixteenth and seventeenth centuries can be ignored' (Raven, 1953:7). It is as naive as seeing history as a simple procession of good and bad rulers whose alliances and jealousies wholly controlled the fates of their dependants.

Moreover our understanding of creation can be attributed to an environmental succession just as valid as that of physical scientists, with Francis of Assisi as its patron saint, and Konrad Gesner, John Ray, Gilbert White, Richard Jefferies, John Muir, Henry Thoreau, Aldo Leopold, Rachel Carson, Eric Ashby, Arne Naess, and Jim Lovelock as its prophets. And to confuse matters and detracting from the latter sequence, there is also the influence and authority of Lynn White as the Venerable Bede of the environmental movement, charting the traducing of Christian naturalism by technology and greed.[1] White's thesis has become almost the standard way of interpreting the development of modern environmental attitudes, despite criticism from historians, sociologists and theologians (Sheldon, 1989; Oeschlager, 1994; Bakken, Engel and Engel, 1995; Harrison, 1999). We shall have to return to it.

In seeking to identify key issues and assumptions, it is difficult to avoid attributing too much to a few particular individuals and missing lesser luminaries. In the review of history and ideas which follows, my aim is to draw attention to the major influences and conflicts that have led to modern confusions. In doing this, I have tried to avoid giving the impression that our attitudes depend upon simple insights or single achievements. Every landmark has multifactorial roots.

Ancient Times

One of the most detrimental influences on biology and probably on science as a whole has been that of Plato (429–348 BC) with his notion of essential forms and essences. Platonism imposed a numbing assumption of stasis, and diverted attention away from variation, one of the key concepts of biology; variation was interpreted as nothing more than an imperfect manifestation of determining essences. If Whitehead is right in asserting that 'the safest general characterisation of the European philosophical tradition is that it consists in a series of footnotes to Plato' (cited by Mayr, 1982:30), it is a condemnation of the clarity and independence of those in that tradition. Toulmin and Goodfield comment:

> Once the axiom was accepted that all temporal changes observed by the senses were merely permutations and combinations of 'eternal principles', the historical sequence of events (which formed a part of the [Platonic] 'flux') lost all fundamental significance. It became interesting only to the extent that it offered clues to the nature of the enduring realities ... philosophers concerned themselves instead with matters of *general principle* – the geometric layout of the heavens, the mathematical forms associated with the different material elements ... More and more they became obsessed with the idea of a changeless universal order, or 'cosmos': the eternal and unending scheme of Nature – society included – whose basic principles it was their particular task to discover. (Toulmin and Goodfield, 1969:90)

Four Platonic dogmas persisted from classical to early modern times and stifled biology:

1. the belief in a constant *eide*, separate from and independent of appearance;
2. a living animate cosmos, with the implication that change would be disruptive;
3. a creative demiurge, which pervaded nature through Plato's polytheism;
4. a stress on soul.

In addition, the 'principle of plenitude' can also be traced to Plato. In later centuries this was used as an argument against the possibility of extinction or organic change (p. 6).

The other great inheritance from ancient Greece is from Plato's contemporary, Aristotle (384–322 BC). For him the world of Ideas (or Forms, as he called them) coincides with the natural world. Aristotle's god is the Prime Mover, although he is only a final cause, not an efficient one. He is a god absorbed in self-contemplation and does not care for the world; neither is he the creator, since the world, the Forms and matter are all eternal. Aristotle was an excellent naturalist, and some of his observations on embryology and marine life remain valid today. However, more significant for his continuing influence were his views on the 'soul', in which he differed from Plato. For Aristotle, 'matter is identical with potentiality, form with actuality, the soul being that which gives the form or actuality'.

The empirical attitude of Aristotle was generally unattractive to the church fathers. For example, the Cappadocian father, Basil of Caesarea (329–79) argued in his *Hexaemeron* that the behaviour of the elements must be understood in terms of laws ordained by God rather than in terms of their essences; that the heavens are corruptible like the earth, so the same laws should apply to both; and that nature, once created and put in motion, evolves in accordance with its own laws, without interruption or diminishment of energy. Aristotle's greatest influence came in the twelfth to fourteenth centuries following the rediscovery of his work and lasted until the scholasticism built round his writings (rather than his writings as such) was ravaged by Renaissance humanists.

Greek and Jewish culture met in Alexandria, and collided over Gnosticism, which incorporated many Platonic-type ideas, including a dualism between a transcendent God and an ignorant and presumptuous demiurge, and the assumption that matter is fundamentally evil, meaning that God bears no responsibility and cares not for the material world. Its most effective opponent in early Christian times was Irenaeus (130–200). He proclaimed the cosmic significance of the incarnation, death and resurrection of Jesus Christ as expounded by Paul and John in the New Testament, and derived through them a theology of nature contrary to the sub-Christian Gnosticism of his time. He saw the world as humanity's God-given home – blessed, embraced and cared for by the very God who took flesh to redeem a fallen humanity. His starting point was a God who brought the whole creation into being, with the incarnate Word as the ever-present life-giving principle who moves the whole creation towards a divinely intended goal. He interpreted the vocation of Jesus Christ as serving the whole divine creation, not merely fallen and redeemed humankind, until its fulfilment (*telos*), when he will deliver his rule to the Father (Santmire, 1985:35–44).

Irenaeus's battle was with a contemporary threat to young Christianity, much as scholars in our own day attack sexism or Thatcherism. But his assault on the Gnostics can in retrospect be seen as a major stamping on magic and mysticism, and towards modernity, including science and environmental concern (Blumenberg, 1983; Gunton, 1993). Irenaeus argued against the Gnostic belief that the material creation is simply a shadow of the divine light from which the enlightened soul needs liberating. He taught the primacy of created things in their material embodied substance, and the origin of created things in the power and will of God rather than in any pre-existent matter. Against the claim that matter is intrinsically evil, Irenaeus insisted that nature and the material world are fundamentally good and blessed by God, and that any tendencies to evil and discord in the material world have been atoned for and redeemed by Jesus Christ. For Irenaeus, the external God and the temporal creation are linked through the doctrine of the Trinity: 'one God who by Word (*logos*) and Wisdom (*sophia*) created and arranged all things'. Natural evil and corruption result from the fall, and are not inherent in matter itself; salvation and the fulfilment of creation are brought about by the divine *logos*, which both confirms the original goodness of the created order and restores that which needs redemption.

Colin Gunton (1993) has argued that the incarnation and the Trinitarian understanding of creation as expounded by Irenaeus must be central to any ecological and relational ethic in which human and non-human life are conceived as inter-related but distinct, and that the tendency to reject the 'otherness' of nature, to deny the relationality of self to nature, and to remake nature entirely for human purposes, have their origins in the shrivelling of the early Christian idea of the unity of God's creative purposes. Moral value in the Irenaean synthesis lay in the relationships between persons in worship and communal life, in which human life is modelled on the divine life of the Trinity and in the relations of God and humankind to the embodied created order. We shall return to these ideas, in particular to ways in which some modern 'ecotheologians' are experientially recovering part of the Irenaean picture, but first we must trace how the second-century understanding became blurred and distorted.

The clarity of Irenaeus's teaching was clouded by the emerging Neoplatonism of Origen (185–254) and his contemporary, Plotinus (205–70). Their world was dominated by a hierarchical pyramid of being with God at its apex, reminiscent of Aristotle's 'Ladder of Nature' marked by different levels or amounts of 'soul'. Origen saw God as creating the material world as a kind of gracious act, to stop the descent of rational spirits towards ultimate non-being. For him, the fundamental reason for creation was the fall. Matter was created by God and is not evil. It exists largely for the purpose of educating humans through trials and tribulations, before returning to a higher, spiritual destiny. The world is thus a sort of purgatory, reminiscent in different ways of the excesses of hellfire preaching and the reincarnationalism of some of the Eastern religions. Origen equated the forty-two stages that he identified in the wanderings of the Israelites in the wilderness (Numbers 23) with the forty-two generations in the first chapter of the Gospel of Matthew through which the Word of God descended in order to be born of a virgin. He explained, 'In descending to the Egypt of this world, Christ passed those forty-two generations as stages; and those who ascend from Egypt pass by the same number, forty-two stages' (Santmire, 1985:51). Having ascended from the Egypt of this world to the Promised Land above, the soul will return to its rest in paradise.

Origen-type thinking permeated the early Church. By shifting attention from God's redemption of the universe to the salvation of the individual sinner, Origen introduced a distinction between creation and God's saving work, which became ever stronger through Renaissance, Reformation and Enlightenment, and is only now beginning to break down. A similar wedge is seen in the writings of Athanasius (297–373). In his treatment of redemption in *De Incarnatione*, we find no reference to the redemptive power of God for the created order as a whole, since creation is merely contingent and hence unstable. For Athanasius and in sharp distinction to Irenaeus:

> redemption by God in Christ is not directed to the whole created order, not even to sensate animals, but only to the rational race of humans. In this radical divorce between creation and redemption, and in the homin- isation of redemption, the clear imprint appears of Hellenistic, and in particular Neo-platonic assumptions about the corruptibility of matter, bodies and non-rational life which, because they are not eternal but temporal and contingent, are also seen as finite and ever in danger of returning to the non-being from which they originated. (Northcott, 1996:212)

Jaroslav Pelikan (1993) in his Aberdeen Gifford Lectures chronicled the ways in which the triumph of theology over classical culture allowed the invasion of elements of Platonic and Neoplatonic thought into the doctrines of God, creation and redemption. The influence of Plato persists in the distinction between matter and form made by the Cappadocians, Basil of Caesarea (330–79) in *De Spiritu Sancto* and Gregory of Nyassa (330–95) in *De Anima et Resurrectione*, where they argue that Genesis describes the devel- opment of particular embodiments in the cosmos from the heavenly ideals. This adaptation of Platonism encouraged belief that God could be known from creation without the aid of revelation, although only those forms of being nearest to the reason and wisdom of God – the invisible angelic powers and the human soul – can truly reflect the divine nature, for those natures 'of which the senses can take cognisance are utterly alien to deity, and of these the furthest removed are all those that are entirely destitute of soul and of power and of motion' (q.v. Pelikan, 1993:261).

The Cappadocians distinguished between the creative and redemptive work of God by means of the concept of the *economy* of salvation. Thus Gregory used the term 'economy' to distinguish the ineffable transcendence from the necessary immanence of the God who acts as creator and saviour. By this means the Cappadocians sought to preserve the absolute transcendence, immutability and *apatheia* of the eternal God, arguing in relation to Christ that it was his human bodily nature that suffered and died on the cross, while his divine nature was preserved in its unchanging form. This contrasted with Irenaeus's affirmation the unity of God's actions towards the world and humans, from creation through redemption to the eschaton, a Trinitarian economy which mirrors the Trinity of Father, Son and Holy Spirit. Consequently, 'Irenaeus was able to allow history to be itself, by virtue of its very relation to God. Because all that God does is achieved by means of his two hands, the Son and the Spirit, it is done both effectively and in due recognition of the integrity of created being' (Gunton, 1993:159).

This brings us to Augustine of Hippo (354–430), the dominant theologian of the early Church and for many succeeding centuries. Like Origen, he was impressed by the great chain of being, but unlike Origen he focused on God's overflowing goodness rather than the impermanence of life on earth.

For Augustine, God governs and moves all things from within, in such a way that the whole creation remains 'entirely natural, since all things are from Him, through Him and in Him' (Augustine, *De Genesi ad Litteram* 1.17.36). Imperfection for Augustine sprang from the fall, which distorted the original goodness of sexuality, friendship and society, and disrupted the good order and harmony of the cosmos. The divine gift of human freedom was weak because of its created contingency, and Adam's choice was disastrously wrong. This is very different to Irenaeus's doctrine; for him, creation was finite, plural and particular, but inherently good due to the linkage of the creative and redeeming 'hands' of the Father, the Son and the Spirit. But Augustine separated creation from redemption, because his doctrine of creation was Neoplatonic as opposed to Christological (Gunton, 1993:54, 56); for him, creation was the product of an arbitrary divine will and very different from the Christological care and Spirit's providence taught by Irenaeus.

The consequence of Augustine's emphasis on freedom is that the problems of the world lie in human actions; human and creation salvation are opposed. This laid the foundation (developed by the medieval nominalists such as William of Ockham, 1285–1347) for the removal of order and moral significance from the external world. The world became a 'thing'.

Commodification and Commercialisation

The Hebrew tradition was that the world belonged to God, but was separate from him and not sacred (May, 1994). The Christian understanding initially emphasised the value of creation because of its relationship to God, but then as we have seen, downgraded the significance of the material through concentrating on the work of God in human beings. Changes in emphasis and exegesis led to reification.

> The effect of this interpretation of history, which virtually reduced the meaning of Providence to the protection and guidance of the Church, was to empty belief in progress of any reference to the world of nature and of secular affairs. Now with [the decline of the Roman Empire and] the breakdown of civilisation, hope had been transferred from the world to the Church and from this world to the next: when the Kingdom came it would be by miracle and with fire: the earth and all that it contained would be utterly consumed ... It is not surprising that Augustine and the Churchmen of Western Christendom thus rejected the order of nature as a *massa perditonis*, totally corrupt and doomed to destruction. (Raven, 1953:52)

This is the background to Lynn White's 'historical roots of our ecologic crisis' (p. 38). His starting point was the replacement of the scratch plough, which produced shallow furrows and was only useable in light soils, with a new design, incorporating a ploughshare which allowed much deeper furrows (and productivity) but needed a team of up to eight oxen to pull it. Under the old system, fields were distributed in family units, with the presumption of subsistence farming. To use the newer and more efficient plough, farmers had to pool their oxen into large plough-teams. Land distribution became related to the capacity of a power machine to till the soil rather than the needs of a family. Farmers had formerly been part of nature, now they were exploiters of nature.

Part of White's evidence for this was in illustrated calendars. In earlier times, the months were shown as passive events; after *c.*830 the calendars show people coercing the world around them – ploughing, harvesting, chopping trees, butchering pigs.

White's conclusion was that:

> what people do about their ecology depends on what they think about themselves in relation to things about them. Human ecology is deeply conditioned by beliefs about our nature and destiny – that is, by religion ... In its Western form, Christianity is the most anthropocentric religion

the world has seen ... Christianity, in absolute contrast to ancient paganism and Asia's religions (except, perhaps, Zoroastrianism) not only established a dualism of man and nature but also insisted that it is God's will that man exploit nature for his proper ends' (White, 1967)

Scholasticism nourished this duality. Alexander Neckham (1157–1217) and Bartholomew the Englishman (*c.*1260) filled their pages with the fantastic emblems of heraldry, with wonderful tales of plants and beasts usually based on some record of Pliny (23–79) or 'Physiologus' (writing in Alexandria around the second century AD); generations of preachers and story-tellers used them as illustrations of morality. This tradition reached its fullest expression in Thomas Aquinas (1227–74). Like Paul and the Hebrew prophets, Aquinas argued that much can be known about God and about the way we are to live from our natural experience of reason and our observations of the natural order; in other words, from natural theology. He regarded 'being' as of the essence of divinity, but the sense in which God is everywhere is teleological ('things are ordered to the ultimate end which God intends') rather than pantheistic. It is the whole and the interconnections therein which show the wise ordering of the universe by the active being of God.

Through his doctrine of natural law, Aquinas extended Aristotle's belief in the rationality and purposiveness of the created order. God not only caused the universe to come into being but he is also the origin of the purpose which every kind of being pursues in the course of its life. He also sought to limit private actions and property rights by social obligations (*Summa Theologica*, quaestio 66): natural law provides that material things are provided by God for the use of all; human law requires that a system of private property be set up for the management of material things; and the use of property must be limited to that which is reasonable for the individual. In Roman times, possession had not involved any assumption of social responsibility, but that changed with feudalism; responsibility for local government and the administration of justice were important functions of the feudal lords. Medieval agricultural economy, in which much of the land was held in a form of corporate ownership, survived for centuries only because the lord of the manor, through his steward, maintained a close supervision of the villagers and the way in which they worked the land. Without such supervision, the maintenance of fertility would have been impossible, since in any system of commonalty it does not pay the individual to hold back in the interests of future production if his actions are going to be vitiated by those of his competitors.

The transition from the mental atmosphere of the Middle Ages to that of the modern world took several centuries, and incorporated far-reaching changes in resource use, population and economic organisation. The technical control of the environment which had been achieved in Europe at the end of this transition period depended on convergent developments in social and political insti-tutions, and could not have occurred if the principles laid down by Thomas Aquinas had been strictly applied. His ideal society was one whose conduct was to be guided by Christian maxims, with limitations on the ownership of property and condemnation of usury. Herein lay the crunch: Christian rules of social conduct stood in the way of economic development. With the benefit of hindsight, we can see how the areas of human conduct covered by the existing principles were manipulated so that they shrank; economic and commercial activities were gradually removed from the domain of traditional ethics. Tawney (1938) quotes Benvenuto da Ismola, whom he describes as a medieval cynic: 'Qui facit usuram vadit ad infernum; qui non facit vadit ad inopiam' ('He who takes usury goes to hell; he who does not, goes to the workhouse').

Notwithstanding, the underlying theory emphasised that we are responsible to God for the use of the world. In *The Primitive Origination of Mankind* (1677), Sir Matthew Hale, Lord Chief Justice of England wrote:

> In relation therefore to this inferior World of Brutes and Vegetables, the End of Man's Creation was, that he should be the VICE-ROY of the great God of Heaven and Earth in this inferior World; his Steward, *Villicus*, Bayliff, or Farmer of this goodly Farm of the lower World, and reserved to himself the supreme Dominion, and the Tribute of Fidelity, Obedience, and Gratitude, as the greatest Recognition or Rent for the same, making his Usufructuary of this interior World to husband and order it, and enjoy the Fruits thereof with sobriety, moderation, and thankfulness.
>
> And hereby Man was invested with power, authority, right, dominion, trust, and care, to correct and abridge the excesses and cruelties of the fiercer Animals, to give protection and defence to the useful, to preserve the *Species* of divers Vegetables, to improve them and others, to correct the redundance of unprofitable Vegetables, to preserve the face of the Earth in beauty, usefulness, and fruitfulness. And surely, as it was not below the Wisdom and Goodness of God to create the very Vegetable Nature, and render the Earth more beautiful and useful by it, so neither was it unbecoming the same Wisdom to ordain and constitute such a subor-dinate Superintendent over it, that might take an immediate care of it. And certainly if we observe the special and peculiar accommodation and adaptation of Man, to the regiment and ordering of this lower World, we shall have reason, even without Revelation, to conclude that this was one

End of the Creation of Man, namely, to be the Vice-gerent of Almighty God, in the subordinate Regiment especially of the Animal and Vegetable Provinces. (cited by Black, 1970:56–7)

In Hale's view there was no escape from human responsibility towards God for the proper management of the earth, to control the wilder animals and to protect the weaker, to preserve and improve useful plants and to eliminate weeds and, interestingly, to maintain the beauty as well as the productivity of the earth. Was it entirely a coincidence that, like the author of Genesis, he put beauty before utility? Our ability to carry out these duties appeared to him as evidence for the purpose of the creation, and, given Hale's legal background, it is not surprising that he viewed the situation within the contractual framework with which he was in everyday contact, 'steward, *villicus*, bailiff, or farmer'. From this, justification for private property rights was not difficult. As we have seen they were specifically allowed by Thomas Aquinas. Calvin believed strongly that the world was provided for our use: 'God, like a provident and industrious head of a family, has arranged the motions of the sun and stars for man's use, has replenished the air, earth and water with living creatures and produced all kinds of fruit in abundance for the supply of food' (*Institutes* 2.2.19). Nature was treated increasingly in an anthropocentric and instrumentalist way. Although Calvin argued against the abuse of nature, his emphasis on the depravity of nature and on the subjection of natural to human purposes led to treating the land and its products as a commodity.

Passmore (1980) regarded Hale as the sole seventeenth exemplar of the stewardship tradition implicit in the theology of Irenaeus. Whether or not this is true, the eighteenth century introduced radical changes in attitude which enlarged the medieval belief in duality as applied to creation into Enlightenment practices of domination and control of the natural world. Harrison (1999) lists five inter-related factors which operated at this time:

1. the decline of the concept of the human mind as a 'microcosm' of the world;
2. the replacement of Aristotelian vitalism with a mechanical world view;
3. a radical collapse of the 'symbolist mentality' with its assumption of the transcendental significance of natural things (q.v. Thomas, 1971);
4. the ascendancy of Protestantism with its associated work ethic;
5. a hermeneutic of modernity, which replaced allegory with literal analysis (Harrison, 1998).

A key rationalisation was made by John Locke (1632–1704) in his *Two Treatises on Government*, published in 1690 only thirteen years after Hale's book. Locke's concern was with justice; his unfortunate contribution was to justify unequal and unlimited appropriation of natural goods. Individual ownership as the most efficient means of land management was taken for granted, but Locke was faced with the need to justify the accumulation of land additional to the requirements of the owner himself. To do this he had to overcome two objections; the first, that a man should not possess so much property that he wasted some of its products, Locke removed by introducing into the argument the concept of money, which was not itself subject to spoiling. The second objection was that the concentration of ownership in a few individual hands would reduce the resources available to the rest of the population, and this Locke set aside by claiming that large-scale management increased overall production. He based his theory of property on the argument that a man's labour is his own, to do with as he liked (recalling Hobbes's *Leviathan*, 'A man's labour also, is a commodity exchangeable for benefit as well as any other thing'). The importance of this lay in the relation of the individual to the society of which he or she is a member. If individuals own their own labour, to do with as they please, society is not involved; consequently, if the right to unlimited property rests on personal labour, property rights no longer carry social obligations. The way was cleared for the worst excesses of the industrial revolution.

It now became distinctly eccentric, if not quaint, to treat the 'goods' of creation as outside market forces, even if these were tempered by caring landlords. During the seventeenth and eighteenth centuries and into the nineteenth in Scotland, rising commercial interests led to enforced depopulation of rural areas and the enclosure of common lands, primarily to make way for the sheep and game of landowners. The traditional uses of the commons for hunting, grazing and fuel collection were denied to peasants, many of whom were then forced to abandon their subsistence plots since they could not support a family without the associated commons. Enforced enclosures provoked widespread but ineffective protest. Transport and communication developed to facilitate free trade between towns and regions. Land and labour became counters in a money economy. Links to family and place, which had imposed moral constraints, lessened.

These developments forced agricultural workers into rural landlessness or urban squalor, fuelled the expansion of trade, and were the enabling features of the transformation from feudalism to capitalism in post-medieval Europe. The biblical injunctions against usury and the accumulation of profit should have set the Church against the upheavals of the new system. But the Church itself was part of the emerging trading system both as landowner and as economic actor, and this hindered its restraint. On mainland Europe Rousseau's *Discourse on the Origin and Foundations of Equality and Men* (1754) compounded the disruption (Bate, 2000). Consequently,

> the natural resource demands of the growing urban culture were no longer balanced by an awareness of the limitations of soil, rivers and climate, or respect for farm animals and the creatures of the wild. The consequent disembedding of human social structures from the limits and needs of the land, and the loss of a widespread relationality between nature and human life, is a key figure in the modern abuse of the natural world, and may also be linked to a more general demise of virtue in human relations as well as relations with nature in modern urbanised societies. (Northcott, 1996:50)

These social changes were mirrored and deepened by commercial legislation. Individual consciences were submerged by the overriding sanctity of profit-making. The Companies' Act of 1862 made it possible for anyone to found a limited liability company by obtaining signatures to a memorandum of registration. Prior to this, the ability to profit from commercial transactions was restrained by liability for any obligations incurred. This check was now removed. It became possible to grow rich without risk and in complete ignorance of business practices which would have been outrageous if practised by an individual. Arthur Bryant (1940:215) called 'the consequences of the Companies' Act of 1862 perhaps greater than that of any single measure in English Parliamentary history. They completed the divorce between the Christian conscience and the economic practice of everyday life. They paganised the commercial community.'

But two positive notes need inserting into this litany of environmental apostasy. First, the monastic system, particularly the Benedictine rule, provided a model of careful stewardship throughout medieval Europe. Although various scandals marred the system from place to place and its spread was much reduced after the Reformation, the conscious care of creation encouraged successful environmental practices. Lynn White (1967) proposed that Francis of Assisi should be recognised as the patron saint of ecology (Pope John Paul II declared him to be such thirteen years later); René Dubos (1972) suggested that Benedict would have been a stronger candidate.

My other 'positive note' is stronger and increasing. I shall have
more to say about it in later chapters, but it is proper to place it here
in historical context. I refer to the scientific study of nature itself, the
story which we arbitrarily began in 1543, but which was a sub-theme
running through earlier centuries. Charles Raven used to revel in
the irony that some of the most delicate and truly representational
carving was carried out in wood and stone in the thirteenth and
fourteenth centuries during the long submergence of academic
biology in formalised herbals and bestiaries. The artisans who
worked on the great cathedrals were obviously much more familiar
with their native plants and animals than their formally learned
contemporaries.

Worship and practical skill combined may be seen in the two great
Oxford Franciscans, physicist and Bishop of Lincoln, Robert
Grosseteste (1175–1253), and his pupil Roger Bacon (1214–94).
Bacon in particular was condemned for criticising his colleagues
over their neglect of experiment. But things were changing. The
strains which were to lead to the Reformation were starting to have
an effect: obsession with the 'revealed word' (which included much
besides the Bible, notably the writings of Aristotle and Arab scholars
like Avicenna) was beginning to be complemented by attention to
natural history; Albertus Magnus (1193–1280) was a pioneer of this
new wave. However,

> in spite of his great reputation for learning and the influence of his pupil
> St. Thomas [Aquinas], his [Albert's] strenuous attempt to lift the study of
> nature out of an atmosphere of fable and falsehood was wholly unsuc-
> cessful ... He was as helpless as his ill-used contemporary, Roger Bacon,
> to break through the mediaeval indifference to the realities of the natural
> world or to initiate for mankind any scientific movement. (Raven,
> 1953:71)

Another contemporary of Albertus, Frederick II (1194–1250) wrote a
superb treatise on falconry, centuries ahead of its time in its concern
for the biology of birds. His influence was wide. He had some of
Aristotle's works translated into Latin, and perhaps most significantly
was a patron of the medical school of Salerno, where human bodies
were dissected for the first time in more than 1,000 years.

Beginning with Salerno, universities emerged in various parts of
Europe, from Italy (Bologna, Padua) and France (Paris,
Montpellier) to England (Oxford, Cambridge). They had very
different backgrounds, some being originally medical or law schools,
others (like the Sorbonne, founded *c.*1200) schools of theology.

Most of them became centres of scholasticism but some became foci for progressive scholarship in areas such as anatomy – which brings us back to Vesalius, appointed to Padua in 1537.

The Study of Nature

At the beginning of the sixteenth century, five naturalists born within a few years of each other contributed significantly to the revival of biology after the Middle Ages: William Turner (1508–68), father of English botany; Pierre Belon (1517–64); Guillaume Rondel (1507–66); Ulisse Aldrovandi (1522–1605); and most influential, Konrad Gesner (1516–65), whose four-thousand-page *Historia Animalium* was an encyclopaedia in the true meaning of that word. These were all contemporaries of Copernicus and Vesalius; the scientific era had begun.

Gesner was a true Renaissance man. Alongside his scientific interests, he had strong theological connections. He was born in Zurich. His father was killed fighting alongside Zwingli when he was fifteen. He knew the Swiss Reformers, Bucer, Bullinger, Conrad and Samuel Pellican, Marti, Wirt and Zwinger. At one time his life's work seemed to be as a pastor, but he took his MD at Basel and settled down to medicine and science in Zurich. He undertook fieldwork for himself. He wrote:

> I have determined, as long as God gives me life, to ascend one or more mountains every year when the plants are at their best – partly to study them, partly for exercise of body and joy of mind ... I say then that he is no lover of nature who does not esteem high mountains very worthy of profound contemplation. It is no wonder that men have made them the houses of the gods, of Pan and the nymphs ... I have a passionate desire to visit them. (cited by Raven, 1953:88)

The century after Gesner saw great advances in plant classification although few in zoology. Progress was not made until structure replaced function or habitat as the criterion for classifying. This was first done by Francis Willugby (1635–73) in his posthumously published *Ornithologiae libri tres* (1676), although probably it was mostly the work of his friend and editor, John Ray, properly called the father of natural history (Berry, 2001).[2]

With Willugby and Ray, we move from the continuing pedantry of Catholic Europe to the increasing intellectual activity of Reformed Britain. This raises significant questions about the way the

Reformation unlatched new interpretations (Hookyaas, 1971, 1999; St Andrews Gifford Lecturer, 1975–7). Raven notes that:

> the strongholds of Catholicism – Spain, Rome and Paris – produced hardly any outstanding scientists in the sixteenth century ... It is too easy to ascribe this solely to the contrast between the natural and the supernatural, or to the power of tradition and legendary law ... There is more in it than this. Catholicism had been a religion of authority: only the ecclesiastics were entitled to expound its teaching or to understand its mysteries; it was for the layman to hear and obey. When Luther raised the standard of revolt, it was upon the right of every Christian to study the open Bible that he based his policy ... the reign of prescription and privilege was over; the common man had the right to learn and to study for himself. (Raven, 1953:90)

Galileo's contretemps with the Pope had been an argument within what we now call the Establishment. Over the following two centuries the 'new knowledge' spread to all levels of society. Men and women found themselves in an ever-widening cosmos, regulated by laws being discovered and made known by the 'new philosophers'. The newer world still had many unknowns and was not necessarily less frightening than the older version where magic and divine fate ruled. But it was an existence where God was less obviously obtrusive. When the Marquis de Laplace (1749–1827) told Napoleon that he had no need for the hypothesis of God in his science, he was not denying the existence of God but recognising that there was no place for a God who was little more than a treadmill operator.

John Ray's *The Wisdom of God Manifested in the Works of the Creation* (1691) has been described as the best work on natural theology ever written (albeit by one of Ray's biographers, who may not be an impartial judge); it knit together the works of God in creation, redemption and providence in a seamless way, with God treated as a benevolent dynamo as distinct ·from a distant mechanic or a Cartesian *deus ex machina.* A hundred and fifty years later Paley plagiarised Ray without acknowledgement, and wrote of a creation running under God's governance, but largely independent of him. The Reformation had detached God from the clutches of the ecclesiastical hierarchy, but the Enlightenment sent him back to the beginnings of time, relegating him to little more than the First Cause.

Darwin and Divinity

Charles Darwin (1809–82) is apparently far removed from the world of early Church theologians, medieval philosophers or industrial entrepreneurs, but the revolution he provoked has profoundly affected the way we view the natural world and (as we have already seen, pp. 9f) our understanding of natural theology. We need to explore how (and whether) twenty-first-century naturalism relates to the nineteenth-century pietism of Gifford's time. It involves us in one more journey into history.

Darwin was born and brought up in Shrewsbury, the son of a prosperous general practitioner. As a young man, his world was that of Paley. In his *Autobiography*, he commented on the old argument from design in nature 'which formerly seemed to me so conclusive'. When he began his notes on evolution (or transmutation as he called it), he started from a Paleyian belief that the creator creates by laws; his theory developed from ideas of harmony in nature, which stemmed directly from Paley (Ospovat, 1979). His Unitarian connections were congruent with Paley's deism. And deism was peculiarly ill-fitted to cope with the mechanism for evolutionary change which was Darwin's crucial contribution, and which removed the need for a divine watchmaker.

Darwin himself recognised the impossibility of reconciling Paley's ideas with his own, and the debates sparked by *The Origin* did not centre on Paleyian natural theology (Moore, 1979; Numbers, 1992). Indeed the British Association debate between Bishop Wilberforce of Oxford and T. H. Huxley in 1860, which is the one bit of Darwinian history known to almost everybody, was not about religion and science at all, despite all the conflict stories that use it as their icon. Wilberforce's worries were ecclesiastical, and his aim was to stamp as hard as possible on anything that legitimised change – as, of course, did evolution. It is wrong to portray him as a blinkered cleric: he had a first-class degree in mathematics and was a Vice-President of the British Association. His concerns were threefold: *sociological* – the conventional church-going habit was being disrupted by the movement of people into towns, where they proved less likely to be worshippers; *theological* – the triumphant progress of manufacture, engineering and colonialism contrasted and apparently conflicted with the Bible's picture of human weakness and the need for redemption; and *ecclesiological* – questionings of the authority of the Bible (and hence, of the Church) were beginning to spread, fuelled by the 'higher criticism' of German scholars and stimulated by the recent publication in England of *Essays and Reviews* (Jowett *et al.*, 1860), a collection of essays by authors who rejected the verbal inspiration of Scripture. Wilberforce's attack on evolution was secondary to his main aim of protecting the status quo of society and Church.

Likewise, Huxley's main target was not Christianity but what he regarded as the illegitimate authority of church leaders, holding on to offices of secular power and thus excluding the voice of science, which to Huxley represented objective truth as opposed to superstition. His aim was (and remained throughout his life) the secularisation of society.

There are no verbatim reports of the meeting. Huxley was certain that he had 'won' and that he was 'the most popular man in Oxford for full four and twenty hours afterward'. In contrast, Joseph Hooker (Director of Kew Gardens) reported to Darwin that Huxley had been inaudible, and that it was he (Hooker) who had carried the day. Wilberforce went away happy that he had given Huxley a bloody nose. As far as the audience was concerned, many scored it as an entertaining draw (Desmond and Moore, 1991:497). The tragedy has been a legacy of inevitable conflict between science and faith, a conflict encouraged by Huxley himself[3] and fuelled by two much-read manifestos: (*History of the Conflict between Religion and Science*, by W. Draper (1875) (Draper was one of the main speakers in the British Association meeting; Hooker called him a 'Yankee donkey ... [spouting] flatulent stuff'); and *A History of the Warfare of Science with Theology*, by A. D. White (1886). The influence of the latter two still persists, despite their many factual errors and their long-discredited tradition of positivist, Whiggish historiography. They were New World crusaders at a time when science seemed triumphant at home and abroad, and each had his particular reasons for settling old scores with organised religion.

As we have already noted, evolution was generally accepted in Britain by the time of Darwin's death (p. 10). Ironically, it was not liberal theologians, but orthodox believers with a firm hold on God's providence that felt least nervous about Darwinism (Livingstone, 1987). In the United States, three scientists who were evangelicals (James Dana and George Wright, both geologists; and Asa Gray, America's leading botanist) ensured that Darwin's ideas had a fair hearing; in denominational journals George Macloskie, a Presbyterian, and Alexander Winchell, a Methodist, argued their understanding of God and evolution; and evangelical theologians such as Warfield, Orr, A. A. Hodge, Iverach, Pope and McCosh all embraced the new biology. Ironically in view of later history, several of the authors of the eponymous 'fundamental' booklets produced between 1910 and 1915 to expound the 'fundamental beliefs' of Protestant Christianity as defined by the 1910 General Assembly of the American Presbyterian Church were sympathetic to evolution. For example, James Orr (Professor of Systematic Theology in the Glasgow College of the United Free Church of Scotland) argued that the Bible is not a textbook of science, that the world is 'immensely older than 6000 years', that the first chapter of Genesis is a 'sublime poem' which science 'does nothing to subvert', and that although evolution was not yet *proved*, there was growing evidence for some form of evolutionary origin of species. George Wright declared that 'if it should be proved that species have developed from others of a lower order as varieties are supposed to have done, it would strengthen rather than weaken the standard argument from design'. And Princeton theologian B. B. Warfield, well known (or notorious) as an authoritative defender of the inerrancy of the Bible, believed that evolution could supply a tenable 'theory of the method of divine providence in the creation of mankind', and that Calvin's doctrine of the creation 'including the origination of all forms of life, vegetable and animal alike, including doubtless the bodily form of man [was] ... a very pure evolutionary scheme'.[4]

By the time of the fiftieth anniversary of the publication of *The Origin of Species* in 1908, the fact of evolution was almost universally accepted both on the grounds of circumstantial evidence collected by Darwin himself and others, and through the power of the idea to explain the uneven geographical distributions of different living forms, the possibility of rational biological classification, and the persistence of vestigial organs. On the other hand, Darwin's real contribution was to devise a plausible mechanism for evolutionary adaptation. There has been a continuing and wholly proper scientific debate about this, but it was only through the work of R. A. Fisher in the 1920s on the effects of substituting genes that the 'neo-Darwinian synthesis' between genetics, palaeontology and classical biology finally took place, eponymised by the publication of Julian Huxley's *Evolution: The Modern Synthesis* in 1942 (Berry, 1982, 2000*b*). One of the consequences of this delayed synthesis was that natural selection (i.e. Darwinism *sensu stricto*) was regarded as of little importance for at least the first third of the twentieth century, and this misunderstanding has remained more widespread than it should have been through its propagation in three widely read histories of biology written before the synthesis (by Nordenskiold, 1928; Radl, published in English in 1930; and Singer, 1931).

Dissent about Evolution

However, there seems to be a continuing desire among many religious people that evolution may be somehow disproved. Time after time we hear that it is 'only' a theory. This betrays a complete misunderstanding of the scientific use of the word. In science, a theory is used to distinguish between a set of ideas subject to experimental test (a 'hypothesis') and the accumulated synthesis of tested hypotheses, which is a 'theory'. It is thus quite distinct from the speculative rationalisations which are called theories in detective novels. A valuable theory combines a host of observations and conclusions into a single whole (sometimes called a 'paradigm'). It may incorporate some apparent anomalies, which are tolerated for the sake of the synthesis (just as physicists accepted Newtonian mechanics although the orbit of Mercury never fitted its predicted path), and suggests experiments for further research. The accusation that evolution is *only* a theory betrays an ignorance of scientific language; evolutionary 'theory' is a corpus of ideas as firmly grounded as any other in biology.

The grumbling distaste for evolution was reflected in a book *Darwinism Today* written for *The Origin*'s Jubilee (Kellogg, 1907), which began: 'Ever since there has been Darwinism there have been occasional death-beds of Darwinism on title pages of pamphlets, addresses, and sermons.' J. B. S. Haldane headed a 1927 essay 'Darwinism is dead – Mr. H. Belloc', referring to attacks on evolution by the Roman Catholic apologists Hilaire Belloc and G. K. Chesterton. He changed this in his 1932 book *The Causes of Evolution* (one of the seminal works of the neo-Darwinian synthesis) to 'Darwinism is dead – Any sermon'.

But in parallel to these debates, what has been called the New Catastrophism but more commonly just creationism, was born in the United States, largely begotten by the Adventist George McCready Price (1870–1963). He was wont to call his *Outlines of Modern Christianity and Modern Science* (1902) the first fundamentalist book. His clarion call was 'No Adam, no fall; no fall, no atonement; no atonement, no Saviour.' He regarded his magnum opus to be *The New Geology* (1923), featuring the Genesis flood as the central geological event in the history of the earth.

By the end of the 1920s, three states (Tennessee, Mississippi and Arkansas) had passed laws banning the teaching of evolution in government-funded schools, under one of which John Scopes, a teacher in Dayton, Tennessee was tried and convicted. He was fined $100 although the sentence was later overturned on a technicality, because the judge had set the fine, rather than the jury as the law required. There is considerable irony in the fact that modern 'creationism' springs from a dogma of Seventh Day Adventism, and does not have direct historical roots in either biblical or Darwinian ideas or debates.

There have been periodic bursts of enthusiasm for creationism, notably in North America and Australia. A major stimulus for the creationist cause was a book *The Genesis Flood* (1961) by John Whitcomb, a Bible teacher, and Henry Morris, a hydraulics engineer. This is not the place to record the arguments and methods of the creationists. They have tended to be spurned as ridiculous by the scientific community except in moments of frustration (Plimer, 1994).[5]

But the question in the context of understanding attitudes to the natural world is why creationism persists and arouses the passions that it does. The answer to this seems to be sociological rather than scientific or theological. For the creationist, God fixed the world and determined its ways; he declared the order that he had established was 'very good'. Any deviation from it becomes automatically heretical. Consequently, change is seen to be inevitably wrong, whether it is technological (destroying a traditional farming economy), political (replacing one – usually local – method of decision making with another which tends to be distantly based) or sexual (the legitimisation of any other form of family structure than the so-called nuclear family). All these anathemas are expressed to the point of caricature in the 'religious right', representing a set of attitudes peculiar to those who fear and therefore resist change, a reflection of the position adopted by Bishop Wilberforce in 1860. In fact the anti-evolution of the 'creationists' is more a reaction against the Social Darwinism of railway surveyor turned philosopher, Herbert Spencer (1820–1903) who argued that human society could be regarded as an organism, so that damage to any part affected the whole, than against Darwin's own ideas. Ernst Mayr (1982:36) condemns Spencer: 'It would be quite justifiable to ignore Spencer totally in a history of biological ideas because his positive contributions were nil. However, since Spencer's ideas were much closer to various popular misconceptions than those of [his contemporary] Darwin, they had a decisive impact on anthropology, psychology and the social sciences.' Spencer's ideas were immensely popular with North American liberals, because they apparently justified individual freedom and unfettered capitalism.[6]

> Whereas Darwin offered a theory of evolutionary change, Spencer offered a metaphysic based on change; whereas Darwin's universe was at the mercy of time and chance, Spencer's had a clear and comforting direction; and perhaps above all, where Darwin detected only the amoral processes of reproduction, competition and selection, Spencer discussed in nature the foundations of right conduct – evolution was, to use his term the 'survival of the *fittest*'. (Durant, 1985:21)

The leaders of the late-nineteenth-century religious establishment embraced Herbert Spencer's evolutionism with enthusiasm. The natural order of things was God's will, they argued. Yale's William Graham Sumner summarised the intellectual convention of the time: 'Let it be understood that we cannot go outside of this alternative: liberty, *inequality*, survival of the fittest; not liberty, *equality*, survival of the unfittest.' In practical terms, this meant:

> The millionaires are a product of natural selection, acting on the whole body of men to pick out those who can meet the requirements of certain work to be done ... It is because they are thus selected that wealth – both their own and that entrusted to them – aggregates under their hands.

This was obviously welcome news to the rich but not to the poor, who were disinherited now by God as well as by an often rapacious economic system. It generated the unlikely phenomenon of industrial barons claiming to be philosophers, writing books and articles to celebrate the congruence of God's will, natural law and their own prosperity. In 1900 John D. Rockefeller epitomised their pious claims: 'The growth of a large business is merely survival of the fittest [forcing small companies out of business] ... it is not an evil tendency in business. It is merely the working-out of a law of nature and a law of God.'

Spencer's Social Darwinism gave birth to a North American version of the divine right of kings, 'proving' it scientifically for the age of technology. People who opposed the scientifically intellectualised social order often became explicitly anti-scientific. Told that both God and Darwin decreed popular misery and that evolutionary law ordained the direction in which they were 'naturally' headed, many resented and opposed the new doctrines of inequality. They thus rejected Darwin and turned to 'conservative' churches, unsullied by Social Darwinism. Darwin's biology was not necessarily the issue, except to the extent that Social Darwinists (including many biologists) misused it to rationalise as 'natural progress' the headlong rush into brutal industrial society. Anti-evolutionist analyses of social and political ills were naive in their understanding of the processes of history when they believed that the solution was to return to a mythical golden age. But they accurately perceived that their troubles were caused by other people, and not by the immutable will of God or nature.

The paradox is that arch-conservative politics in the United States are today often associated with anti-evolutionism. The populists who opposed World War I because they saw in it the results of belief in progress and technology would be amazed to see their anti-evolutionist conclusions preached from 'electronic pulpits' via satellite television relays and accompanied by the message that intercontinental missiles and unbridled capitalism are God's will. Populists past and present exemplify a range of discontent whose anti-establishmentarianism can be perceptive, irrational and bigoted at the same time. But activist right-wing religious movements such as the 'Moral Majority', and the political sophistication of allegedly non-partisan groups such as the Institute for Creation Research have proved to be effective lobbies for religious and social conservatism. Their success belies the liberal myth that the Scopes trial settled once for all the issues of evolution, education and the value of intellectual rigour (Larson, 1997; Miller, 1999). Mary Midgley has labelled Spencer's Social Darwinism and not Darwin's scientific Darwinism as the creation myth of our age.

This brings us full circle: the revolution of 1543 brought in observation, test and considered learning; we are now back to an era ruled by myth and pseudo-authority. Fundamentalism, whether it be religious, nationalistic or racial, is in the ascendant. It would not have been a word known to Adam Gifford; its first appearance was in 1923 according to the *Oxford English Dictionary*. But Gifford's ethos and endowment were directed against fundamentalism – not explicitly to fight it, but to undermine it as comprehensively as possible.

NOTES

1   In a paper originally given at the 1966 meeting of the American Association for the Advancement of Science on the 'Historical roots of our ecologic crisis' (White, 1967).

2   The author declares he has 'wholly omitted what we find in other Authors concerning *Homonymous* and *Synonymous* words, or the diverse names of Birds, *Hieroglyphics, Emblems, Morals, Fables, Presages* or ought else pertaining to *Divinity, Ethics, Grammar,* or any sort of Humane Learning.' Harrison (1998:2) comments: 'The list may seem a curious one – not for the fact that Ray chose to exclude this information – but because it was ever thought pertinent to the subject of natural history in the first place. Yet we do not have far to look to find the "other authors" who are the subject of Ray's reproach.'

3   He wrote: 'Extinguished theologians lie about the cradle of every science as the strangled snakes besides that of Hercules; and history records that whenever science and orthodoxy have been fairly opposed, the latter has been forced to retire from the lists, bleeding and crushed if not annihilated; scotched if not slain' (1893:II, 52).

4   Warfield's views have been examined in detail by Noll and Livingstone (2000), who show that Warfield distinguished carefully between the scientific understanding of evolution (with which he had no difficulty) and philosophical extrapolations from Darwinism (which he deplored).

5   For example Harvard geneticist Richard Lewontin (1981) has written: 'It is time for students of the evolutionary process, especially those who have been misquoted and used by the creationists, to state clearly that evolution is a *fact*, not theory, and that what is at issue within biology are questions of details of the process and the relative importance of different mechanisms for evolution. It is a *fact* that the earth, with liquid water, is more than 3.6 billion years old. It is a *fact* that cellular life has been around for at least half of that period and that organised multicellular life is at least 800 million years old. It is a *fact* that major forms of the past are no longer living. There used to be dinosaurs and *Pithecanthropus*, and there are none now. It is a *fact* that all living forms come from previous living forms. Therefore, all present forms of life arose from ancestral forms that were different. Birds arose from nonbirds and humans from nonhumans. No person who pretends to any understanding of the natural world can deny these facts any more than she or he can deny that the earth is round, rotates on its axis, and revolves round the sun.'

6   Joseph Hooker regarded Spencer's writing as 'noisy vacuity'. James Moore (1985:90) described it as 'the political economy of English middle-class dissent with an evolutionary twist'. Aubrey Moore (1889:60) comments on a 'reconciling' proposal by Spencer to recognise science as the product of reason and religion as the outcome of faith, that 'if anything in the world could make religion hate and fear science and oppose the advance of knowledge, it is to find itself compelled to sit still and watch the slow but sure filching of its territory by an alien power'.

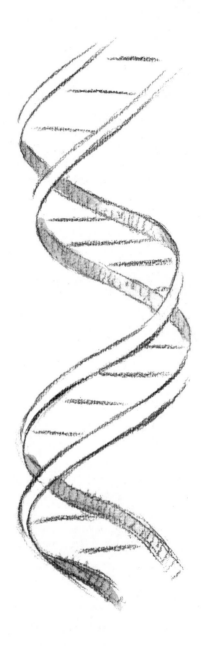

4
Theology of DNA

Darwin has a throwaway sentence near the end of *The Origin of Species*. He wrote 'In the future I see open fields for far more important researches ... Much light will be thrown on the origin of man and his history.' He was, of course, aware of the implications of 'dethroning' humanity from its assumed place as the pinnacle of creation, and deliberately sought to play down its importance in *The Origin*; he returned to the subject in depth twelve years later in *The Descent of Man*. His declared purpose was 'first, to show that [the human] species had not been separately created, and secondly, that natural selection had been the chief agent of change, though largely guided by the inherited effects of habit, and slightly by the direct action of the surrounding conditions' (Darwin, 1871:143). He was clear that 'there is no evidence that man was aboriginally endowed with the enabling belief in the existence of an Omnipotent God', although he rapidly qualified this by pointing that that 'the question is of course wholly distinct from that higher one, whether there exists a Creator and Ruler of the universe'. Notwithstanding, 'belief in unseen and spiritual agencies seems to be universal with the less civilised races'.

Darwin's friends and contemporaries had their own ideas about the nature of human-ness. The geologist Charles Lyell fought against the evidence of evolutionary change in his own work, because he was disturbed at the prospect that we would be 'degraded' through a link with animals. However, by the time that he wrote *The Antiquity of Man* (1863), he accepted the archaeological evidence for 'sub-humans' and had to face the prospect of human evolution. He admitted the plausibility of Darwin's conclusions, and was prepared to acknowledge a gradual evolutionary progress through history – something he had been arguing against for decades. Where he baulked was at the appearance of humans as a continuous development from their closest animal relatives; he believed that our distinctive qualities must have been produced by a sudden leap in organisation, taking life to a new and higher plane. Alfred Russel Wallace, co-discoverer with Darwin of natural selection, came to a similar conclusion (Kottler, 1985). It led him to assume that we possess a soul capable of existence independently of the body, and he became a spiritualist (or perhaps it was the other way round – that his spiritualist convictions produced his dualist beliefs). In his Bampton Lectures, Frederick Temple (1885) believed that the 'enormous gap' separating human from animal nature might be due to a 'spiritual faculty ... implanted by a direct creative act'.

There are thus two interlinked questions: are we what we are by the same evolutionary processes that produced slugs from snails and birds from reptiles, and is our 'religious sense' anything more than a rationalisation (or even, as Richard Dawkins has it, a viral infection)? In past decades these questions were explored by anthropologists, whose comparative methodology can never give an unequivocal answer. More recently molecular and reproductive biologists have unravelled the 'mystery' of life, and shown that it can be understood in fairly straightforward physico-chemical terms without the necessity of invoking divine intervention at the individual or (by implication) the species level.

It is here that gaps appear between those who investigate our origins, those who explore and worry about our relationships with other living beings, and those who believe we are divine and individual creations. Are we merely vehicles for selfish genes or do we have a responsibility for and a need of respect towards the world in which we live? The latter can be dressed up in philosophical or religious language: does it have any support from science other than the narrowly pragmatic one that we depend on our environment for food and survival? Thinkers as different as the deep ecologists (such as Arne Naess and Warwick Fox), the 'ecofeminists' (like Val Plumwood and Sally McFague), and religious writers (particularly Orthodox Bishop Paul Gregorios and Pope John Paul II) use arguments based on the characteristics and worth of 'life'. This becomes practically important when used to justify opposition to artificial methods of birth control. Once we divest 'life' of its mystical component, can we use it as a counter in moral argument? We need to examine the nature of humankind both as a general issue at the edge of science, and more particularly to clarify our relationship to the world about us. In some respects, this chapter is a digression from my response to Adam Gifford, but it is an essential base for understanding our place as human beings in the divine economy, and hence our proper role in relation to nature.

Genetics and Epigenetics

One of the commonest assumptions about human biology is that we are nothing more than the sum of our genes, or put another way, that we are imprisoned by our genes: that the blueprint laid down when our father's sperm fertilised our mother's ovum determines not only our sex and size and liability to disease, but also our desires, abilities and moral quirks. This is a gross over-exaggeration, owing more to Aldous Huxley and *Brave New World* (first published in 1932) than to the science of genetics, but it is very widespread. Although it is true that if two particular gametes (sperm and egg) had not fused nine months before I was born, I would not be here, it does not follow that the 'genetic code' of the 30,000 or so genes on the forty-six chromosomes of my body gives a complete or even adequate specification of me. There is both scientific and moral evidence for the falsity of this assumption.

The DNA of the chromosomes is 'translated' into sequences of amino acids (polypeptide chains), which in turn form proteins and enzymes. But the production of polypeptide chains is not an automatic process that goes on throughout life. Genes are subject to precise control or regulation, with many (indeed, most) being switched off most of the time. The genes in every cell in the body are affected by the history and environment of that cell, and the bulk of the chromosome set which is replicated and found in the nucleus of most body cells is inactive. Cells in which this control process breaks down are liable (if they survive) to be cancer-producing.

The development and functioning of a whole organism is even more complicated. Some of the proteins that are primary gene products are recognisable in a normal body; they turn up as enzymes controlling vital processes or antigens affecting particular immuno-logical reactions. But the primary products of most genes interact in the body to form secondary compounds, which are the real building-blocks for most growth and maintenance, hormones and so on. These interactions are highly complex and ordered; in no way can the human body be regarded as the inevitable consequence of a set of randomly assembled chemical specifications. Although virtually all our characters can be regarded as affected by genes, their inheri-tance and control should be described as epigenetic rather than genetic; in other words, they are the result of processes acting subsequently to the primary action of the genes themselves.

The primary gene products are the direct consequence of a rather simple chemical process worked out in the revolution of molecular biology begun in 1953 with the elucidation of the structure of DNA by James Watson and Francis Crick. At this level, inherited characters can truly be said to be determined by the genes carried by an individual. Once we leave the primary gene product level, however, the occurrence, speed and direction of the chemical processes in the body are affected to varying extents by environmental influences. This is of considerable importance in clinical medicine, because inherited defects in metabolism can often be corrected once they have been identified. For example, diabetes can be treated with insulin, haemophilia with anti-haemophilic globulin, and phenylketonuria and galactosaemia by withholding from the diet phenylalanine and galactose respectively. One of the aims of the Human Genome Project is to advance these possibilities. It is not true that genetic disease cannot be treated, as used to be believed.

The interaction of genes and environment applies throughout normal development. Prenatal growth is slowed if the mother smokes, and maternal drinking may reduce the intelligence and size of a baby at birth (foetal alcohol syndrome). Childhood growth can be affected by nutrition. Intelligence (as measured – inadequately – by IQ) is higher in first children, and higher in small families than in larger ones.

It is difficult fully to disentangle the details of interactions between genes and environment in humans, where experimental breeding and environmental control cannot be carried out. Comparison of the behaviour and achievements of identical and non-identical twins, and of adopted and natural children, can go some way to helping us understand these processes, but unchallenged conclusions are few, as the recurring debates about intelligence show. Criminality and sexual deviation have often been attributed either to family or to inherited influences, but the grounds for distinguishing between these tend to be equivocal. Notwithstanding, there can be no doubt at all that we are affected radically by our environments as well as by our genes.

The genetic control of behaviour has been much discussed in recent years. For my purpose, all that it is necessary to note is that very, very few behavioural traits are irrevocably determined by genes; virtually all human behaviour (and associated characteristics, like intelligence) can be unintentionally or consciously influenced by the environment. Although it is true that we can speak of behaviour as being inherited, it is equally true and perhaps more helpful to recognise that there is no one gene for any specific behaviour.

This is well shown by identical twins (that is, genetically identical individuals), who are often strikingly alike in both behaviour and physical traits even when reared apart, but may differ markedly in some characteristics. Genes cannot express themselves in a vacuum; even in cases where our genes predispose us towards certain characteristics (as a shallow hip-joint to congenital hip dislocation, or an extra Y chromosome to mindless aggression), there is no automatic association between a gene and the physical or behavioural trait that finally emerges.

There is also no simple relationship between a fertilised egg and survival to adult life. For every 100 eggs subject to normal internal fertilisation, 85 on average will be fertilised if intercourse is frequent, 69 implant, 42 are alive a week later, 37 at the sixth week of gestation, and 31 at birth. Between a third and a half of the foetuses that abort spontaneously in the first few weeks of pregnancy (that is, with no human intervention) have an abnormal chromosomal complement; 97 per cent of foetuses with a single sex chromosome (Turner's syndrome) and 65–70 per cent of those with Down syndrome miscarry by the eighteenth week. It seems likely that a large proportion of embryos with anomalies of the central nervous system (anencephaly, spina bifida and so on) are spontaneously aborted. Survival to birth is not the norm; it occurs in only a minority of conceptuses, and many of those eliminated are recognisably abnormal in their genetic complement.

When we consider together interactions between different genes, and interactions between genes and the environment, it is obvious that we are determined by our genes only in a very loose sense. Some of the differences between us result from different genetic complements, but these differences can be magnified or shrunk by family, social, educational, cultural or other environmental influences. Even people with a hereditary make-up that irrevocably fixes a particular trait – such as those with Down syndrome – nevertheless show a wide range of behavioural responses (in the case of a Down syndrome individual, from gross mental defect to near normality).

Clearly there is a sense in which we must be regarded as the sum of the genes we acquire at conception, but in another sense we are considerably more than that sum. Just as the wetness of water cannot be predicted from the atomic properties of its constituent hydrogen and oxygen, so human beings cannot adequately be described by their genes, even if we knew the details of all the DNA of an individual.

Genes and Morals

Moralists traditionally argue that ethical decisions cannot be controlled by genes. One reason for this is that positive virtues might hinder their possessors in the struggle for existence. Charles Darwin himself spelled out the problem in *The Descent of Man* (1871):

> It is extremely doubtful whether the offspring of the more sympathetic and benevolent parents, or of those who were the most faithful to their comrades, would be reared in greater numbers than the children of selfish and treacherous parents belonging to the same tribe. He who was ready to sacrifice his life, as many a savage has been, rather than betray his comrades, would often leave no offspring to inherit his noble nature. The bravest men, who were always willing to come to the front in war, and who freely risked their lives for others, would on average perish in larger numbers than other men. Therefore it hardly seems probable that the number of men gifted with such virtues, or the standard of their excellence, could be increased through natural selection, that is, by the survival of the fittest.

Half a century later, J. B. S. Haldane (1932) qualified this, pointing out that if the unselfishness (even to the point of self-sacrifice) of an individual had an inherited basis and helped near relatives, then 'altruistic genes' could be selected in families; there could be situations where cooperation (that is, unselfishness) is an advantage to a group of relatives, even if particular individuals were disadvantaged. Haldane's argument was formalised in 1964 by W. D. Hamilton as the concept of 'inclusive fitness' or (as it has since become known) 'kin selection'; it is now assimilated into general biology as the mechanism underlying 'sociobiology'.

The 1950s and 1960s saw much interest in biology and behaviour, shown in popular writings by Konrad Lorenz, Niko Tinbergen, Vero Wynne-Edwards, Robert Ardrey and Desmond Morris, and later expressed in such television series as David Attenborough's *Life on Earth* (1979). The word 'sociobiology' entered common parlance with the publication of a book with that name by Edward Wilson (1975), a distinguished entomologist who had spent many years studying social insects (such as ants, termites and bees). In his book, Wilson ranged widely through the animal kingdom, concluding with a chapter entitled 'Man: from Sociobiology to Sociology', in which he extrapolated conclusions about genes and behaviour from (mainly) invertebrates to human beings. He later expanded this chapter into a book called *On Human Nature* (1978). In this, Wilson expounded sociobiology as providing a biological underpinning for all the human sciences: 'Biology is the key to human nature, and social scientists cannot afford to ignore its rapidly tightening principles'[1] (for the response to this by philosophers, see Camilo Cela-Conde and Gisele Marty, and Nancey Murphy, in Russell, Stoeger and Ayala, 1998:446–62, 463–89).

Wilson has been attacked by both sociologists and socialists, who see his ideas as contrary to their dreams of improving society by manipulating the environment.[2] We are not concerned with these here; they are driven more by political conceptions and correctness than by science. What we are concerned with is the attempt to portray sociobiology as a complete and satisfactory basis for ethics. The Australian philosopher Peter Singer has written:

> 'Sociobiology ... enables us to see ethics as a mode of human reasoning which develops in a group context ... so ethics loses its air of mystery. Its principles are not laws written up in Heaven. Nor are they absolute truths about the universe, known by intuition. The principles of ethics come from our own nature as social reasoning beings. (Singer, 1981:49)

It must be emphasised that this statement has no support from science. Our behaviour is affected by our genes but is certainly not controlled by them. The argument is too often heard that a person cannot be held responsible for some action because of his or her inherited disposition – towards alcohol, academic work, homosexual acts or even traits such as punctuality or tidiness. When a high proportion of tall men committed to institutions for the criminal insane on account of their aggressiveness were found to have an extra Y chromosome (that is, to be XYY instead of the normal XY), their disability was hailed as proving the inheritance of original sin – until other XYY men were found living perfectly normal lives in the community. This illustrates the general point that behaviour is the result of interaction between a flexible reacting substrate (the genome) and a complex of environmental components. There is no such thing as a behavioural gene; and among the environmental factors that interact with the genes are all the constraints regulating society.

It is pertinent here to quote the apostle Paul. He was well aware of the tensions producing immorality: 'What I do is not the good I want to do; no, the evil I do not want to do – this I keep on doing' (Romans 7.19). His distinction between temptation and sin (e.g. 1 Corinthians 10.13 ['So far you have faced no trial beyond human endurance; God keeps faith and will not let you be tested beyond your powers, but when the test comes he will at the same time provide a way out and so enable you to endure.']) may perhaps be taken as describing much temptation as the consequence of inherited disposition. Although not the main point here, it is worth noting that different people have different problems, some of which may need medical correction (e.g. depression or schizophrenia), but yielding to these problems is still moral weakness, whatever its underlying cause.

Genes, Character and Talents

Genetic orientation reduces neither moral responsibility nor culpability, but we all know that genes influence our talents and characters. This was notoriously described by Francis Galton (1822–1911), Charles Darwin's cousin. Galton took from contemporary encyclopaedias details about leading jurists, statesmen, military commanders, scientists, poets, painters and musicians. He found that a disproportionately high proportion of those in each category were blood relatives, and concluded that 'families of reputation' were much more likely to produce offspring of ability than average families. He documented this in his *Hereditary Genius* (1869). It convinced him that it would be 'quite practicable to produce a highly gifted race of men by judicious marriages during several consecutive generations'. He believed that talent was rarely damaged by social disadvantages, because men of achievement frequently came from humble families; conversely removal of disadvantage does not produce talent by itself. He wrote: 'Culture is far more widely spread in America than with us [in Britain], and the education of their middle and lower classes far more advanced; but for all that, America most certainly does not beat us in first-class works of literature, philosophy or art.'

Such considerations led Galton to propose the importance of 'eugenics', the encouragement of breeding for good traits and selecting against deleterious ones. The sorry history of eugenics, particularly when linked to Herbert Spencer's 'Social Darwinism' (p. 57) and the perversions of a pantheon of racialists, is outside this discussion, although it is relevant as indicating the dangers of building too much upon an incomplete understanding of science. For example, talk about 'inferior races' is nonsense: there are greater genetic differences between individuals than between races. From the present perspective, the problem is that inherited characteristics and human reproduction are combined and confused in popular understanding (Gould, 1981; Kevles, 1985). The unravelling of the genetic code and the possibilities of genetic manipulation have put genetics (and geneticists) on the hit list of many ethicists and sociologists (never mind some theologians).

The Nature of Human-ness

Can we make any positive affirmations about the nature and worth of individual human life? Biology is not particularly helpful. There is general agreement that the human line diverged from its origin in Africa, and spread widely through Eurasia, with at least one offshoot, the Neanderthals, becoming extinct. The change from ape to human involved a degree of neoteny: that is, retardation in the rate of sexual maturation, so that juvenile features persist into adulthood, giving us the flat face of modern humans (as distinct from the prognathous ape one) and, more importantly, allowing brain size to increase after birth because the skull bones are slow to ossify. There were other changes which have nothing to do with neoteny: for example, the skeletal alterations which gave rise to bipedalism. Nevertheless, we are genetically very close to the great apes. Our DNA (or genetic code) is only 1.6 per cent different to that of the chimpanzees, and 2.3 per cent different to that of the gorilla. The two chimpanzee species (common and pygmy) differ from each other by only 0.7 per cent of the total. Jared Diamond (1991) has pointed out that on strict criteria of genetic relatedness, we ought to be classified as a third species of chimpanzee.

Diamond hastens to note that no one seriously suggests we should be regarded as 'nothing but' (p. 23) chimpanzees. He identifies the key difference between us and the chimpanzees as the ability to communicate in a spoken language with a large vocabulary, as opposed to that of the apes who are apparently incapable of uttering some of the commonest human vowel sounds. For Diamond, the significant step towards human-ness:

> seems to involve the structure of the larynx, tongue and associated muscles that give us fine control over spoken sounds ... The missing ingredient [which prevented the chimps developing more complex speech] may have been some modification of the proto-human vocal tract to give us finer control and permit formation of a much greater variety of sounds. (Diamond, 1991:47)

Such detailed adjustments would almost certainly not be detectable in fossil skulls.

Other workers agree. Although many criteria have been proposed for the significant feature(s) of human-ness – bipedalism, opposable thumbs, tool-making, learning ability, abstract thought, play, artistic sense – all have fallen to our increasing knowledge of animal life and behaviour. From comparative psychology, two things stand out. The first concerns language. In their different ways, Robert Hinde and William Thorpe have both identified this as one of the crucial distinguishing features of human-ness. Writing on 'Animal–Human Comparisons' in *The Oxford Companion to the Mind* (1987), Hinde concluded that the main human characteristic is the complexity of language. He argued that animal communication falls so far short of human language that the difference is best seen as one of *quality* rather than *quantity*. Coming at the same issue from the point of view of a neuropsychologist and a comparative anatomist respectively, both George Ettlinger and Richard Passingham conclude that it is aspects of language such as 'the ability to represent information *within* an individual's mind' (Ettlinger, 1984) and 'our ability to represent words to ourselves; to manipulate internal systems' (Passingham, 1982) that are the basis of the crucial difference between humans and non-human primates.

Perhaps the most detailed analysis of human–animal difference(s) in recent years has been that of W. H. Thorpe (1974) in his 1971–2 St Andrews Gifford Lectures. He agrees with Diamond about the anatomical problems of the great apes, stating 'I believe it is safe to conclude that if chimpanzees had the necessary equipment in the larynx and pharynx, they could learn to talk, at least as well as children of three years of age and perhaps older' (Thorpe, 1974:298). He accepted that there is no single attribute that can be unequivocally identified as unique to the human species, but there is such a tremendous chasm – intellectual, artistic, technical, moral, ethical and spiritual – 'there comes a point where "more" creates a "difference"' (1974:301).

Two questions immediately arise about our differences from the apes:

1. Given that there is a rather small amount of genetic distinction between the chimpanzees and us, can we regard the genes carried by our distinguishing DNA as contributing all the characteristics of human-ness? Is the 1 per cent or so of our apparently unique genetic content the equivalent of the medieval assumption of the 'soul' that was supposed to reside in the pineal gland? If we sequenced the code in this human section of DNA (which would in principle be relatively easy), would we have the essence of human-ness and the means of creating humans by injecting this genetic element into the genome of an ape?

   The unequivocal answer is 'no'. Although our genes can be described as a blueprint of our inherited characteristics, the translation of blueprint to body requires a four-dimensional building of materials into a whole, as we have seen. It is just as foolish to equate a length of DNA with human-ness as the old sermon illustration that we are simply 65% oxygen, 18% carbon, 10% hydrogen, 3% nitrogen, 1.5% calcium and 1% phosphorus; that does not mean that we can build or calculate the worth of a human being merely from our constituent chemicals. Human-ness does not reside in genes – or any other aspect of biology. It is not sufficient to argue that we would not exist without our genes and the body they produce; our genes are *necessary* for us, but they are not *sufficient.*

2. Can consciousness emerge from simple physico-chemical reactions, or as the question is commonly asked, can a brain (or super-computer) in which all the contributing (neural) actions are describable think? The answer to this seems to be 'yes'. Donald MacKay argued this point at length in his 1986 Gifford Lectures (published as *Behind the Eye* [1991]). Although there are still occasional advocates for a dualism to explain a 'ghost in the machine', the consensus among neurologists and psychologists is that this is unnecessary (Jeeves, 1994:106). Malcolm Jeeves has summarised the conclusions of Nobel Prize winner Roger Sperry (Sperry, 1990):

a. Consciousness is a dynamic emergent property of brain activity, neither identical with nor reducible to, the neural events of which it is mainly composed;

b. Consciousness exerts 'potent causal effects in the interplay of cerebral operations';

c. At the highest levels in the hierarchy of brain organisation, subjective properties exert control over the biophysical and chemical activities at subordinate levels;

d. Conscious phenomena are not 'nothing but' neural events;

e. The relationship between body and brain is not best described as an 'interaction'.

These conclusions are important in discussions about whether we can be regarded wholly as the result of 'blind' and random evolutionary forces. Richard Dawkins has elegantly shown that adaptation through natural selection produces consequences 'purpose-built' for a particular environment. 'Natural' processes may produce a far more complicated result than the simple contingency of an apparently fortuitous evolutionary history.

Does this help in deciding whether we are 'nothing but' apes? John Polkinghorne (1986:92) points out that for a thorough-going reductionist the answer is easy, since 'mind is the epiphenomenon of brain, a mere symptom of the physical activity . . .' The trouble is that 'the reductionist programme in the end subverts itself. Ultimately it is suicidal. If our mental life is nothing but the humming activity of an immensely complexly connected computer-like brain, who is to say whether the programme running on the intricate machine is correct or not?' J. B. S. Haldane was equally scathing when he considered his own consciousness (p. 24).

We have already seen that experimental reductionism is a necessary strategy in science, but that it has to be distinguished from ontological reductionism which assumes that a system is 'nothing but' the sum of its parts (p. 23). The key is in the two words 'nothing but': we need repeatedly to emphasise that there is a logical distinction between mechanical and teleological causation, and that there is no necessary problem for an event having more than one cause. As far as humans are concerned, there is no reason to expect that ethical behaviour would arise from our evolutionary past, but equally no reason to dissent that our ethical concerns may result from factors operating in our history. Ayala (1998) has argued that the emergence of ethical behaviour can be regarded as equivalent to the emergence of language, not as a primarily selected trait (in the way that animals may be selected for camouflage as a protection against predators), but as an incidental result of other genetical changes. Such correlated or pleiotropic characters are common in evolution. Ayala suggests that the biological basis of ethical behaviour depends on three reasonable conditions:

1. the ability to anticipate the consequences of one's own actions;
2. the ability to make value judgements, i.e. to recognise the connection between means and ends;
3. the ability to choose between different causes of action.

Ayala distances his own analysis from other attempts to find the grounds of morality in biological evolution. He regards Spencer (1893), Huxley (1953) and Waddington (1960) as falling into the naturalistic fallacy, since they use as their criterion for good or evil the contribution particular actions may make to evolutionary progress, which in turn is determined by value judgements about what is progress (Gould, 1996). It is not clear why the promotion of evolutionary change by itself should be the standard to measure what is morally good, a point made on a number of occasions by Richard Dawkins.

The attempt by Edward Wilson (and the sociobiologists he has inspired) to 'biologicise' ethics differs from that of the evolutionary 'progressionists', because it is based on the premise that altruistic (i.e. ethical) behaviour is directly selected under specifiable conditions, so that altruists leave more offspring than non-altruists; in other words, that reproductive success is a direct consequence of moral choice.

This is intuitively unappealing, but worse since it confuses ethics with biological strategies which could include euthanasia, racism, genocide, homophobia, and so on. It recalls the suggestion by Jonathan Swift (1667–1715) in his satire *A Modest Proposal* that killing and eating babies is a sensible practice in a time of famine. Horrific as this may sound, it reflects what has been accepted in some communities, including the Inuit, Australian Aborigines and the city states of Ancient Greece, since the survival of the parents' other descendants becomes more likely. The point is that it is not a species-specific behaviour, because only a few human groups have resorted to it.[3] The historical trend has been to accept some form of the commandment, 'Thou shalt not kill'. The link between biology and morality is not a matter of mechanism or reproductive calculations; ethics cannot be automatically or easily 'biologicised'.

Imago Dei

The overall conclusion from the preceding discussion is that it is insufficient to describe us as 'nothing but' our genes, whether they be selfish or unselfish. Religions tend to describe the necessary added dimension as the soul. Although this has been (and often still is) regarded as a separate and detachable element of the body, the Bible's understanding is of God's image, impressed in some way on our biological components; it is that which separates us from other animals. We do not *bear* or *have* an image; we *are* the image of God, created by God (Genesis 1.26–8). Theologians interpret this as meaning that we are to mirror and represent God, so the essence is of relationship, not substance (reviewed Theissen, 1987; Jeeves and Berry, 1998). C. F. D. Moule (1964) concluded: 'The most satisfying of the many interpretations, both ancient and modern of the image of God in man is that which sees it as basically responsibility (Ecclus 17:1–45 ["The Lord created human beings from the earth and to it he returns them again. He set a fixed span of life for mortals and gave them authority over everything on earth. He clothed them with power like his own and made them in his own image. He put the fear of them into all creatures and granted them lordship over beasts and birds"])' H. D. MacDonald (1981) goes one stage further: 'image should be taken as indicating "sonship" which holds together both the ontological and relational aspects of the image'.

How does God's image affect us? I turn again to W. H. Thorpe, as one of the most distinguished students of animal behaviour. He refers to the six levels of mental activity described by Hobhouse

(1913), of which four can be discerned in animals, while the remaining two Hobhouse regarded as characteristic of humans.[6] Hobhouse called these two 'the correlation of universals' and 'the correlation of governing principles'. They involve a recognition of abstract moral law or, in Thorpe's words, 'eternal values which are in themselves good'. He qualifies this by saying that:

> of course we can find in the higher social animals, such as wolves, behaviour which appears altruistic, unselfish, indeed 'moral'. Nevertheless I believe at this level we can see a difference between the minds of humans and of present-day animals, and that in Hobhouse's last two categories we have reached a distinction which we can for the time being at least regard as fundamental (Thorpe, 1961).

Genetic Engineering

The recurring theme of the examination of 'life' (including human life) in this chapter is that DNA is neither sacred nor determinative of the characteristics of life. This leads us to practical questions. As we have moved from the human as an ape (perhaps a third chimpanzee species) to a being made 'in the image of God' – what we can call *Homo divinus* (p. 228), we need to consider our relation and responsibility to other living creatures. Is it legitimate or immoral (perhaps even sinful) to seek to change living nature?

The first point to make is that domestication of both animals and plants has been going on for millennia, and that this involves intense genetic selection and change. Although some domesticates are distorted or distressed (the commonest targets of criticism are tame dogs and poultry) and concentration on a few favoured varieties reduces the natural genetic diversity in particular crop species, most argument has been directed against the legitimacy of using molecular techniques to introduce or remove particular genes into or from commercially valuable plants or animals. Some of the debates about this are misinformed. For example, species are not separated from each other by an impenetrable barrier to 'foreign genes'. Genes may be 'naturally' transferred from one species to another by cross-breeding and introgression, or by straightforward infection attached to a bacterial or viral vector. The extent of these processes varies between groups and there is as yet no way to determine how important they are. Again, as we have seen for the great apes and human beings, different species may share a high proportion of their genetic constitution. We have 80 per cent of our genes in common with rats, and 50 per cent with bananas. Although it may be possible to state that a particular gene product (usually a protein) is from (say) a cow or a mouse, this statement is usually based on fairly small chemical differences.

Secondly, the most heated debates tend to be about the 'risks' of particular procedures. Clearly there are practical issues of containment, but these are primarily pragmatic issues. In 1974, in the early years of work with 'recombinant DNA' (i.e. DNA with new sequences introduced using enzymes which cut DNA strands in particular places and thus allow the insertion of novel sequences), all research was suspended by worldwide agreement among scientists until the hazards could be evaluated (the Berg moratorium), but was restarted within a couple of years when the relevant scientific and safety bodies were satisfied than an acceptable regulatory framework was in place.

In Britain this involved the establishment of a Genetical Management Advisory Group (GMAG) under the auspices of the Health and Safety Executive. The Royal Commission on Environmental Pollution devoted its Thirteenth Report (1989) to the 'Release of Genetically Engineered Organisms to the Environment'. It concluded that most genetically engineered organisms are likely to be no more harmful than plants and animals bred by traditional or widely used techniques. Some, however, might pose significant risks either as 'super-weeds' (aggressively replacing naturally occurring forms) or by acting as a source for 'dangerous' genes (i.e. ones conferring resistance – or susceptibility – on existing predators or pathogens). Notwithstanding, the Commission saw 'no justification on environmental grounds for a ban or moratorium on releases', although these should only be permitted under strict supervision and formal permission. In other words, the Royal Commission took the same view as the previous review, that genetical engineering was a technique to be used with care, not an illegitimate interference with 'nature' nor, by implication, an immoral involvement with a divine prerogative (although official committees do not use that sort of language).

Such an approach is wholly in accord with the understanding set out in this chapter. Genes are a key part of natural life, but in no way can – or should – they be regarded as sacrosanct or untouchable. The genetic composition of organisms changes in individual lives as well as in evolutionary time: most cancers and ageing are the results of genetic changes, and new genes can be incorporated by infection. This does not mean that genetic manipulation can be unrestricted. Genetic change is likely to be detrimental, as is any random change in a functioning mechanism; it may introduce unanticipated effects. Some manipulations may be better outlawed unless or until we can better control them, but this does not make them intrinsically immoral.

This is an important conclusion, because it places a clear responsibility on fallible humans, rather than facing us with an impenetrable *deus ex machina*. Our dilemma is not unlike that experienced by Bishop Wilberforce in the Oxford Museum in 1860. His reaction when faced with inexorable change was to deny its possibility. Our problem is how to handle change for good rather than ill.

There is, unsurprisingly, a plethora of Wilberforcean-type arguments against any form of genetic manipulation. Michael Reiss and Roger Straughan comment:

> many religious believers reject genetic engineering not because of concerns specific to the moral status of animals,[7] but simply because it clashes with their understanding of God's action in the world ... someone who believes in the literal creation of the universe in six days is presumably less likely to support genetic engineering than someone, whether religious, agnostic or atheistic, who accepts the theory of evolution. (Reiss and Straughan, 1996:87)

Notwithstanding, the most frequent response of religious writers is caution or hesitancy. Whilst this is reasonable, we also need to be theologically positive. Phil Challis has commented:

> We are co-creators with God, 'fearfully and wonderfully made' (Psalm 139:14). With our finite freedom we are called by Him to act responsibly as we continue the process of genetic manipulation of domestic organisms. A theology that emphasises embodiment rather than body–spirit dichotomy, that emphasises becoming rather than immutability as an essential part of God's nature, that emphasises relationship within the web rather than domination from outside the system, such a Christian theology may provide a critical framework that can realistically embrace the potential of genetic engineering for good. (cited by Reiss and Straughan, 1996:88)

Perhaps we should link genetical engineering with a theological imperative to attack imperfections in the natural world, including those in humans. Some see this as the thin edge of a eugenic wedge, but the key is surely to do good rather than simply accepting evil. The accusation that genetical engineering is 'playing God' is an objection widely expressed by many who have no belief at all in a divine plan. If the emphasis is to outlaw 'playing', well and good, but as Jonathan Glover has pointed out from the perspective of a philosopher:

> The prohibition on playing God is obscure. If it tells us not to interfere with natural selection at all, this rules out medicine, and most other

environmental and social changes. If it only forbids interference with natural selection by the direct alteration of genes, this rules out negative as well as positive genetic engineering. If these interpretations are too restrictive, the ban on positive engineering seems to need some explanation. If we can make positive changes at the environmental level, and negative changes at the genetic level, why should we not make positive changes at the genetic level? What makes this policy, but not the others, objectionably God-like? Perhaps the most plausible reply to these questions rests on a general objection to any group of people trying to plan too closely what human life should be like. (Glover, 1984:46)

Reiss and Straughan conclude

it is difficult to maintain fundamental theological objections to all aspects of genetic engineering *per se*. The notion that in some sense to be human, some would say to exist in the image of God, is to be called to participate responsibly in the ongoing work of creation, is a persuasive one, though not to be undertaken lightly. (Reiss and Straughan, 1996:89)

Can we divide natural theology into the positive (taking responsibility) and the negative (accepting or discovering God in nature)? I rather think Adam Gifford would like the distinction.

NOTES

1   In a later book, *Consilience* (1998), Wilson divides humans into 'transcendentalists' and 'empiricists'. He writes, 'The choice between transcendentalism and empiricism will be the coming century's version of the struggle for men's souls. Moral reasoning will either remain centred in idioms of theology and philosophy, where it is now, or it will shift toward science-based material analysis' (p. 240). Wilson suggests that the distinction between these types will be resolved 'by the continuance of biological studies of complex human behaviour' (p. 246). He is certainly right to claim that 'if empiricism is disproved and transcendentalism is compellingly upheld, the discovery would be quite simply the most consequential in human history. That is the burden laid upon biology as it draws close to the humanities' (p. 258).

2   For example, the 'social ecologist' Murray Bookchin (1994:52): 'The work of Wilson and his collaborators, some of whose views approximate pure fascism, must be singled out as a new attempt to give the interface between biology and society the halo of a scientific authority that defies mere theorising and speculation. We are no longer dealing here with the Ionian philosophers, Parmenides' and Heraklitos' 'Dike', Plato's *Demiurgus*, Aristotle's tour de force in the *Physics* and the *scala natura*, Demokritos, Epikurus, the Stoics, or for that matter, with Bruno, Leibnitz, Hegel,

Kropotkin, Bergson, and the like ... The opening chapter of Wilson's *Sociobiology* is titled "Morality of the Gene" – and it is the book's reductionist and ugly ethos viewed as a key to society and human behavior, that must never be permitted to elude us.'

3   This highlights the problem of extrapolating from animals to humans (Barnett, 1988). One animal species may be quite peaceful, another sometimes dangerously violent; but, in either case, all social interactions are typical of the species and depend on standard signals. No species, except our own, has a code of morals or of laws based on what is held to be right or socially necessary; nor do neighbouring animal populations differ widely, or debate what code is best. Ayala stresses the distinction that should be made between ethical *behaviour* (which can be regarded as biologically based) and ethical *norms*, which can be described as culturally derived, but are only loosely related to biology. (Culture is part of our environment, and therefore affects our breeding behaviour and success.)

4   Hobhouse (1913: ch. 5) regarded the key property of 'mind' (which he interpreted as incorporating both neural process and consciousness) as the ability to coordinate or correlate different functions. He saw behaviour as produced by heredity, adaptation to environmental conditions, and experience. Experience could change behaviour as the result of:
1. a modified susceptibility to stimuli (such as hunger);
2. acclimation;
3. reactions to objects (including acquiring skills and habits);
4. development of ideas ('articulate correlation').
The next two levels which impressed Thorpe were the ability to correlate universals (i.e. the ability to analyse and synthesise) and 'the correlation of the principles underlying the activity of correlation itself' – in which 'experience is organised into bodies of thought and action subordinated to wide and permanent ends' both personal and social.

5   Andrew Linzey (1990:180) argues that genetical engineering is a form of slavery: 'genetic engineering represents the concretisation of the absolute claim that animals belong to us and exist for us. We have always used animals, of course, either for food, fashion or sport. It is not new that we are now using animals for farming, even in especially cruel ways. What is new is that we are now implying the technological means of absolutely subjugating the nature of animals so that they become totally and completely human property.'

5
Green Religion

For some, Judeo-Christianity cannot form a viable basis for either a stable environment or a caring environmentalism, because it is too closely associated with a pietism that isolates and thus emancipates us from fluctuations in our surroundings, and then unleashes the tyrannies of technology. Nature, such critics argue, is found in identification with it, in the protection of life rather than its manipulation.

Dominion and Devastation

We have seen in Chapter 3 how the world (or nature, or the environment) changed from being accepted and treated as a divine creation to being regarded as a 'thing', subject to misuse and valued only for its productivity. Recent commentators have interpreted this 'dedivinisation' of creation as the inevitable expression of Judeo-Christianity and condemned Jews and Christians for all they see wrong in the world. In the essay already quoted (p. 38), Lynn White wrote, 'We are superior to nature, contemptuous of it, willing to use it for our slightest whim ... We shall continue to have a worsening ecological crisis until we reject the Christian axiom that nature has no reason for existence but to serve man' (White, 1967). Ian McHarg believes that the Genesis story

> in its insistence upon dominion and subjugation of nature, encourages the most exploitative and destructive instincts in man, rather than those that are deferential and creative. Indeed, if one seeks licence for those who would increase radioactivity, create harbours and canals with atom bombs, employ poisons without constraint, or give consent to the bulldozer mentality, there could be no better justification than this text ['God blessed them and said to them, "Be fruitful and increase, fill the earth and *subdue it, have dominion* over the fish in the sea, the birds of the air, and every living thing that moves on the earth"' Genesis 1.28]. When this is understood the conquests, the depredation and the despoliation are comprehensible ... Dominion and subjugation must be expunged as the biblical injunction of man's relation to nature. (McHarg, 1969:26)

For pioneer conservationist Max Nicholson:

> the first step must be plainly to reject and to scrub out the complacent image of Man the Conqueror of Nature, and of Man Licensed by God to conduct himself as the earth's worst pest. An intensive spell of environmental repentance is called for ... The core of the cultural complex disseminating and maintaining errors of attitude and practice on these matters has been organised religion. (Nicholson, 1970:264)

Poet Laureate Ted Hughes was appalled by Nicholson's diagnosis: 'The subtly apotheosised misogyny of Reformed Christianity is proportionate to the fanatic rejection of Nature, and the result has been to exile man from Mother Nature' (Hughes, 1994:129).

There are two answers to these accusations, one defensive, one positive.

The defensive response is that the critics have misunderstood Bible teaching. The command to have dominion and subdue the Earth was given by God in the context of beings *made in his image*. It was not a licence for unfettered exploitation, but an obligation to look after God's work responsibly on his behalf (Hall, 1986; Reichenbach and Anderson, 1995). Our role is to act as God's stewards, not to behave as children given toys for play (cf. the proper attitude to genetic engineering, p. 79). The word translated 'dominion' implies rule, but the Israelite ideal of kingship was of a servant king (like David, or Jesus himself), not oriental despotism. The Hebrew understanding was of a ruler totally responsible for his subject's welfare – caring, feeding, protecting (e.g. Psalm 72.1–2 ['God, endow the king with your own justice, his royal person with your righteousness, that he may govern your people rightly and deal justly with your oppressed ones']):

> As Lord of his realm, the king is responsible not only for the nation; he is the one who bears and mediates blessings for the realm entrusted to him. Man would fail in his royal office of dominion over the earth were he to exploit the world's resources to the detriment of the land, plant life, animals, rivers and seas. (Westermann, 1971:52)

Christ came to serve (Matthew 20.28 ['The Son of Man did not come to be served but to serve, and to give his life as a ransom for many']; Philippians 2.6–7 ['He [Jesus Christ] was in the form of God, yet he laid no claim to equality with God but made himself nothing, taking on the form of a slave']); human dominion equates with responsible authority.

This is not to deny that generations of Christians have interpreted the Genesis commands as almost mandating an exploitative and totalitarian dualism. The seventeenth-century Puritans who fled to New England saw themselves as entering a Promised Land, which had to be cleansed and tamed in the same way that God commanded the Israelites to subdue the wilderness of Israel. They were frightened by the great forests; early settlers wrote how wonderful it was to remove enough trees to see the stars or, even better, to see a neighbour and know that you were not alone (Lillard, 1947). The distortion gave birth to a heroic archetype, opening new lands to settlement through his courage, skill and derring-do. The frontiersman and his surrogates, the mountain man, the cowboy, the logger, the flatboat man, came to represent in an exaggerated way valuable and desirable characteristics (Golley, 1993*b*).

Historian Donald Worster has described the seductive power of this myth:

> The key American environmental idea, and at once the most destructive and most creative, the most complacent and most radical, is the one that ironically has about it an aura of wonderful innocence. America, we have believed, is literally the Garden of Eden restored. It is the paradise once lost but now happily regained. In Judeo-Christian mythology the first humans, Adam and Eve, discovering evil after yielding to the Devil's temptation had to be kicked out of the Garden on their nearly naked bums. But *mirabile dictu*, Americans of the eighteenth century found a way to sneak back into the garden. A band of their ancestors had made their way to the New World and there rediscovered it, with the gate standing wide open, undefended. What a blessed people. They brought along with them some Africans in chains to help enjoy the place, and by and by they let in a few others from Asia, but mainly it was a fortunate band of white Europeans that destiny allowed to re-enter and repossess the long-lost paradise. No other people in the world have ever believed, as Americans have, that they are actually living in Eden. (Worster, 1993:9)

And lest Europeans become too smug, Robin Grove-White has given an essentially similar picture of the European way of viewing the world, albeit in a sort of mirror reversal:

> Particular industrial societies like ours have become progressively more locked into a vast range of commitments, which have developed over decades and which are economic, industrial, infrastructural, geopolitical, technological and social. These have been underpinned by, and work to reinforce, a dualistic picture of man and nature. Most of the commitments (to individual motorised mobility, to ever higher levels of energy use, to social, moral and cultural norms encouraging increasing levels of material consumption) have tended to be producer-led. They have been entered into without prior analysis of their cumulative potential impact. They are

commitments which help define and shape our collective social and political identities ... The disclosure of 'environmental' problems, expressed in terms of the same man–nature dualism as industrialism itself, is one key manifestation of this ... The sense of unease experienced by those who argue with energy or traffic forecasts, or about regulatory myopia or scientific uncertainties, is social and moral, quite as much as physical.

It is now widespread – as the escalating memberships of NGOs and the unpredictable ebb and flow of green politics, suggests. It arises from a particular, unprecedented set of historical contingencies, in which new configurations of technology and capital, linked to bureaucratic and corporate power, can be seen as presenting societies with a Faustian bargain – goods and 'welfare', in exchange for subtle (and not so subtle) manipulations of man's self-understanding and moral identity. Perhaps the most corrosive dimension of this bargain is the escalating encroachment into sensitive moral and human territory concerning life itself – witness the intensifying conflicts over biotechnologies. (Grove-White, 1992:26–9)

Grove-White's solution is a radical revision of the widespread dualism he identifies, giving a new theological understanding of the human person and his or her needs.

However, there is a positive side to the diagnoses of McHarg, White, and the like: all the critics agree that a necessary key to both past and future is a right attitude to nature. For example, McHarg has written:

In the history of human development, man has long been puny in the face of overwhelmingly powerful nature. His religions, philosophies, ethics and acts have tended to reflect a slave mentality, alternatively submissive or arrogant towards nature. Judaism, Christianity, Humanism tend to assert outrageously the separateness and dominance of man over nature ... these same attitudes become of first importance when man holds the power to cause evolutionary regressions of unimaginable effect or even to destroy all life.

Lynn White is explicit: 'Since the roots of our trouble are so largely religious, the remedy must be essentially religious, whether we call it that or not ... What we do about nature depends on our ideas of the man–nature relationship.'

Even more compelling is the 'confession' of American philosopher Max Oeschlaeger that he had been led astray by White's 1967 essay, into believing that religion is the primary cause of the ecological crisis. He says his confidence was destroyed by 'the demystification of two ecological problems – climate heating and the extinction of species' and the realisation that it was not religion *per se* that causes ecological problems, but us:

> it is primarily our philosophies, economies and governments that motivate and direct the devastating onslaught against the earth. The pervasive idea that there are 'green saviours,' who occupy the environmental high ground and 'evil exploiters' who are rapaciously abusing nature is not useful ... Creating a binary opposition between 'good guys' who protect nature and 'bad guys' who destroy it assigns blame to some groups and excuses others ... Environmentalists like myself can be sanctimonious. People who portray themselves as nature's champions and corporations as evil villains are not always contributing positively to efforts that lead the way beyond ecocrisis .... (Oeschlaeger, 1994:3)

In practice Islam seems to have been no better than Judaism or Christianity. The Qur'ān teaches like the Bible that we are stewards or trustees (*khalifa*) answerable to God:

> He is the One who made
> you inheritors of the earth:
> Subsequently, whoever chooses to disbelieve
> does so to his own detriment.
> The disbelief of the disbelievers
> only augments their Lord's abhorrence towards them.
> (Qur'ān, 35.39)

The *khalifa* is to help in sustaining, not destroying the 'due balance' put in place by Allah to enable all creatures to support one another in an interdependent way. Serageldin (1991:62) notes 'God's grace is conditioned on the proper execution of stewardship', but adds, 'the concept of "stewardship of the earth" ... is curiously under-represented in the scholastic tradition of Islamic theology, although references are plentiful in the Qur'ān'. Commentators have pointed out the earth is only a temporary home for Muslims, and it is God who orders and wills; the environment is merely the platform for God's work (Forward and Alam, 1994; Timm, 1994). This removes any urgency from creation care. But the same considerations apply to Christians.

Religion can legitimately be blamed for some of our environmental problems, but it may be doing no more than serving as a whipping horse for the factors that determine our attitudes to the environment. Although these are influenced by our philosophical and religious background or world view, they tend to be shaped also by selfishness, greed and perhaps lust.

Is it possible to learn from these attitude-forming factors? How do history and reason (or science) affect the way we (as individuals and as societies) treat our environment? How do we come to an acceptable environmental ethic?

Environmentally Friendly Religion

Are the monotheistic religions peculiarly hostile to the environment? Are the Eastern religions more environmentally friendly than the attitudes produced by our frenetic Western lifestyle, which has sprung from Judaism and Christianity even if most of us now disown any formal religious allegiance? The honest answer is that there is no evidence that any religion has been better or more successful than any other when faced with hard environmental decisions. For example, vast tracts of China were deforested despite Taoism and its aim of recovering the 'primordial harmony of heaven and earth'. This devastation contradicts the claim that 'the Taoist passivity in relation to social and political processes restrained Taoists from preventing the ecologically destructive practices of others' (Cobb, 1972:30). Former European Community President Jacques Delors has commented that 'the Oriental religions have failed to prevent to any marked degree the appropriation of the natural environment by technical means ... despite differing traditions, the right to use or exploit nature seems to have found in industrialised countries the same favour, the same freedom to develop, the same economic justification' (Delors, 1990). Cobb (1972:30) confesses that 'it is Communist China which shares the Western passion for mastery and use, that is engaged in widespread efforts of reforestation'.

Failure to protect the environment is not a modern phenomenon. The demands of urban-based civilisations for agricultural products ruined many ancient civilisations, and turned the lands on which they relied to desert; their ecological footprint became an army's boot stamp. This pattern recurred in Mesopotamia, Central America, the Indus Valley and the Roman Empire (Ponting, 1991). Similar disasters have struck many areas of Africa and Central America in more recent times. The densely wooded areas described in ancient Chinese poetry were being cleared before the time of Christ to control wild animals and to provide fuel for industry and cremations; in Japan, the Buddhists felled trees to build huge wooded halls and temples:

> Overgrazing, deforestation, and similar errors of sufficient magnitude to
> destroy civilisations, have been committed by Egyptians, Assyrians,

Romans, North Africans, Persian, Indians, Aztecs and Buddhists ... 'Early' hunters used fire to drive out their game. Agricultural people everywhere clear fields and dam streams and wipe out stock predators and kill plants that get in the way of their chosen crops. (Derr, 1973:19)

Eastern religions can be described as biocentric in contrast to the attitudes characteristic of Judaism, Christianity and Islam. In the Orient, humans are part of nature; in the West, the monotheistic religions are more anthropocentric. Notwithstanding, in practice religious biocentrism seems to have been as ineffective as anthropocentrism in preventing environmental failures. Counterintuitively, an enlightened anthropocentrism may be the best approach for forming proper environmental attitudes. This is because it underpins, as Lynn White recognized, 'the nature of the man–nature link'. The essential point is that it is religion which defines and motivates that link.

The World Wide Fund for Nature (WWF) tacitly accepted the importance of religion when it held its twenty-fifth anniversary celebration in Assisi in 1986 and called upon the world's great religions to proclaim their attitudes to nature. In his presidential address to the gathering, the Duke of Edinburgh (1986) distinguished between the practice and rationale for environmental conservation:

> It is not enough just to be concerned about the conservation of nature, neither is it enough to have the scientific expertise to enable us to achieve the conservation of nature: we also need a clear and sufficient motive to ensure that our hearts as well as our minds are committed to the cause. We need the knowledge plus commitment. We need a credible philosophy. What we need is to establish the practical and moral reasons why conservation is important, and to clarify the motives that will help people to commit themselves to the cause of conservation ... the economic argument ... the scientific argument ... the moral argument, the relationship between man and nature. There can be little advantage in attempting to save our souls or to seek enlightenment or salvation, if our very existence in this earth is threatened by our own destructive activities.

WWF called upon the major world religions to declare their attitudes to 'man and nature', and were answered by leaders of Buddhism, Christianity, Hinduism, Islam and Judaism (and later by Baha'i) (*Assisi Declarations* [1986]). All the statements produced are worthy, and have been acted upon to various degrees by the religions concerned. Following the Assisi event, WWF established a 'Network on Conservation and Religion'. In Britain ICOREC (International Consultancy on Religion, Education and Culture) organised or stimulated various events, including a number of 'Creation Celebrations' in cathedrals, which were aesthetically successful but also strongly criticised on the grounds of syncretism and pantheism, seeming to imply that ecology was the key to theology.

Disenchantment and Alternatives

We return in Chapter 9 to the role of the established religions in caring for the environment, but for the moment we need do no more than note that there is a general agreement that the environment is part of the religious agenda but that there is no consensus about how to deal with it. The result has been a widespread search for answers from other sources than mainstream religion, much of this lumped together in the so-called New Age.

A major problem with the New Age is defining it. It is:

> a vast umbrella movement embracing countless groups, gurus and individuals, bound together by a belief that the world is undergoing a transformation or shift in consciousness that will usher in a new mode of being, an earthly paradise ... By dismissing logical argument, by putting intuition above intellect and feeling above theory, the New Age happily embraces wildly differing creeds. The New Age is not 'either/or' but 'both/and' as its proponents so often insist. (Storm, 1991:91)

Douglas Groothius (1986) calls it 'a smorgasbord ... heralding our unlimited potential to transform ourselves and the planet so that a "New Age of peace, light and love" will break forth'. Perhaps its clearest trait is an assumption that there are no barriers between ideas and things, a belief reminiscent of Nietzsche, the prophet of chaos (Osborn, 1990:20).

Groothius (1986:18–31) identifies six characteristics of New Age thinking:

1. *All is one* (monism). All is interrelated, interdependent and inter-
   penetrating; perceived differences between separate entities are
   only apparent. This is where a practising scientist might be
   expected to part company, but New Agers give high credence to
   quantum physics, since they see there the disappearance of any
   distinction between matter and energy. This allows them to think
   of mind and matter as being effectively interchangeable. They

frequently quote the physicist Fritjof Capra (1982:371) who identified the ultimate state of consciousness as one 'in which all
boundaries and dualisms have been transcended and all individuality dissolves into universal, undifferentiated oneness'. This
approach has some similarities to that of Rupert Sheldrake, a
former Cambridge cell biologist, who in his *A New Science of Life*
(1981:93) wrote: 'chemical and biological forms are repeated not
because they are determined by changeless laws or eternal Forms,
but because of a *causal influence from previous similar forms* [his
italics]. This influence would require an action across space and
time unlike any known type of physical action'; he calls this action
'morphic resonance'.

2. *All is God.* This follows from all-pervading monism and means that
   pantheism is a basic tenet. Moreover, if everything dissolves into
   a cosmic unity, then so does personality because it can only exist
   when defined in relation to other beings or things. If all is one,
   there is only one being – the One which is beyond personality.
   This means that God is more an 'it' than a person; the idea of a
   personal God is abandoned in favour of an impersonal energy,
   force or consciousness. Ultimate reality is god, in all and through
   all; in fact, god is all.

3. *Humankind is divine.* This also follows. Only ignorance keeps us
   from realising our divine reality. Theodore Roszak (1977:225)
   argues that our goal should be 'to awake to the god who sleeps at
   the root of the human being'. Christianity is viewed

   as a shallow surface-religion 'esoteric' cult, concerned with the past-
   historical – or mythical – figure of Jesus, correct moral behaviour and
   belief in God; the 'esoteric' traditions found in all non-Christian religious
   and handed down in some areas of the Judaeo-Christian tradition
   (Gnosticism, the Kabbalah, Rosicrucianism, Freemasonry) are believed to
   convey the real or 'deeper' truths. (Seddon, 1990:5)

4. *A change in consciousness.* We need to open 'the doors of
   perception' so that we recognise that our limitations as
   individuals are nothing more that a seductive illusion. There are
   many names claimed for this process: cosmic consciousness, God-
   realisation, enlightenment, illumination, Nirvana, Satori,
   at-one-ment, satchitananda. Once true knowledge (*gnosis*) is
   achieved, higher powers are activated.

5. *All religions are one.* There may be various paths to the one truth,
   but all the differences are superficial and external. The 'god
   within' or the 'perennial philosophy' as Aldous Huxley called it,

undergirds the experiences throughout history of Hindus, Buddhists, Jews, Taoists, Christians and Muslims. All claims of uniqueness and exclusivity must be submerged into the cosmic unity.

6. *Cosmic evolutionary optimism.* This is somewhat different from the other marks, but it follows that there must be a progress towards greater perfection, greater realisation. Julian Huxley (1957:236) described 'Man as that part of reality in which and through which the cosmic process has become conscious and begun to comprehend itself. His supreme test is to increase that cosmic comprehension and to apply it as fully as possible to guide the course of events.' Groothius includes Teilhard de Chardin and his notion of progression towards the Omega Point as arguing the same point: at Omega all consciousness is fused, and all become one with the One.[1] Julian Huxley wrote a laudatory Preface to the English translation of Teilhard's *The Phenomenon of Man* (1959), although he later regretted his enthusiasm (H. B. D. Kettlewell, pers. com.).

Once we accept the New Age assumption of boundarylessness, other beliefs follow. For example, health becomes 'a dynamic and harmonious equilibrium of all elements and forces making up and surrounding a human being' (Weil, 1983:51). This becomes an explicit reaction against scientific (= reductionist) medicine, and implies a notion of 'holistic health' (and healing).

The significance of the New Age is not its intellectual rigour, but the size of its following, which shows that there are large numbers of people who are concerned about themselves and the world in which they – and we – dwell. There seems little doubt that at least some of Western unease arises from the widespread perception that the world is 'only' a machine with a geological and biological history, which can in principle be explained by known mechanisms – and we are trapped in the machine. God has become not so much impossible as unnecessary. On this interpretation, Adam Gifford's bequest to 'Promote, Advance, Teach and Study the Knowledge of God ... and the knowledge of the Relation which men and the whole universe bear to him' can be regarded as having hit the rocks, particularly if God has been dissolved into an impersonal life force without relationships.

Is this so? Is God still credible, and is it orthodoxy which has failed by misunderstanding the nature of God revealed (or excluded) by advancing knowledge? I feel sure Adam Gifford would have approved of the idea that his bequest should be applied to exploring how and if human aspirations and divine reality can meet. Is there common ground between God and the Way(s) of the world religions, and the yearning of men and women for 'meaning'? Do the assumptions and practices of the New Age meet in any way the reality of the world as understood by science (accepting that it may be impossible fully to comprehend reality)?

These questions can be approached from either end, asking:

1. How has orthodoxy responded or how should it respond to the gap revealed by the successes of the New Age?
2. How does the New Age justify itself in terms of our understanding of scientific processes?

A Sharing and Suffering God

There are those in all religious traditions who argue from society to God, seeking ways to bring their God to meet the needs of the poor, the oppressed, the sick. Such a God has to be one who can come alongside those with problems to share and suffer together. The Christian tradition is that God came to society: Christ is the one who lived with us and who has sent his Spirit to work in human communities (as well as in non-human ones: Romans 8.19–23 ['The created universe is waiting with eager expectation for God's sons to be revealed. It was made subject to frustration, not of its own choice, but by the will of him who subjected it, yet with the hope that the universe itself is to be freed from the shackles of mortality ... Up to the present, as we know, the whole created universe in all its parts groans as if in the pangs of childbirth']). This does not necessarily involve any alteration in God himself, although there are those who argue that God cannot be impassive to suffering and therefore must change with time and experiences (Fiddes, 1988).

The notion of process in theology (associated particularly with the philosophy of Alfred North Whitehead, Edinburgh Gifford Lecturer, 1927–8, and the theology of Charles Hartshorne) was introduced into environmental debate in a book by John B. Cobb, *Is It Too Late?* (1972). Cobb argued like Lynn White that ecological problems arise through treating nature as a commodity, and that they can only be dealt with by overcoming the twin dualisms of God and nature, and humankind and nature. Cobb's solution was a sort of re-divinisation, that we should regard matter and the organisms from which we have evolved as having intrinsic value, because these sub-human elements existed '*in* themselves as something *for* themselves'. Instead of the normal assumption that human experience is the measure of our existence, Cobb suggested that a better yardstick would be the degree of richness of each event in the evolutionary process. The events in this process are guided by God at every point. God is *in* every event and is affected by, suffers or is enriched in all that happens, and consequently coerces and compels the processes of life in certain directions. This is a very different understanding of God from the transcendent God of Christian tradition, as Cobb recognises. We might, he says, be better to abandon the word 'God' and speak instead 'of Life, of Nature, or of Creative Process'.

Cobb has developed his ideas in later books, particularly with the Australian biologist Charles Birch (Cobb and Birch, 1981) where they claim that 'Life may be called God, and that God and the world – by which is meant the universe – are coterminous because "God includes the world" and "there is no God apart from some world"'.[2]

Cobb's theology is a radical departure from traditional Christian theism, and approaches the holism and mysticism of the New Age on the one hand and the attempts of evolutionary ethicists like G. G. Simpson, Julian Huxley and C. H. Waddington to derive 'humanness' from evolution on the other. None has found widespread sympathy in Britain. The problem is that Cobb's immanent suffering God is by definition also a God who is the progenitor of all evil and suffering. He is diminished when species become extinct or when the oceans and the air which sustain life are polluted or when animals are subjected to pain by our insensitivity. A God who is totally identified with all life is a God who has to be seen as committing a tremendous amount of harm, including not only natural evils such as parasitism but also human evils such as genocide and species extinction. This poses much greater problems for theodicy than historic Christian theism, for the traditional Christian belief that humanity and the world are in some ways corrupted by the fall means that humanly originated evil does not have to be seen as part of God's original good will and design of the cosmos.

The American theologian Jay McDaniel (1988) has attempted to answer this charge of inadequate theodicy within process theology by arguing that natural evil and predation, and the life process which underlies them, are not under God's domain or control. For McDaniel, the events which make up the evolutionary process are inherently creative and spontaneous; there is a creativity in matter and in life, which is not predetermined or ordered by God. This independence from God is inherent in the original chaos of energies from which God fashioned the world. God creates order out of this chaos, but the universe and each individual energy event retain the possibility of novelty, and hence of choosing either an harmonic or a discordant path. God's intention for all matter and life is relational harmony and integration, but this intention is merely an offer of possibilities. The creatures themselves – from atoms and cells to mammals and humans – must make the choice. McDaniel's model means that God was unable to prevent animals and humans from evolving in ways which lead them to cause pain to one another, because of a 'necessary correlation' in the very nature of life between the capacity for intrinsic good and the capacity for intrinsic evil.

The problem is that McDaniel gets rid of the theodicy problem by introducing a dualism, which is what Cobb sought to avoid in the first place. Indeed, McDaniel's approach is reminiscent of early Christian Gnosticism where matter was regarded as inherently evil, and which in turn led to the Docetic need to disallow the embodiment of God in the human person Jesus Christ. Redemption in McDaniel's schema is a long way from a traditional Christian understanding of it.

The theologies of Cobb and McDaniel are panentheist; that, they are based on 'the belief that the Being of God includes and penetrates the whole universe, so that every part of it exists in Him but (as against pantheism) that His being is more than, and is not exhausted by the universe' (*Oxford Dictionary of the Christian Church* definition). It is a concept particularly associated with process theology, but is used by other theologians in an attempt to hold together the transcendence and immanence of God in relation to the world (Peacocke, 1993:371–2). It is probably better avoided because of the danger of confusing it with pantheism, which is a creed, in C. S. Lewis's words 'not so much false as hopelessly behind the times. Once, before creation, it would have been true to say that everything was God. But God created; He caused things to be other than Himself' (Lewis, 1947:86). Process theology makes a problem for itself by postulating an association between creator and creation which is both contentious and unrequired on an informed theistic understanding of God's ways of working (p. 27).

A more traditional exponent of panentheism is Jürgen Moltmann, particularly in his 1984–5 Edinburgh Gifford lectures published as *God in Creation* (1985) and his subsequent work *The Spirit of Life* (1992). His central theme is that God as Spirit is indeed *in* creation; he inhabits the world of matter and ecosystems, plants and birds, animals and humans. But this immanence does not mean that God is entirely identified with the creation; although God as Trinity is related to the creation as Son and Spirit, he is distinguished from it as Father. This Spirit-driven cosmology is consonant with the mechanistic approach of modern science, and has the advantage of helping understand less mechanistic and more developmental and holistic interpretations of life on earth. Thus the immanent Spirit can be said to work through matter and organic life by creating new possibilities of being, and at the same time the Spirit is the holistic principle, which creates and harmonises the interactions of life forms into a community of life (Bauckham, 1995:182–98). The Spirit is thus the principle of both individuation and of differentiation, guaranteeing the ontological significance of all the myriad life forms in the cosmos and their relation to the one holy and transcendent God.

However, Moltmann's ideas generate their own problems, particularly when we try to assign values to creation and the environment since, according to Moltmann's avowed 'panentheism', God as Spirit is in everything, including presumably the smallpox virus and the louse. Moltmann comes very close to biocentrism in his way of stating the relation of the Spirit to life on earth, though at other times he appears very humanocentric (as, for example, when he discusses the image of God).

If Moltmann is a relatively orthodox exponent of panentheism, Matthew Fox is a highly heterodox one, providing a link (albeit a convoluted and contentious one) between the mysticism of some forms of traditional Christianity and that of New Age syncretism. Fox's starting point is God's blessing on all life at creation. To him, all forms of dualism are anathema; dualism he identifies as original sin, and transcendence as the worst sort of dualism. His solution is 'synthesis'. Redemption is not overcoming evil, but uniting good and evil. Consequently, syncretism is to be welcomed. Fox argues that environmental abuse arises from the desacralisation of nature; a particular *bête noire* for him is Augustine's doctrine of original sin, which he regards as condemning creation and humanity as inherently sinful. Fox suggests that the primary Christian doctrine with regard to creation and life ought to be original blessing (Fox, 1983). Such a doctrine would encourage us to take pleasure in our bodies and in the earthiness and fertility of creation: it releases in us the power of Eros and fertility to order our own lives without the numbing power of priests who gain control over the lives of the faithful under the guise of providing a solution to original sin; this freedom enables us to reorder our relations with nature and so share in its cosmic harmony, beauty and justice. Participation in the original blessing and justice of creation is Fox's key to human fulfilment. We are not called to transform nature but rather to integrate our life and society into the prior order and harmony of the cosmos.

Fox rejects what he calls 'fall/redemption' theology because he sees in it a false dualism between subject and object, human and non-human, body and soul, God and nature, blessing and sin.

Instead of dualism Fox proposes relationality, balance, harmony and blessing as the real basis of the cosmos and of human life. This leaves him with the problem of both human evil and natural evil. He resolves this with a new kind of dualism, or as he prefers to call it, dialectic: he opposes good and evil, harmony and disharmony, life and death, pleasure and pain, interpreting these as equal options created by God for the creation to follow in all its parts. Fox identifies these options with the two traditional paths of spirituality, the Via Positiva and the Via Negativa. The Via Positiva emphasises blessing, awe, harmony, fertility, pleasure, beauty; the Via Negativa affirms the reality of pain, suffering, nothingness and death, which are the shadow-side of God and of original blessing. God is both light and darkness, the creator of blessing and of nothingness.

For Fox, the biblical God is a sadistic 'fascist' deity. In his thinking, 'we are we and we are God'. Our divinity is awakened through ecstasy – drugs, sex, yoga, ritual drumming or Transcendental Meditation; 'the experience of ecstasy is the experience of God'. Crucifixion and resurrection are transferred from the historical Jesus to Mother Earth; Easter is the life, death and resurrection of Mother Earth, a constantly sacrificed paschal lamb. Fox's religion is one in which Christ becomes just one among many players on the world's stage. Fox asserts a pantheism where everything is holy and therefore to be worshipped, although he continues to insist that his God is bigger than the universe and that his faith is really panentheistic.

Fox's affirmation of joy, pleasure and praise in the wonder, fertility and diversity of creation is a powerful corrective to the corrosive pessimism of so much Christian worship and doctrine which emphasises the corrupting potential of natural instincts and the joyless suspicion of pleasure. Perhaps for this reason, it has attracted considerable following, particularly in North America. However, Fox's theology has fundamental problems: the duality of good and evil which is read into the being of God; the location of salvation in the balancing of these tendencies in human and non-human life rather than in the redemption of both humanity and nature in the life, death and resurrection of Christ; the adulation of erotic power as exemplified in Fox's frequent references to the writings of Starhawk and Wiccan ritual with their embrace of eroticism and pain, and their worship of nature as representations of God; and the sacralisation of the created order as the body of God. Fox's version of panentheism, like that of McDaniel, reduces God to an almost entirely immanent entity whose identity with the cosmos is so complete that we cannot really distinguish his good will for creation and human life from the occurrence of ever-present evil and suffering.

The ethic which emerges from Fox's creation spirituality is primarily an aesthetic one, where we are charged as co-creators to participate in what he sees as harmony in the natural order. He is rarely explicit about precise environmental issues and conflicts, or about the relative rights of different orders of life.

Ecofeminism

The ecotheological tradition of panentheism has keen advocates amongst theologians who propose that the most effective cosmological model for our ecologically endangered times is to conceive of the world as the body of God. Many of these are feminists. For example, Grace Jantzen rejects the traditional Christian distinction between an eternal, immaterial, invisible, timeless God and a contingent, material, embodied cosmos: 'the model of the universe as God's body helps to do justice to the beauty and value of nature' (Jantzen, 1984:150). She argues that we need to re-sacralise the world of matter to counter the Western Christian tendency to oppose divine being and material substance.

But it would be wrong to take this Christian understanding as diagnostic of ecofeminists. There are many who ground their beliefs in specifically non-Christian religions, often seeking a sort of primitive romanticism. In this they link with a common New Age emphasis on medicine women – women of power and wiccans (witches who do not wish to harm others and who practise so-called 'white magic'). Since these approaches, often incorporated in anthologies of ecofeminist writing, are based on animism or animalism (spirits or supernatural beings appearing in animal form), one might assume they have abandoned all social and divine hierarchy, but this is not always the case.

For example *The Medicine Woman* trilogy by Lynn Andrews (1981, 1984, 1985) inverts the myth of the priests of the 'good' sky god who destroy the sacred groves of the 'bad' or 'weak' mother goddess, and instead tells tales of righteous women who protect nature through disciplined magic. For Andrews environmental care is a male–female power battle, where good medicine women struggle against depraved men who do not have a proper respect for nature or for spiritual power. Any transcendent form of the divine disappears in a horde of animist spirits. Andrews is not a theologian, but she represents a common form of ecoreligious reaction against Christianity.

Another goddess-feminist is Starhawk, a wiccan who sometimes uses theological language, although she advocates earth-based spirituality. Proclaiming herself improbably as a practitioner of a religion going back to the last Ice Age, more ancient than Judaism or Christianity, Starhawk rejects any image of a god external to nature in favour of a goddess who is the world, and who 'fosters respect for the sacredness of all living things' (Starhawk, 1989:10). Her goddess is not transcendent; she cannot rule 'over', because she is the earth itself. The planet, as in the Gaia hypothesis (p. 120), is a living being. For Starhawk, 'witchcraft is the religion of ecology', which strives to develop interconnectedness and community, both among humans and between humans and the natural world. Perhaps because she has a strong interest in heterosexual activities, Starhawk's cosmology incorporates both the goddess and the god, the latter taking the form of the 'horned god' of witchcraft, whom she claims has been distorted as the Christian devil.

Not all worshippers of such a goddess are wiccans, and some have abandoned the supernatural so that the goddess becomes an extension of their own femininity. Jungian analyst Jean Shinoda Bolen (1984), for example, uses archetypes of Greek divinities such as Hera to help women investigate their own psyches. For her, the divine is neither transcendent nor immanent because it is a product of the human mind.

In contrast to the wiccans and women of power, there are ecofeminists who profess to remain within Christianity or Judaism, whilst reinterpreting its theology. Anna Primavesi (1991), for example, wants to keep the canon of Christian Scripture whilst engaging in 'deconstruction', by which she means inserting feminist alternatives to sexist or otherwise unjust language, social structures or human relationships. Primavesi proposes 'reimaging transcendence', which she believes is necessary because 'we view transcendence through the distorting lens of a certain Christian conception of reality as a hierarchy of being. Through this, Jesus is regarded not only as a normative human male, but as *the* normative divine male.' According to Primavesi, this can best be countered by getting rid of the hierarchy and recognising 'all beings live in a relationship with God' (Primavesi, 1991:152).

Another Christian ecofeminist is Rosemary Ruether (1992). She rejects the idea of an Eden ruled by a goddess, and concentrates on the 'domination and deceit' which she sees embedded in the culture of Europe and North America. She suggests this has developed in three stages: the male 'co-opts' the power of his mother and of the earth by making himself 'king of the universe'; then he separates, as in Platonic thought, 'the immortal soul or spirit from the mortal body'; finally, he attempts to sterilise the power of nature altogether, treating it as dead stuff wholly malleable in the hands of men in power.

Ruether believes that this 'competitive alienation' can be overcome by incorporating covenant and sacrament from the Christian tradition, and here she rejoins more orthodox under-standing. Both Ruether and Primavesi want to target the weak social responses of conventional organised Christendom. Primavesi wants to dissolve all hierarchy by 'resouling' nature, and portrays this as an addition to human spiritual status. Ruether could also be said to be 'resouling' nature, but for her this requires removing the possibility of any dominance in relationships by redefining the notion of soul as something that is completely shared, and not something that belongs to an individual. She also wants to replace the idea of divine purpose with cosmic recycling; in doing so, she abandons the concepts of final judgement and of Christian 'saints'. Ironically, although Ruether blames Platonism as a source of dominance, her notion of the Great Self is reminiscent of Neoplatonic mysticism.

Probably the most influential ecofeminist theologian is Sally McFague (1993, 1997). Like most feminists, she argues that the relationship of God to the world is best envisaged as 'embodiment', although she specifically distances herself from the materialist immanentism of ecofeminists such as Grace Jantzen. She suggests that both God's immanence and transcendence can be conceived as being embodied in the world: God is an 'embodied spirit', the 'inspirited body of the entire universe'. She adopts this model because it is consistent with and sustains an organic model of the world in which all the parts of the world are interconnected, and hence (she believes) it is more likely to produce ecological respect for the environment than a cosmology which conceives mechanisti-cally of the world and its inhabitants, with God outside and distant from the material and embodied cosmos.

Such an ecological theology of God's embodiment interprets sin as not so much rebellion against God as a refusal to 'stay in our place, to recognise our proper limits so that other individuals of our species as well as other species can also have needed space'. Consequently, ecological sin causes us to devalue and harm animals and inanimate nature, and to misunderstand the distinction between us and the rest of creation. The recognition of the legitimate otherness of nature should lead us to restrain our demands and hence allow the rest of creation space to be.

A key element in ecofeminism is its approach to the immanence–transcendence tension. Immanence is seen as truly feminine, while transcendence is characteristic of distant managerial males. Susan

Bratton (1994) has identified a series of problems with ecofeminist approaches, particularly as they seek to deal with this divide.

First, both New Age and goddess thinkers are selective in their use of religious systems (such as those of native people), ignoring either the relationship of gender to the spirit world in those systems, or whether the original deities in these systems were transcendent. For example, creative acts in different religions often employ both male and female imagery, with some emphasising the feminine, others the masculine. Many cosmologies portray the earth as mother, but cultures with an Earth Mother creation myth usually have numerous other environmentally oriented myths that do not identify all portions of the non-human world as feminine. Non-Western cultures do not necessarily identify women as 'nature-wise' and men as 'nature-stupid', or women as being primary defenders of spiritual good.

Attempts to justify the goddess as the most ancient and universal deity have often resulted in oversimplifications of complex cosmologies. For example, among Native Americans, the Wind River Shoshoni recognise an Earth Mother in the sun dance, but in their original Great Basin mythology, they had a supreme being called 'father' who 'supervises the world', either in human form or as a wolf; the Seneca belief system has creator twins, both male, who bring good and evil into the universe; among strongly agricultural tribes, mythologies of female, earth-oriented deities are more common (Baring and Cashford, 1991).

Secondly, in their eagerness to get rid of patriarchal hierarchies, many ecofeminists de-divinise virtually everything and end up with demi-gods or earth spirits. Rosemary Ruether's concept of the divine has converged to such an extent with scientific cosmology, that her earth goddess appears to be an analogue of day-to-day biophysical functions. Susan Bratton describes this deity as 'a stolid male process philosopher trying to squeeze into a dress'. Ruether's appeal to biblical covenants and her concern for human gender sit uneasily with a cosmological position verging on monism. In adopting a very modern process model, she loses the lure and environmental attachment of the ancient goddesses, who had strong associations with places, seasons or social and economic activities, such as planting and weaving.

Thirdly, ecofeminists tend to use 'immanence' to describe everything from biophysical processes to animal spirits and human desires. The immanent goddess is presented as several different beings, some spirit and some not. This creates an ecotheological tangle, especially when applied to biblically oriented western religion.

Fourthly, by divesting God of transcendence, goddess worshippers and animists effectively ignore the possibility of an omnipotent deity, whom they might need to please or placate. The goddess is not able to express herself independently of her followers. The personal, loving, all-powerful deity of Christianity and any divine entity similar to the Holy Spirit, are absent, together with any need for human repentance or appreciation of divine grace.

Fifthly, ecofeminist theologians tend to conflate gender as it operates in nature with the question of determining what God is like. They are so interested in human gender issues that they spiritualise sexuality and ignore actuality. The argument that hierarchical ranking degrades both women and nature (since women and nature are either of lower status or mere instruments of males) is common, but the conclusion that all hierarchies must therefore be disposed of does not follow. Whilst it is true that ecological hierarchies, like food chains, have been used to justify abusive human behaviours, we cannot therefore assume all food chains in (say) a marsh or forest have a valid human social match.

As far as the Bible is concerned, creation is seen as a whole, from the creeping things to the great whales and human beings. Noah included both genders in the Ark (in pairs, no precedence being given to males). The creation in Genesis 1 is instigated by Yahweh's 'Word' (masculine) and also by 'the spirit' (*ruach* – feminine) that moves over the waters.

Sixthly, ecofeminist thought is so obsessed with gender roles that it touts gender where divine neutrality might be better. The principle dualism in Christian theology is creator–created, not male–female. The basic theological problem is whether there is a god who is separate from the biophysical universe and/or the human mind; the key environmental issue is whether God must be 'in nature' for nature to be properly valued. One does not have to give God a gender for God to be found in nature; many forms of pantheism do not bother to gender-type the divine. Conversely a transcendent God does not mean a misogynist one.

From a Western religious perspective, transcendence is better defined as 'wholly other' or completely ineffable, than as necessarily masculine. Although both Jewish and Christian theology portray God as an independent creator who maintains prerogatives concerning the creation, both traditions also portray God as loving or sympathetic.

Finally, a common ecofeminist interpretation of history treats transcendence as a recent, sexist innovation in religious thought; the primitive idea (it is claimed) is of a 'matriarchal paradise'. The irony here is that religions with primarily or exclusively immanent deities or sources of spiritual power or enlightenment often do not have large numbers of (or any) women in their upper echelons of leadership. In practice, both Buddhism and Hinduism have as many sexist practices and social structures as Christianity. Major religions of all types, including those with an immanent deity or deities, have oppressed women in the name of God, especially when the religious hierarchies become aligned with 'worldly' power and pursuits.

In general, ecofeminists seem more attracted by revisionist ideas of God and associated problems, than with the specifics of environmental care. Feminism is largely fuelled by concerns of injustice, and hence with the development and maintenance of proper attitudes. Susan Bratton suggests the way for ecofeminists to

> make a real difference environmentally is to seriously attack the actual environmental problems and deconstruct unjust gender relations as they get in the way of getting things done ... Ecofeminism is often ecologically facile and unrealistic about the function of natural and social hierarchies. Ecofeminism makes a major contribution, however, when it is sensitive to destructive social structures and to environmental abuses. (Bratton, 1994)

Metaphysical Reconstruction

One of the patron saints of environmentalism is the economist Fritz Schumacher. Although he is best known for his arguments that 'small is beautiful' (and for the book of that name [1973]), his other persistent call was for some kind of 'metaphysical reconstruction'. He was convinced that major reorganisations of perspective are needed if the world is to have a viable future. In an epilogue to *Small is Beautiful* he quotes a UK Government Report written for the Stockholm Conference (*Pollution: Nuisance or Nemesis?* [1972]) which talked about the need for 'moral choices' since 'no amount of calculation can alone provide the answers [to effective pollution control]. The fundamental questioning of conventional values by young people all over the world is a symptom of the widespread unease with which our industrial civilisation is increasingly regarded.'

Schumacher asked:

> But how is it to be done?[3] What are the 'moral choices?' Is it just a matter, as the report suggests, of deciding 'how much we are willing to pay for clean surroundings'? Mankind has indeed a certain freedom of choice: it is not bound by trends, by the 'logic of production,' or by any other fragmentary logic. But it is bound by truth. Only in the service of truth is

perfect freedom, and even those who today ask us 'to free our imagination from bondage to the existing system' fail to point the way to the recognition of truth. (Schumacher, 1973:248)

Oelschlaeger (1994) has tried to identify the components needed for Schumacher's 'metaphysical reconstruction'. He compares what he calls the 'Dominant Social Matrix' with a 'New Social Matrix'. Both have six components. The dominant matrix comprises:

1. Nature has instrumental (anthropocentric) value only; biocentric values, such as the preservation of endangered species, are meaningless.
2. Short-term economic interests override long-term issues like intergenerational equity; future generations of human beings will be able to fend for themselves.
3. If environmental risks caused by habitat modification, consumption of resources, and the emission of pollution are economically beneficial (as measured monetarily), then they are acceptable.
4. Environmental risk poses no limits to growth, just problems that require engineered solutions (for example, restoration of habitat, resource substitution, and pollution-control technologies).
5. The strategy of managing planet Earth is feasible: through biotechnology and other sciences, humankind will ultimately be able to control biophysical processes on the planet.
6. The politics of interest is sufficient to guarantee that the best available technology to restore habitat, devise resource substitutions and control pollution will be employed.

The new matrix is very different:

1. Nature has intrinsic value (value in its own right apart from human interests) as well as instrumental value; a healthy economy cannot be sustained by a sick environment.
2. Long-term issues, such as intergenerational equity, are at least as important as short-term economic interests; sooner or later someone pays the costs associated with short-term greed, and that someone is our children and the infra-human species adversely affected by actions motivated solely by economic self-interest.
3. Economic activity always entails risks, but risks that entail either unpredicted or irreversible ecological consequences are not acceptable no matter how profitable; when in doubt– and especially when human action affects fragile ecosystems, endangered species, or has global implications – act conservatively.

4. There are biophysical limits to growth that no human technology can overcome in the long term, though these limits can be exceeded in the short term; accepting limits to growth does not mean that human beings live in degraded conditions of poverty. A life of relative plenty is possible even in delicate ecosystems.

5. Creating a sustainable society is a feasible alternative to the modern project that attempts to manage planet Earth; the modern project is in fact driving the Earth towards ecocatastrophe. Hubris sustains the illusion that humankind can control the biophysical processes that govern life on Earth.

6. A citizen democracy, attentive to local geography and environmental issues as well as to global issues, is required to build a sustainable society that is also consistent with democratic life.

We have already touched upon some of these points. We will return to them in more detail in the following chapters. For the moment, my purpose is to agree with Oeschlaeger that the differences are not single issues, but are elements in a multifactorial whole, which means that reconstruction rather than a serial technological fix is needed.

For some, the reconstruction is an aesthetic process, seeking inspiration from some of the 'ecological saints' of old, like Francis of Assisi, Meister Eckhart or John Ray, or more modern gurus like John Muir, Henry Thoreau, Richard Jefferies, Aldo Leopold, Rachel Carson or Peter Scott. There is indeed much to be learned from such people, especially the ways they faced dilemmas and solved problems. Their experiences show clearly that reason by itself is inadequate for 'metaphysical reconstruction'. As Richard Austin wrote in his biography of the pioneer American conservationist John Muir:

> Knowledge alone will not protect nature, nor will ethics, for by themselves they do not arouse motivation strong enough to transform the exploitative patterns to which we have become accustomed. The protection of nature must be rooted in love and delight – in religious experience ... Muir's own religious ecstasy and the depth of his communion with nature challenge our capacity to follow. (Austin, 1987:3)

But 'religious experience' must be grounded in reason.[4] Our subjective awe and wonder relate to real animals and plants, real ecological and geological and biogeochemical processes. Passion without rationality is insufficient. Muir himself moved from a Calvinistic Christianity as a boy to a pantheism close to Buddhism in later years (although his wife remained a devout Methodist). In contrast Fritz Schumacher moved from a fascination with Buddhism to Roman Catholicism.

Albert Einstein famously said: 'Science without religion is lame, religion without science is blind.' As we have seen, Lynn White wrote at the end of his 1967 paper: 'Since the roots of our trouble are so largely religious, the remedy must also be religious.' Six years later he returned to the point:

> Christianity ... recognises the progressive unfolding of truths inherent in an original doctrine of revelation. The Christian wants to know what Scripture says to him about a puzzling problem ... In my 1967 discussion I referred to St. Francis's abortive challenge to the anthropocentric concept of God's world. Scattered through the Bible, but especially the Old Testament, there are passages that can be read as sustaining the notion of a spiritual democracy of all creatures. The point is that historically they seem seldom or never to have been so interpreted. This should not inhibit anyone from taking a fresh look at them. (White, 1973)

Such an approach is not so far different from the need for continuous reinterpretation of the Bible which John Calvin called accommodation and about which preachers have always agonised in their search for integrity in hermeneutics[5] (Berry, 2000*a*).

And this is the challenge. American biologist Fred van Dyke has written:

> In his call for a new ethic toward the biotic community, Aldo Leopold portrayed Judeo-Christian ethics as a 'primitive deficient system which could not speak to environmental dilemmas ...' Christians have been lazy, ignorant and apathetic about environmental concerns. But only Christians possess an ethical system strong enough to bring conviction, courage, correction and direction to the environmental dilemma. (van Dyke, 1985)

NOTES

1   Bookchin (1994:62) labels Teihard de Chardin's "noosphere" as 'modern Neoplatonism writ large'.
2   Nevertheless, 'there is enough in process thought to justify something more than a "take it or leave it" approach. Whatever else it offers, it can surely provide a very useful incentive to re-think the relationships involved in confessing faith in God the Father Almighty, Maker of Heaven and Earth, who, if with St. Augustine we may add, has made us for himself' (Shaw, 1975).
3   Schumacher's own proposals in *A Guide for the Perplexed* (1977) were largely a restatement of Thomas Aquinas's position, and have had little impact.
4   I find it difficult to relate to or empathise with the position of ecotheologians who effectively ridicule reason in their environmental passion. For

example, the widely read American author Thomas Berry (1988) has written, 'The very rational process that we exalt as the only true way to understand is by a certain irony discovered to be itself a mythic dream experience. The difficulty of our times is our inability to awaken out of the cultural pathology.'

5   Paul Santmire (1985:189–90) regards the Bible as containing 'a new option ... an ecological reading of biblical theology'. He believes 'it is possible to construe [the historical categories of biblical theology] ... not in terms of God and humanity over against nature, but in terms of God and humanity *with* nature. This could be called an ecological hermeneutic of history. It is predicated on the assumption of a divine and human concomitance with nature, rather than a divine and human disjunction from nature.' This is exactly the point that Aubrey Moore made about the effect of Darwinism on our understanding of God (p. 17). Santmire (2000) has begun to face his own hermeneutical challenge in a further book, *Nature Reborn. The Ecological and Cosmic Promise of Christian Theology.*

6
Green Science

The place(s) where green religion meets green science is the test-bed of natural theology. If there is a God who is creator and sustainer of the material world, one whom we worship because of his works both past and present, then there is a reasonable expectation that we might expect to detect him or her in these works. If we find no traces of such a God, it might mean that we are using the wrong tests, but more seriously that he (or she) does not exist. Green science is obviously an important enterprise for a natural theologian. St Paul, in his only recorded address to pagans, rather surprisingly did not preach Jesus as Lord or proclaim the significance of the resurrection, but used the regularity of nature as evidence for God's work ('[God] has not left himself without some clue to his nature, in the benefits he bestows: he sends you rain from heaven and the crops in their seasons, and gives you food in plenty, and keeps you in good heart' Acts 14.17). This does not appear particularly convincing to us. Can we do better? Can we find God in nature, and if not, what do we conclude?

We have seen (p. 6) that the recognition that the world is old and that it has changed through time destroys the naive assumption of a world created by a benevolent being who assigned a place and function to everything. But the traditional belief involved more than the mechanical assembly we associate with Paley's divine watch-maker; it included the idea of self-regulation, often using the analogy of a living body as a microcosm of the world.

The Balance of Nature

Commonly associated with the notion of self-regulation is that of an equilibrium or 'balance' in nature. This is a favourite of politicians, who profess themselves upset about disturbing this balance and urge the need to return to it, as if there were some ideal state, presumably akin to the biblical Paradise. In her Royal Society address in 1988, which testified her acknowledgement that the environment could not be left wholly to 'market forces', Margaret Thatcher spoke of 'the fundamental equilibrium of the world's systems and atmosphere' (Thatcher, 1989).

But such balances and equilibria almost certainly do not exist; they owe more to obsolete theology than to scientific understanding. Clarence Glacken (1967:230) cites Aquinas as teaching a concept of balance and harmony in nature. This led Glacken to conclude: 'modern ecological theory, so important in our attitudes towards nature and man's interference with it, owes its origin to the design argument: the wisdom of the Creator is self-evident, everything in the creation is inter-related, no living thing is useless, and all are related one to the other' (p. 423).

The reality is less mechanistic and, if we want to invoke religious faith, owes more to sustaining providence than deistic regulation. The world and its processes are so vast that it is difficult to shift them, but we should not confuse inertia with intrinsic stability. Egerton (1973) identified three ideas which have led to the myth of a balance in nature:

1. a commonly applied parallel between the microcosm of the body and the macrocosm of the living world;
2. the *scala naturae* or chain of being, linking all organisms together (p. 6);
3. a divinely ordered balance, derived from Stoic ideas of the creator's wisdom and benevolence.

All these recognise some sort of relationship of interactions in the natural world, and this, of course, is the science of ecology. To understand natural processes it is necessary to delve somewhat into the content and history of the science.

The name 'ecology' was proposed by the German biologist Haeckel (1866); he introduced the word so as to free 'biology' to be used in its modern sense (i.e. as the study of morphology or anatomy, plus physiology or function). Natural history is centuries old but 'the first sketch of a science of ecology', is attributed by Egerton (1973) to an essay on *Oeconomia naturae* by Carl Linnaeus (1749), little more than a hundred years before Haeckel. In it, Linnaeus used reproduction, cooperation and mortality as the key elements in the 'economy' of an organism. This well describes the British pursuit of ecology, which is sometimes described as 'scientific natural history' particularly when contrasted to the more physiological German and North American traditions. This is not a claim that ecology sprang from – or worse, is synonymous with – European Romanticism, the transcendental naturalism of Ralph Emerson or Henry Thoreau, or the preservationist movement represented by John Muir and John Burroughs, although there is a proper sense in which ecology has what Donald Worster (1985) calls 'Arcadian roots' of awe and respect in the writings of people like John Ray (*The Wisdom of God Manifested in the Works of Creation* [1691]), William Derham (*Physico-Theology*) [1713]), and even John Wesley (*Survey of the Wisdom of God in the Creation* [1763]).

In its modern guise, ecology surfaced at the same time as genetics, around the turn of the century. The British Ecological Society was founded in 1913 as a direct descendant of the Central Committee for the Survey and Study of British Vegetation, a group of botanists who came together to use their passion for collecting wild flowers and swapping rarities as a means of determining the distribution and characteristics of different species and hence their limits and preferences; the Ecological Society of America was founded two years later.

The British Ecological Society received an enormous impetus from the fashionable collecting and recording habits of the Victorian era (Allen, 1976; Barber, 1980). For most it was a hobby, but there were certainly some who saw it as a specifically religious quest (Armstrong, 2000). Indeed, natural history (in its wide sense) can be regarded as an expression of a search for order and purpose in the world paralleling the speculations of philosophy through diverse times and cultures: Herodotus on predators, St Basil on forest succession, José de Acosta on the biogeographical problems raised by the animals and plants of the New World, Benjamin Franklin on the control of insect pests by birds.

In the early years of professional ecology, most ecologists took it for granted that communities of animals and plants existed as natural, repeated, internally organised units with a considerable degree of integration. Such a community was commonly called a super-organism or quasi-organism. The American botanist Frederic Clements (1874–1945) used to stress the existence of ecological succession to argue for an inevitable development towards an end point or climax community (Clements, 1936). His ideas were developed philosophically by the Edinburgh-born botanist John Phillips, who sought to show that 'in accordance with the holistic concept [of Jan Christian Smuts, 1870–1950] the biotic community is something more than the mere sum of its parts; it possesses a special identity – it is indeed a mass-entity with a destiny peculiar to itself' (Phillips, 1931:20). However, this was too great an extrapolation for the leading British ecologist of the period, Arthur Tansley (1871–1955), and he responded with a trenchant criticism of

Phillips's views including coining a new word 'ecosystem', defined as:

> the whole system (in the sense of physics) including not only the
> organism-complex, but also the whole complex of physical factors forming
> what we call the environment of the biome – the habitat factors in the
> widest sense. It is the systems so formed which, from the point of view of
> the ecologist, are the basic units of nature on the face of the earth. [They]
> are of the most various kinds and sizes. They form one category of the
> multitudinous physical systems of the universe, which range from
> the universe as a whole down to the atom. (Tansley, 1935:299)

Patterns in Nature

Sadly, ecosystems, which Tansley introduced as a descriptive gener-
ality, have spawned a whole sub-discipline with ascribed properties of
resilience, persistence, resistance and variability. Ecosystems are said
to have health and needs and to suffer damage, designations properly
attributed to organisms. This is hyperbole; more realistically,
ecosystems are 'self-organising systems in which random disturbance
and colonisation events create a heterogeneous landscape of diverse
species, which then become knitted together through nutrient fluxes
and other forms of interaction ... some simply having to do with
chance and geography ...' (Levine, 1999:38, 80).

In fairness to scientists within ecology, there has been a long-
continued and unresolved debate between the advocates of
structured communities and those more impressed with contingency
and adventitious opportunism in nature (McIntosh, 1995). This is
not the place to rehearse details of internal ecological debates, but it
is relevant to note that ecology suffers from the same problems of
lack of cohesion experienced by evolutionary biology before the neo-
Darwinian synthesis of the 1930s, and by implication needs its own
synthesis. Ecologists have, of course, attempted to find key principles
in their science. In a widely used textbook, Allee *et al.* (1949)
indexed twenty-five such principles, whilst Odum (1953) had more
than thirty. Watt (1971) listed only fifteen, but increased this two
years later to thirty-eight (Watt, 1973). Notwithstanding, the picture
is still terrifyingly like that painted by Charles Elton (1949) who
wrote of his experience at ecological meetings that 'the dominant
impression retained is of the extreme range and fragmentation of
ecological knowledge ... I think the ocean of ecological facts has
reached a dangerous tide level, [needing] a raft to float on.'

Half a century on, the situation is still unresolved (Berry,
1989). Elton himself, one of the founders of animal ecology, was

instinctively suspicious of tidy models for the complexity of nature. He wrote: 'The "balance of nature" does not exist, and perhaps never has existed. The numbers of wild animals are constantly varying to a greater or less extent, and the variations are usually irregular in period and always irregular in amplitude' (Elton, 1930); although twenty years later he was more circumspect, accepting that: 'A general equilibrium in nature ... does exist, even though it is subject to recurring fluctuations of all sorts, and even complete breakdowns of the ecosystem such as the poisoning of lake faunas by outbreaks of blue-green algae and the desolation of vegetation by field mice, locusts and caterpillars' (Elton, 1949).

This equivocation is perhaps a true representation of reality. It is almost trivial to state that patterns of species and individuals exist in natural situations: recognisable successions recur in time and space; although population numbers vary, they tend to be within understandable limits; there are density-dependent interactions which damp extreme variations; and so on. The challenge and problem of these perceptions of pattern is that they depend on the scale by which they are observed.

For example, tropical forests are almost the epitome of a stable, multi-species system but detailed studies of tree death and replacement convinced Connell (1979) that 'they represent an open, locally non-equilibrium system that may or may not be in regional equilibrium'[1] (i.e. large-scale or short-term surveys may give an illusory impression of uniformity and therefore of equilibrium). His repeated sampling of the same patches of coral reef showed likewise that 'the relationship between disturbance and species richness is similar in coral reefs to that in tropical forests' (Connell, 1978). These processes are highlighted and magnified by the biota of oceanic islands which strongly reflect the apparently chance sequence of colonisation and subsequent change rather than any deterministic progress towards an 'ideal' community (Williamson, 1981; Grant, 1998). This does not detract from the undeniable existence of predictable successions or of well-defined associations; what it does is to shift the appropriate questions from descriptive statics to dynamic processes, with the focus on the ordering mechanisms rather than the results of that process.[2]

Detailed knowledge of the interactions controlling community structure (the word 'ecosystem' is often used synonymously) is surprisingly weak (Law and Watkinson, 1989). For example, the comprehensive descriptions of food webs routinely illustrated in elementary textbooks are 'caricatures of nature' (Pimm, 1982). Most food-chains (i.e. A eats B, B eats C, etc.) are very short, involving only three or four stages. Some links are specific to particular species (e.g. certain hosts and parasites), but the majority are largely non-specific, depending on such factors as size and abundance (Lawton, 1989). Too often advocates of a struggle for existence as producing an adaptively organised community have been driven to postulating competition in the past if it cannot be demonstrated in the present, a tendency described by Connell as invoking the 'ghost of competition past'. Cornell and Lawton (1992) have argued that local communities are controlled by local or biogeographical characteristics, so that 'the key to community structure may lie in extrinsic biogeography rather than in intrinsic local processes, making community ecology a more historical science'. Put another way, this means that contingency plays a major part in ecology just as in evolution. Commenting on ways of linking species and ecosystems, Lawton and Jones agree that

> ecology text books summarise the important interactions between organisms as intra- and inter specific competition, predation, parasitism and mutualism; [but] conspicuously lacking from this list is the role that many organisms play in the creation, modification and maintenance of habitats, although particular examples have been extensively studied. (1995:142)

Coevolution[3]

In fact Jones and Lawton are rather unfair here, because ecological geneticists have devoted a great deal of time and energy to studying organism–environment interactions, and developing a body of knowledge (albeit frequently involving considerable speculation) about the 'fit' or coevolution of interacting species. The problem has been that the approaches of ecologists and evolutionists (geneticists) have tended to run in parallel rather than converge (Berry and Bradshaw, 1992). Do evolutionists have information which shows that biotic communities can be regarded as super-organisms?

The answer is no. To understand this, it is necessary to explore evolutionary mechanisms. The practical problem here is to detect reciprocal change in real situations. It is much easier to recognise genetical changes in a single population in response to an environmental challenge which may or not involve an interacting species, than it is to detect mutually dependent change in two species in the same place. The hard evidence for coevolution is surprisingly small.

1. *Pollination.* Pollination is almost a touchstone example of coevolution. Yet, if the common assumption is right, the early stages of
   the evolution of pollination went as follows: selection against
   beetle damage in flowering plants led to the formation of carpels
   for protection; this was followed by feeding on reproductive
   shoots by animals whose movements coincidentally brought
   about pollination. In other words, pollinating mechanisms in all
   their variety arose originally as a straightforward protective
   response by plants against animals.

2. *Parasitism.* There is no doubt that hosts and parasites adjust to
   each other in a rapid and precise manner. What is less generally
   appreciated is that parasitism is an adventitious relationship, and
   that the idea of a perfect parasite harmless to its host is a myth.
   May and Anderson (1983) have shown that the effect of a parasite
   on a host follows no fixed path, but depends on the virulence and
   transmissibility of the parasite, and the cost to the host of evolving
   resistance. They quote the large amount of data on the virus
   which causes myxomatosis in rabbits which has apparently
   stabilised in both Britain and Australia at an intermediate level of
   virulence after beginning at a very high level.

   The point that parasitism does not represent some ideal state of
   harmonious benevolence is underlined by Rothschild and Clay's
   (1952) conclusion from an extensive survey: 'Parasitism can
   develop gradually or suddenly. It can be the outcome of complicated interactions or the result of isolated accidents which
   occurred a million years ago or only this morning ... There is
   only one vital factor in the genesis of a parasitic relationship, and
   that is opportunity.'

3. *Mimicry.* Much ink has been wasted over definitions of mimicry
   and its distinction from straightforward concealment (Berry,
   1981). In practice, both are simply devices to deceive. Batesian
   mimicry involves one (or more) species coming to resemble
   another, otherwise protected form: there is no advantage to the
   latter. In contrast, Mullerian mimics gain by resembling one
   another, and there is selection for similarly confusable patterns in
   Mullerian situations. However, and this is the point I wish to
   emphasise, similar selection pressures may result in resemblance
   to some non-living feature in the environment, such as a stone;
   and this may involve (as in industrial melanism) selection
   following an environmental change resulting from non-biological
   causes. In other words, selection (and adaptation) is a possible
   consequence of any factor in the environment, biotic or abiotic;
   there seems no reason to single out any particular element,

although coevolution *sensu stricto* can, of course, be produced only by biotic components in the environment of a population.

An often forgotten – and very important – factor about adaptive genetic change is that it is opportunistic and pragmatic, not optimising and perfecting. This, of course, introduces another degree of indeterminancy into the understanding of coevolution, particularly understanding based on analytical models.

For example, industrial melanism in Lepidoptera tends to be written about as an inevitable consequence of smoke pollution, but other factors are involved. In many cases species have become locally extinct in the absence of available melanics: the rosy minor moth *Miana literosa* was extinct for many years in the industrial Sheffield area of England, and only managed to recolonise the city in the mid 1940s through a newly arisen mutant. Even the 'type species' of industrial melanism, the peppered moth (*Biston betularia*), has shown considerable genetical change and adjustment in the century since its black *carbonaria* form became common and then decreased in Britain (Lees, 1981; Berry, 1990). Examples of sudden change are common in the occurrence (and loss) of inherited pesticide resistance in a wide variety of species. Variation is normally not limiting, but a population faced with a new environmental challenge may be unable to respond until an appropriate variant occurs (Berry and Bradshaw, 1992).

Dog whelks (*Nucella lapillus*) are extremely common on rocky shores. Most of them have white shells yet round the west coast of Britain there are many places where uniquely banded forms have persisted locally for more than a hundred years (Berry, 1983). Under conditions and in a species where genetical equilibrium would be expected to occur without hindrance, geographical heterogeneity exists on a significant scale.

Dog whelks underline the fact that adaptation does not tend towards an obviously predictable end point, although individuals experience strong selection, with populations losing up to 90 per cent of their shell shape variation on wave-exposed shores (Berry and Crothers, 1968). Selection is directed towards survival, not perfection or some theoretical optimum. Both genetics and ecology reveal contingency rather than cohesive cooperation in natural populations.

Towards an Ecological Synthesis

I have suggested already that ecology lacks the focus provided in the physical sciences by the Periodic Table and quantum theory and in most of the biological sciences by neo-Darwinism. The difficulty

within ecology has been to provide a realistic theory which incorporates the massive data from natural populations with the historical and
local specificities of particular situations. One obvious simplification is
to concentrate on the fitness of individuals, that is their reproductive
success. This is determined by the interactions of the individual with
its environment, both biotic and non-biotic. Adaptation is the
response of the organism towards its total environment, involving a
reduction in any 'stress' imposed by the environment. I use the term
'stress' conscious of the controversy that surrounds it, and the
difficulty of defining it. Notwithstanding, it clearly represents a biological reality involving a cost to an organism which can be lessened
behaviourally, biochemically, physiologically or morphologically.

Southwood (1978, 1988) has traced the interactions of the factors
defining the relationship between organism and habitat in both time
and space, and derived a 'reproductive success matrix' depending on
five habitat and three organism characteristics and their variances
(which involve inherited components both for the organism traits,
and also for those habitat traits that involve other species).

A link between this matrix and traditional genetic models is
provided by Wallace's (1975) concept of 'hard' and 'soft' selection.
This terminology comes from economics where 'soft currency' is
usable only within a particular country, whereas 'hard currency'
maintains its value in all countries. In Wallace's sense, hard selection
acts on phenotypes under all conditions (for example, lethal genes
[genotypes] are invariably fatal to their carriers), whereas soft
selection involves different probabilities of survival (or death) as
conditions change. This means that the fitness of certain phenotypes
will vary with density and population composition. Hard selection is
both density and frequency independent. The key to evolutionary
ecology is not simple population dynamics or gene frequency
change, but a complementation of perceptible genetical processes
(involving appropriate ecological variables) with an appreciation of
the effects of stressful conditions on different phenotypes.

All this produces pattern in nature, which is apparent to even the
most casual observer. The analysis of the pattern has spawned a
dictionary of descriptive concepts: mutualism, parasitism, competition, symbiosis, commensalism, antagonism, *ad nauseam.* All of
these are valuable in their own contexts. But when we seek the
processes that make up the pattern, there is no better starting point
than that given to us by Darwin (1858):

Nature may be compared to a surface on which rest ten thousand sharp
wedges touching each other and driven inwards by incessant blows. Fully

to realise these views much reflection is requisite. But let the external conditions of a country alter ... can it be doubted from the struggle each individual has to obtain subsistence, that any minute variation in structure, habits, or instincts, adapting that individual better to the new conditions, would tell upon its vigour and health? In the struggle it would have a better chance of surviving; and those of its offspring which inherited the variation, be it ever so slight, would also have a better chance. Yearly more are bred than can survive; the smallest grain in the balance, in the long run, must tell on which death shall fall, and which shall survive.

Darwin's great achievement was to change the focus of biologists from the 'much reflection' on pattern to the processes that determine the pattern. Or as Paine (1980) has put it: 'Pattern is generated by process. The former embodies static description, the latter more subtle and dynamical events.' In other words, we are merely confusing ourselves when we compound pattern with process: we shall do much better to begin our investigations with the consequences of variation in organisms, and see how these knit together into a pattern. The danger is that we become so involved with the details that we lose sight of the whole; somewhat literally, we fail to see the wood for the trees.

But the natural world is composed of parts which add together, with the whole probably constituting much more than the sum of the parts: to understand the pattern, we need to know the processes which constitute it; but knowing all the processes does not necessarily mean that we will fully understand the pattern. Meanwhile, it is worth emphasising that, despite all the efforts of scientific ecology and the vast amount of knowledge we have accumulated, in the end science itself needs to be truly holistic (or, in view of the overtones of the term 'holism' stemming from its use from Smuts's philosophy to New Age syncretism, much less reductionist). Ecology will only come of age when it is perceived as a synthesis and not as a specialism in its own right (Berry, 1989).

Gaia

My digression into the history, content and state of scientific ecology makes it apparent that contemporary theory does not understand 'nature' as a massive super-organism in its own right with ourselves as small-part players, perhaps even dispensable parasites. Modern ecologists do not support the implicit assumptions of many green religionists, where reincarnation, process thought, pantheism, feminism all assume some integral and often organic connection between human beings and the wider living world. Whereas this lack of congruence between science and faith is of little importance to most green worshippers, it could be regarded as indicating a final break between reason and traditional faith, and an irrevocable end to natural theology. This fracture was referred to by the Prince of Wales in his Reith Lecture:

> The idea that there is a sacred trust between mankind and our Creator under which we accept a duty of stewardship for the earth, has been an important feature of most religious and scientific thought throughout the ages. Even those whose beliefs have not included the existence of a Creator have, nevertheless, adopted a similar position on moral and ethical grounds. It is only recently that this guiding principle has become smothered by almost impenetrable layers of scientific rationalism. (Patten *et al.*, 2000:81)

Notwithstanding, any robust relationship we have with our environment must be based on the reality of the natural world, in other words, on reason as well as moral commitment. Consequently, it is pertinent to examine Lovelock's 'Gaia theory' which has been claimed as showing a functional set of interactions between ourselves and our world, and hence could more than replace the illusory interactions claimed within ecological systems.

Lovelock developed his theory following a request from NASA to devise a test for detecting life on Mars. He reasoned that the atmosphere of a lifeless planet would be in equilibrium with the physical composition of that planet, and would consist mainly of carbon dioxide, with a small amount of nitrogen and almost no oxygen. Such a planet would have a very high surface temperature due to the blanketing (or greenhouse) effect of the carbon dioxide. Any deviation away from this equilibrium situation would indicate the presence of a disturbing influence, which could be regarded as 'life'. Lovelock's definition of life, based on his own discipline of physical chemistry, is 'a member of the class of phenomena which are open or continuous systems able to decrease their internal entropy at the expense of substances or free energy taken in from the environment and subsequently rejected in a degraded form ...' (Lovelock, 1979:4). Mars has an atmosphere expected from its geological structure but – and this was the point that set Lovelock thinking – the earth's atmosphere is radically different from expectation.

Now the traditional interpretation of the origin of life on earth about 4,000 million years ago is that it was an outcome of chemical processes involving adaptation to contemporary atmospheric conditions, which were initially reducing but then became oxidising. Lovelock turned these ideas upside down, and proposed that the atmosphere changed in response to the life developing in it. In other words, that life (or the biosphere) regulates or maintains the climate and the atmospheric composition, and thus provides an optimum for itself. If this is true, the whole geobiochemical system can be regarded as a single gigantic, self-regulating system. William Golding (the novelist and a neighbour of Lovelock) suggested the name 'Gaia' for this system, after the earth goddess of ancient Greece.

Lovelock's description of the 'recognition of Gaia' is eerily reminiscent of Archdeacon Paley's walking across a common and finding a watch – which, of course, meant to Paley that there must have been a watchmaker:

> Picture a clean-swept sunlit beach with the tide receding; a smooth flat plain of golden glistening sand where every random grain has found due place and nothing more can happen ... Now let us suppose that our otherwise immaculate beach contains one small blot on the horizon: an isolated heap of sand which at close range we recognise instantly to be the work of a living creature. There is no shadow of a doubt, it is a sand-castle. Its structure of piled truncated cones reveals the bucket technique of building. ... We are programmed, so to speak, for instant recognition of a sand-castle as a human artefact, but if more proof were needed that this heap of sand is no natural phenomenon, we should point out that it does not fit with the conditions around it. The rest of the beach has been washed and brushed into a smooth carpet; the sand-castle has still to crumble; and even a child's fortress in the sand is too intricate in the design and relationship of its parts, too clearly purpose-built, to be the chance structure of natural forces. (Lovelock, 1979:33)

Lovelock continues much as did Paley, analysing possible disturbing factors that might have produced apparent design on the beach. Gaia can be treated as a scientific or a metaphysical theory. As the former, it has been a great success whether or not it is true, because of the research it has stimulated. Lovelock (1990) has claimed five predictive successes for the theory:

1. prediction of the lifeless state of Mars made in 1968, confirmed 1977;
2. carbon dioxide influence on climate through the biological weathering of rock predicted in 1981, shown in 1989;
3. the constant 21 per cent of oxygen in the environment for the last 200 million years could be due to fire and phosphorus cycling, for which the biological input is important;

4. the transfer of elements necessary for life on land predicted in 1971 to be mediated through algae, shown 1973;
5. a link between dimethyl sulphide produced by phytoplankton in the deep oceans has an effect on cloud cover.

The last claim has been contested because dimethyl sulphide in Antarctic ice cores decreased at the end of the Pleistocene when it might have been expected to increase due to the rise in temperature. However this is exactly the sort of anomalous result that research produces and which leads to further work. In itself it should not be regarded too negatively.

More serious criticism has come from biologists because of the apparent absence of any Gaian mechanism for producing evolutionary adaptation in biological organisms. Dawkins has written:

> Homeostatic adaptations in individual bodies evolve because individuals with improved homeostatic apparatuses pass on their genes more effectively than individuals with inferior homeostatic apparatuses. For the analogy [that the whole Earth is equivalent to a single living organism] to apply strictly, there would have to be a set of rival Gaias, presumably different planets. Biospheres which did not develop efficient homeostatic regulation of their planetary atmospheres tend to go extinct. The Universe would have to be full of dead planets whose homeostatic regulations had failed, with, dotted around, a handful of successful well-regulated planets of which Earth is one. (1982:236)

Lovelock has responded to this criticism by producing a computer model called Daisyworld which shows, he believes, that regulatory behaviour such as he postulates for Gaia can develop simply as a property of the complex processes which link organisms to their environment (Watson and Lovelock, 1983; Lovelock, 1989). There is certainly truth in the idea that living organisms (as defined in the normal as opposed to the Lovelockian way) modify their environment and this may lead to natural selection (Lenton, 1998). The jury remains out on the extent and rates of such effects.

However, exploring Gaia as metaphysics is to enter a world of speculation and pantheism. The physicist Fritjof Capra sees the emergence of Gaia as a sign of a universal change of attitude, the earth 'not just functions *like* an organism, but actually seems to be an organism ... the new paradigm is ultimately spiritual' (Capra, 1982:308–9). Baring and Cashford (1991:304) write:

> The name of Gaia is now everywhere heard. There is the 'Gaia Hypothesis' of the physicist James Lovelock ... there is 'Gaia Consciousness', which urges that the Earth and her creatures be considered as one whole; and

there is simply the term 'Gaia', which expresses a reverence for the planet
as a being who is alive and on whom all other life depends.

Celia Deane-Drummond (1996:106–10) identifies four different
Gaias: influencing or regulatory Gaia; coevolutionary Gaia; homeo-
static Gaia; teleological Gaia. She welcomes Gaia as a positive
challenge to mechanistic science and technology and the power-
lessness of humans, comparing its holism to that of Aldo Leopold
(Deane-Drummond, 1993); Hugh Montefiore (1985:57) sees Gaia as
a manifestation of the Anthropic Principle (p. 12) and links it to
Paul's description of the coordinated body in 1 Corinthians
12.14–26 (Montefiore, 1997:123); Michael Northcott (1996:196)
finds a 'close fit between the covenant and Torah and aspects of the
land ethic, of Gaian order and the relationality of self, nature and
society'. These responses are much more realistic than the sort of
excited attitude expressed by Peter Russell, a one time Maharishi
Mahesh Yogi disciple, who believes that continuing evolution of the
human consciousness will produce a shared Gaiafield, that there are
millions of Gaias in the cosmos which will all eventually network
together through something like ESP and form a super-Gaia so that
the whole universe will become a conscious being which he calls
Brahman, with cyclical expansion and contraction and repeated
reincarnation of Brahman, 'each time being a more perfect
Universal being ... the ultimate goal of Universe upon Universe
might be the enlightenment of Brahman – the perfect cosmos'
(Russell, 1982:218).

Lovelock himself professes surprise at the religious implications
that many see in his hypothesis. He writes:

> For every letter I got about the science of *Gaia: a New Look at Life on Earth*
> [his 1979 book] there were two concerning religion. I think people need
> religion, and the notion of the Earth as a living planet is something to
> which they can obviously relate. At the least, Gaia may turn out to be the
> first religion to have a testable scientific theory embedded within it.

His long-time collaborator, Lyn Margulis is more forthright, quoted
as saying, 'The religious overtones of Gaia make me sick!'; although
she later conceded: 'Gaia is less harmful than standard religion. It
can be very environmentally aware. At least it is not human-centred'
(Joseph, 1990:70–1).

Gaia as a scientific hypothesis may prove to be true or not. From
the point of view of theology it is of no great import; the existence or
working of God does not depend upon a scientific theory. However,

it seems worth insisting on a clear distinction between Gaia as science and Gaia as metaphysics. Herbert Spencer wrought long-term damage to the proper understanding of biological evolution by his unwarranted extrapolation of so-called social Darwinism. It would be easy for both natural science and natural theology to be harmed by failing to separate Gaian science from Gaian speculation.[4]

The 'New' Physics

Another science that has been claimed for 'green' religion is sub-atomic physics, particularly Einsteinian relativity and quantum theory. Four advocates are frequently cited: Fritjof Capra, author of *The Tao of Physics* (1975) and *The Turning Point* (1982), Gary Zukav (*The Dancing Wu Li Masters* [1979]), A. de Riencourt (*The Eye of Shiva* [1980]); and, in rather a different category, Paul Davies, author of *God and the New Physics* (1983), *The Mind of God* (1992), and other books.

Capra can be taken as the leader of the first three. He is a strong critic of what he regards as the fragmented dualism of Western science, which he blames on Newton and Descartes. He claims to be a postmodernist in the sense of promoting holism; he finds his inspiration in Buddhism, Hinduism, Taoism and Ch'an (which developed into the Japanese version of Zen): 'The most important characteristic of the Eastern world view – one can almost say the essence of it – is the awareness of the unity and the mutual interrelation of all things and events, the experience of all phenomena in the world as manifestations of a basic oneness.' All things are seen as interdependent and inseparable parts of the cosmic whole, as 'different manifestations of the same ultimate reality' (Capra, 1982:142). He argues that both Eastern mysticism and modern physics are empirical and both draw their observations from realms inaccessible to the normal senses, and hence are complementary ('Mystical experience is necessary to understand the deepest nature of things, and science is essential for modern life. We need not a synthesis but a dynamic interplay between mystical intuition and scientific analysis' [Capra, 1983:339]), with physics supporting Eastern mysticism (Capra, 1983:126, 247).

Two ideas from science recur throughout Capra's writing. The first is the impossibility of attaining any absolute, detached vantage point within the universe. This follows directly from Werner Heisenberg's Principle of Indeterminacy and from Relativity Theory. The second is that there is some sort of underlying connection between apparently distinct objects ('paired polarities' or the Bell Effect; this was first pointed out by Einstein and two of his co-workers, Podolsky and Rosen, and is sometimes called the Einstein-Podolky-Rosen, or EPR paradox). Bohm has suggested that this implies an 'implicate' (or enfolded) order in the universe, so that 'everything is enfolded into everything. This contrasts with the *explicate order* now dominant in physics in which things are *unfolded* in the sense that each thing lies only in its own particular region of space (and time) and outside the regions belonging to other things' (Bohm, 1952).

Neither of these ideas necessarily carries religious or metaphysical implications, but they do suggest the inadequacy of the mechanistic notion of the universe as a collection of separate particles. For Capra:

> Relativity theory has made the cosmic web come alive, so to speak, by revealing its essentially dynamic character; by showing that its activity is the very essence of its being. In modern physics, the image of the universe as a machine has been transcended by a view of it as one indivisible dynamic whole whose parts are essentially interrelated and can be understood only as patterns of a cosmic process. At the sub-atomic level the interrelations and interactions between the parts of the whole are more fundamental than the parts themselves. There is motion but there are, ultimately, no moving objects; there is activity but there are no actors; there are no dancers, there is only the dance. (Capra, 1982:91–2)

This leads Capra to argue that since matter and energy are equivalent in the Einsteinian equation $E=mc^2$, matter is only transient and energy is the ultimate reality, and thence that human consciousness plays a part in creating reality (because *how* we look at an entity – or at least, an electron – determines *what* we see).

In fact Capra and those who argue like him fall into two different traps. They legitimately criticise the reductionism of modern physics, but then force their own interpretations on it ('Quantum mechanics tells us', 'Modern physics forces us to believe', etc.) whilst ignoring the mass of confirmatory results obtained by physicists using traditional interpretations of experimental results. But more corrosively, they use Eastern mysticism selectively to support their case. They tend to treat all Eastern traditions as representing a single world view, although (for example) the interconnectedness of all things is alien to Advaitan Hinduism; the distinction in Buddhism between reality as it is and as it usually seems to be is not the same as that between virtual and 'real' particles; energy in any recognisable scientific sense is not dealt with in any classical Asian religious tradition, so there can be none of the confusion between matter and energy claimed to exist in the West (Clifton and Regehr, 1990; Lucas, 1996). Despite the popularity of Capra, Zukav and de

Riencourt, it is hard to disagree with Robert Jones (1986:202) that their reasoning is based on the obvious *non sequitur* that 'because science and mysticism each have difficulty with language, they are talking about the same thing'.

The approach and interpretation of Paul Davies is very different to that of Capra and his ilk. Davies

> always wanted to believe that science can explain everything, at least in principle ... but even if one rules out supernatural events, it is still not clear that science could in principle explain everything in the physical universe. There always remains that old problem about the end of the explanatory chain. However successful our scientific explanations may be, they always have certain starting assumptions built in ... Sooner or later we all have to accept something as given, whether it is God, or logic, or a set of laws, or some other foundation for existence. Thus 'ultimate' questions will always lie beyond the scope of empirical science as it is usually defined. (Davies, 1992:15)

Notwithstanding:

> Most scientists have a deep mistrust of mysticism. This is not surprising, as mystical thought lies at the opposite extreme to rational thought, which is the basis of the scientific method. Also, mysticism tends to be confused with the occult, the paranormal, and other fringe beliefs. In fact, many of the world's finest thinkers, including some notable scientists such as Einstein, Pauli, Schrödinger, Heisenberg, Eddington and Jeans, have also espoused mysticism. My own feeling is that the scientific method should be pursued as far as it possibly can. Mysticism is no substitute for scientific inquiry and logical reasoning so long as this approach can be consistently applied. It is only in dealing with ultimate questions that science and logic may fail us. I am not saying that science and logic are likely to provide the wrong answers, but they may be incapable of addressing the sort of 'why' (as opposed to 'how') questions we want to ask. (Davies, 1992:226)

Davies wants answers to his questions: he writes, 'Personally I feel more comfortable with a deeper explanation than the laws of physics [but] whether the use of the term "God" for that deeper level is appropriate [as is also whether] this postulated being who underpins the rationality of the world bears much relation to the personal God of religion.'

Naturalism – or More?

The assumption – or perhaps better, the question – behind 'green science' is that there is something beyond (and perhaps even, within) conventional science that makes necessary 'green religion'. The conventional expressions of green religion are in terms which do not encourage or attract traditional scientists to develop their thinking, but the widespread belief of both biologists and physicists that they have to expand their understanding further than their scientific results warrant is a clear pointer. It is exactly the same conclusion as that of Peter Medawar in recognising that there are limits to science (pp. 13–14). It could, of course, be interpreted as tentative hypothesis-making in the normal practice of scientific method, but the difficulty of explaining evolutionary progress, ecological complexity and particularly what Paul Davies calls 'the mind of God' ought to prevent us denying 'something' which our ancestors would have described as 'natural revelation' – unless like Hume, Monod, Atkins and Dawkins we have profound faith (as opposed to reason) in our denial.

This faith-denial diathesis tends to be highlighted by the rationalist scorn poured on those who claim the reality of this 'natural revelation' (for want of a better description). For example, Richard Dawkins (1993) has described religion as a viral disease. John Bowker (1995) castigates Dawkins's proposal as a 'weak theory based on analogy', while Keith Ward (1996:97) has no doubts: 'God is not a tentative hypothesis which one should always be seeking to test to destruction by actively seeking for counter-evidence. That is rather like saying that a good marriage is best achieved by always seeking evidence of infidelity.'

But there is another and even more sweeping attack from a philosophical attitude that rejects conventional science as inadequate because it empties the universe – and especially life – of all value and meaning. This commonly manifests as an anti-evolutionism founded on a belief in an interfering rather than an upholding creator. The most distinguished exponent of this approach is the philosopher Alvin Plantinga, but it has been popularised in a series of books by a lawyer, Phillip Johnson (Plantinga, 1991; McMullin, 1993; Pennock, 1996; q.v. Scott and Padian, 1997; a powerful response has been made by Willem Drees in Russell, Stoeger and Ayala, 1998:303–28).

Johnson and his supporters have promoted 'Intelligent Design Theory' as an alternative to what they regard as the atheism implicit in scientific naturalism. Their main complaint is not evolution as such, but the assumption that belief in evolution leads inexorably to atheism. Now it is true that Darwin (or, for that matter, Dawkins) showed that atheism was not inconsistent with biological science, but in no way did he show that one required or implied the other. Johnson seems to accept this, writing 'The blind watchmaker thesis [i.e. neo-Darwinism] ... does not make it obligatory to be an atheist, because one can imagine a Creator who works through natural selection' (Johnson, 1995:77); but his emphasis is on the incompatibility of religious (or at least, Christian) belief and scientific practice: '*Naturalists* ... assume that God exists only as an idea in the minds of religious believers' (1995:7); 'From a naturalistic standpoint ... the Creator God of the Bible is every bit as unreal as the gods of Olympus' (1995:39).

In fact Johnson misses the nub of the question that he seems to be attacking. By concentrating on two antithetical positions (that God could not be a creator, either because he does not exist or because he is impotent; and that he created everything by some unexplained mechanism), he ignores two other possibilities: the *reductio ad absurdum* that God could have created all things but did not; or that God could have created all things, and did so through the evolutionary mechanism (Johnson, Lamoureux *et al.*, 1999; Miller, 1999; Pennock, 1999).

The last interpretation seems to me the only valid one to an honest believer faced with a world which has changed radically in past ages (in other words, evolution has occurred) and with a God who claims to be both creator and sustainer (i.e. a God who works in the world as immanent as well as outside the world as transcendent). Ways in which this could be envisaged are described in Chapter 2. The God of the Bible is one who works in history and experience through processes which can be perceived as divine by the eye of faith. ('*By faith* we understand that the universe was formed by God's command, so that the visible came forth from the invisible', Hebrews 11.3). The atheism of Dawkins *et al.* is more credible than the antinaturalism of Plantinga, Johnson *et al.*, but atheism only survives intact if the indications reviewed in this chapter are wrong, in other words if we fail – wilfully or not – to search beyond science for a full explanation of the world in which we live (Berry, 2000*b*). There is not an explicitly green science which justifies and validates the extravagances of green religion; but there are signs within orthodox science that there is something more than naked naturalism.

NOTES

1   Although the point is different, it is worth recording that large areas – perhaps most – of the Amazonian forest have a layer of charcoal below them, indicating that at some time in the past the forest has burnt (or been burnt), and the present trees are not the original ones (or necessarily their direct descendants).

2   John Polkinghorne (1988:6) notes that the recognition of 'pattern and process' is a key to natural theology (p. 12):

> The twin discernment of both pattern and process in the workings of the world, of being and becoming, lie at the heart of any attempt to construct a natural theology in true accord of the way things are. There has been a perpetual temptation in religious thought to concentrate on one pole or the other of this dialectic – the static perfection of the God of the philosophers, in all his remoteness; the living God of Abraham, Isaac and Jacob, in all his dangerous anthropomorphism. A true account will hold the two in balance. It is interesting that a similar complementarity of being and becoming is necessary in the scientific story of the world.

3   Coevolution is the interdependent evolution of two or more species within an ecological relationship.

4   Murray Bookchin (1994:29) comments, 'For the ecology movement [i.e. environmentalism, not ecological science] to become frivolous and allow itself be guided by various sorts of mystics would be unpardonable – a tragedy of enormous proportions ... The misanthropic strain that runs through the movement in the name of biocentrism, antihumanism, Gaian consciousness, and neo-Malthusianism threatens to make ecology the best candidate we have for a dismal science.'

7
Running Out of World

There is a common myth that the environmental crisis dates from the first pictures of the earth from space, and the sudden realisation that we live on a finite globe with finite resources. This is not true. Although the impact of the idea of 'Spaceship Earth' was sharpened by those remarkable photographs and the 'one small step for a man, one giant leap for mankind' of Neil Armstrong in 1969, environmental crises of one sort or another have been occurring throughout recorded history. An astonishingly modern perception was penned over two centuries earlier than Neil Armstrong's 'giant leap' by the Reverend Otto Lütken, Rector of a parish on the island of Fyn, Denmark. He wrote in 1758:

> Since the circumference of the globe is given and does not expand with the increased number of its inhabitants, and as travel to other planets thought to be inhabitable has not yet been invented; since the earth's fertility cannot be extended beyond a given point, and since human nature will presumably remain unchanged, so that a given number will hereafter require the same quantity of the fruits of the earth for their support as now, and as their rations cannot be arbitrarily reduced, it follows that the proposition 'that the world's inhabitants will be happier, the greater their number' cannot be maintained, for as soon as the number exceeds that which our planet with all its wealth of land and water can support, they must needs starve one another out, not to mention other necessarily attendant inconveniences, to wit, a lack of the other comforts of life, wool, flax, timber, fuel, and so on. But the wise Creator who commanded men in the beginning to be fruitful and multiply, did not intend, since He set limits to their habitation and sustenance, that multiplication should continue without limit. (cited by Cohen, 1995:7)

Environmental problems are not a phenomenon of the modern world, nor of the exponential population growth over the past few decades. Overpopulation was described in a Babylonian history dating from before 1600 BC. The Babylonian gods created humans on the earth to do the work of the lesser gods, but problems soon arose:

> Twelve hundred years had not yet passed
> When the land extended and the people multiplied.

> The land was bellowing like a bull,
> The gods got disturbed with their uproar.
> Enlil heard their noise
> And addressed the great gods:
> 'The noise of mankind has become too much for me,
> With their noise I am deprived of sleep.
> Let there be a pestilence (upon mankind).
>
> (Kilmer, 1972:166)

Lest the problem was repeated, the gods went on to impose religious obligations of celibacy on priestesses and sent a demon to destroy infants.

Whatever the rationalisation for their cause, environmental crises are not new. There were 200 famines in Britain alone between AD 10 and 1846, whilst the Chinese have had nearly 2,000 famines during the past 2,000 years. Even in this century, an estimated 5 to 10 million died in the USSR in 1918–22 and 1932–4; four million in China in 1920–21; and 2 to 4 million in West Bengal in 1943.

Time and again cultures have contributed to their own decline. The early Polynesian population of New Zealand depended on large flightless Moas for food, but after 600 years they had cleared so much forest that a number of bird species including swans, eagles and Moas were virtually extinct. At some stage there must have been an 'ecological crisis' when the increasing difficulty of obtaining enough Moas indicated inadequate recruitment of young birds into the population so that a decline in the number of adults available to be hunted was inevitable.

The decline of the great Babylonian grain-growing civilisation was probably due to the increasing salinity of irrigated areas as a result of imperfect drainage. Again there must have been a time when yields were declining, more and more unsuitable areas were being pressed into cultivation, and irrigation channels required extending and reconstruction, while at the same time the demands of the cities for food would have been increasing (Ponting, 1991:72).

There are plenty of other examples: the Dust Bowl of the southern central United States arose from the practice of growing crops in an area where the rainfall is low and the soil surface is eroded by wind and storm.[1] Sicily was once the 'granary of Italy' but less and less corn is grown there as the soil has deteriorated under excessive cultivation and the grazing of goats. Recently half the population of the Tokelau Islands had to be resettled elsewhere, because hurricane damage on top of overpopulation threatened their continued survival.

Repeatedly crises have arisen and been overcome either by emigration (as from Ireland after the potato blight of 1845–7) or the introduction of new technologies (such as the so-called green revolution in tropical areas following the development of new, high-yielding strains of rice). The easiest assumption about these recurring problems is that they are the result of overpopulation, that there are too many people for the habitable part of the globe to support, and that crowding produces secondary consequences such as epidemic disease and loss of agricultural land. This is an oversimplification, well exposed and reviewed by Joel Cohen in his *How Many People Can the Earth Support?* (1995). Notwithstanding, and whatever one's view about liberty and freedom of choice, parents cannot continue indefinitely to have, on the average, more children than required to replace themselves. The finiteness of the earth guarantees that there are ceilings on human numbers.[2] The practical problem is that the levels of these ceilings are tremendously uncertain.

Carrying Capacity

Perhaps the best way to seek an answer is through the concept of 'carrying capacity' (the number of individuals which can be supported indefinitely or sustainably in a particular habitat), an idea commonly used by ecologists and equally often misapplied by politicians.

The problem is that 'carrying capacity' depends on a whole complex of constraints. If a population of animals has no limitations on food or space, it will grow exponentially in numbers, much as the global human population has been doing until recently. However, the assumption of unlimited food and space is unrealistic, and as numbers increase various intrinsic or extrinsic factors will begin to affect the rate of population growth, until birth and death rates become equal and the population size stabilises. This balance is the carrying capacity of the environment for that population; it was Thomas Malthus's nightmare as he viewed the nineteenth-century world. The error is to refer to *the* carrying capacity of the environment without specifying the conditions that determine it. Cohen (1995) lists 65 different estimates of the earth's total carrying capacity. He separates those which have focused on a single assumed constraint (usually food), and those which recognise that 'man and woman do not live by bread alone. People also require wood, fibre, fuel and amenities.' These needs can be broken down into physical (shelter, food, clean air, and water), economic (transport, shops, work) and aesthetic (space, quiet, access to countryside). Another approach is to examine the link between the quantity and quality of life, explored by Goulet (1995:41), who identifies three goals: optimum life-sustenance, esteem and freedom. 'These goals are properly universalisable, although their specific modalities vary in different times and places. They refer to fundamental human needs capable of finding expression in all cultural matrices and at all times.'

This is an idea to which we shall have to return (p. 206). Sadly it is a factor rarely considered by those who calculate (and worry about) how many people the Earth can support. Perhaps the best known of these is the 'Club of Rome' Report, *The Limits of Growth* (Meadows, Meadows and Randers, 1972), based on a computer simulation of the effects on survival if we carry on growing in number and using non-renewable resources at the same increasing rate as at present. Its conclusions were:

1. If present growth trends in world population and resource depletion continue, the limits to growth on this planet will be reached within the next 100 years.
2. It is theoretically possible to alter these growth trends and to establish a state of global equilibrium; this could be designed so that the basic material needs of each person are satisfied and each person has an equal opportunity to realise their individual human potential.
3. If the world's people decide to strive for this second outcome rather than the first, the sooner they begin working to attain it the greater their chances of success.

The authors reran their model twenty years later (Meadows, Meadows, Randers and Behrens, 1992) with better data, and reached similar conclusions – albeit with a sinister addition that 'business as usual would continue beyond the point where systems could be sustained, and then the overshoot would end with a cataclysmic collapse'.

The *Limits* study has been heavily criticised by economists (e.g. Beckerman, 1995) on the grounds that it ignored market forces and technological developments. Yale economist William Nordhaus (1996) expressed conventional wisdom when he wrote: 'If the earth is reaching ... its limits on land and resources, the increasing stress should be accompanied by rising prices of land, food and energy. But these prices have been declining.' This complaint is off-target. Global market prices are useful for co-ordinating economic activity. They are not reliable as indicators of change for three reasons (Cohen, 1996):

1. Global prices do not reflect the depletion of unowned stocks, such as marine fisheries, the atmospheric ozone, or water in internationally shared rivers.
2. Prices tend not to include all the environmental and social costs of a product, such as atmospheric pollution, restoring used mines, decommissioning nuclear power stations, particularly when these are unknown (e.g. metabolic effects of polychloro-biphenyls [PCBs]).
3. Markets respond to demand, not to human need. The very poor have too little money to buy food, so they cannot drive up its price. Even if there is no global shortage of food relative to effective demand and even if global food prices are falling, there may be chronic hunger, or even serious famine in some parts of the world.

Notwithstanding the economists, *The Limits* resonated widely in drawing attention to the fact that a finite system *must* have limits, even if we cannot agree on what these are or when we will reach them.

The *Limits* approach was taken up in the year it appeared by *A Blueprint for Survival* (Goldsmith, Allen, Allaby, Davoll and Lawrence, 1972). This employed two linked arguments. The first was that the rate of exploitation of non-renewable resources of raw materials which sustain industrial activity threatens them with depletion within the sort of time scale that ordinarily commands political action. The second was that the effects of this exploitation, particularly its waste products, significantly degrade the natural systems which sustain human life.

The *Blueprint* authors argued that industrial societies need to convert themselves into stable societies characterised by a minimum disruption of ecological processes, maximum conservation of materials and energy, and an end to population growth. They outlined a 'green' political programme to achieve these ends.

The Times accorded the *Blueprint* a first leader, 'The prophets may be right'. The leader writer judged 'the thesis is too plausible to be dismissed'. In rather cruder language we can assert that we are 'running out of world'. In past times it was possible to escape from local overpopulation or overdepletion of resources by emigrating. This brought the beaker folk to Britain, and saw the Teutons spreading across Europe, the Vikings sailing west and south from Scandinavia, the peopling of North America in the sixteenth and seventeenth centuries, the expansion of empires in the nineteenth century; on a local scale, it is the basis of slash-and-burn agricultures; more sinisterly, it is the spectre of millions of 'environmental refugees' inexorably spreading across national boundaries in the foreseeable future as existing tracts become uninhabitable through climate change, radioactive contamination, or other anthropogenic activity.

Population, Pollution and Responsibility

'Solutions' to environmental problems have to take a range of factors into account. In the 1960s there was a debate between proponents of 'zero population growth' and those who saw salvation emerging through better and more efficiently used resources. The argument was really about the influence of limiting or critical factors: do population numbers determine pollution levels and environmental quality generally, or can improvements in, say, the management of pollution allow ever-increasing numbers to enjoy better life?

The background to this uncertainty is that:

> there is no simple relation between pollution, population and technology; [However,] population growth is not the main issue facing our nation [Britain]. More important are the concentration of population in cities and in certain geographical areas, and the output [of waste] per head which accompanies a rise in living standards; on a conservative estimate this output could well double over the next 30 years. Failing deliberate measures to control pollution and to repair past damage, there is likely to be a substantial deterioration of the environment in the years ahead and the quality of life in Britain will be correspondingly impoverished, despite an appearance of greater affluence. (Royal Commission on Environmental Pollution, 1971)[3]

Sixteen years after the Royal Commission Report, the Brundtland Commission Report declared:

> The population issue is not solely about numbers. Poverty and resource degradation can exist on thinly populated lands, such as the dry lands and the tropical forests ... threats to the sustainable use of resources come as much from inequalities in people's access to resources and from the ways in which they use them as from the sheer numbers of people. Thus concern over the 'population problem' also calls forth concern for human progress and human equality. (World Commission on Environment and Development, 1987:95)

Religions – particularly Roman Catholicism and some parts of Islam – are traditionally seen as unenthusiastic if not actively antagonistic to contraception. Their opposition is that children are 'God's will' and it is 'unnatural' to oppose the clear workings of nature in marriage. Such an approach could be described as improperly reductionist. From a Christian point of view, marriage was ordained for companionship, not primarily for reproduction (Genesis 2.18, 24; Matthew 19.5); Christ's view of adultery goes far beyond sexual intercourse (Matthew 5.27–28). The Bible uses two words to describe the physical union of a man and woman: *kollao* – to join, glue or cement together, and *ginosko* – to know. These words describe the very deep emotional and spiritual relationship between a man and a woman, the physical vehicle and sign of which is sexual intercourse.

The Old Testament emphasis on the Jews as God's chosen people is a genetic concept, backed by the command to 'increase in numbers and fill the earth' (Genesis 1.28–29; 9.1) and the Levitical teaching on marriage and the importance of families. However, the Old Testament genetical line was abruptly and radically replaced in the New Testament by the spiritual line constituting the Church founded by Christ, which is completely independent for its existence and spread of any genetic link (John 1.12–13; Romans 4.16; 1 Peter 2.9; etc.). Indeed, Paul's exhortations to avoid arguments about 'genealogies' (1 Timothy 1.4; Titus 3.9) can be interpreted as warnings that genetic descent has been superseded by 'the new and living way of Christ'.

The whole thrust of the Bible is that we should be responsible to God for all his creation, and not merely seek to propagate our own genes. In the light of this background, it is depressing that

> Papal encyclicals on ethical issues notably *Veritatis Splendor* and *Evangelicum Vitae* indicate that the humanocentrism of the modern Vatican remains ecologically problematic ... Only human life is [regarded as] the object of the revealed moral law, and of the moral laws of the church and civil society. Amidst the many ringing condemnations of the failure of these laws in modern societies to protect the human embryo or the unborn child, there is no single reference to the immoral treatment and loss of dignity which so many millions of farm animals and birds experience, also at the hands of modern technology, and which technology is visiting on all forms of life throughout the created order.
> (Northcott, 1996:135–6)

Whether we argue from the ecological need to involve a range of factors in calculating the carrying capacity of the earth or from the implication that religious prescriptions have to be inclusive to be convincing, we are faced with the inadequacy of simple unifactorial solutions for overpopulation or wide environmental questions. We will run out of world by default unless we successfully address all the relevant factors.

Environmental Awareness

God made a covenant with Noah after the floodwaters subsided that 'as long as the earth lasts, seedtime and harvest, cold and heat, summer and winter, day and night, they will never cease' (Genesis 8.22). Whether we believe that these regularities are God's providence or merely the way that things are, our experience is of living in a reliable world. Obviously some habitats and some parts of the world are less predictable than others. Retrospectively we can identify some trends or significant fluctuations during history: 10,000–12,000 years ago most of Britain was weighed down by a massive ice sheet; there was a 'Little Ice Age' in the late seventeenth century with much colder winters than normal (Fagan, 2000); during recent decades the southern edge of the Sahara desert has extended significantly further south; the movements of herring shoals around northern Britain are annoyingly variable; and so on. But these are relatively minor fluctuations around our reasonable expectations.

Disasters make us aware that we do not live in a privileged enclosure, but depend on a dynamic system: the volcanic eruptions that destroyed Pompeii and Montserrat; the earthquake that almost obliterated Lisbon; the combination of wind, wave and vibration that broke the Tay Bridge; the iceberg which ripped open the *Titanic*; the near 'silent spring' as songbirds declined following the widespread use of DDT-type insecticides; catastrophic oil spills in many parts of the world; Bhopal; Three Mile Island; Chernobyl – the list is long. The problem is that they are all, almost by definition, the product of rare happenings. Slow deteriorations in our environment are much less easy to detect. Declines in soil fertility are more than matched by better seed quality and fertiliser application. Today's photochemical smog is no worse that last week's and anyway the air is so much cleaner since comprehensive smoke control was introduced; we cannot *see* the reduction in atmospheric ozone, and it does not really inconvenience us since we have been persuaded to apply appropriate sun blocking creams; cod has become expensive, but salmon is much cheaper. Is there, we ask ourselves, any long-term environmental worsening? We play safe and moan about other people's polluting habits, and contribute on occasion to the Worldwide Fund for Nature (as well as Age Concern and a few cancer charities).

The problem about 'running out of world' is recognising that there is a problem; change is so slow and insidious that it is effectively undetectable except at the very local level. Here, of course, we have no difficulty. Some of the earliest recorded laws are regulations to protect game, mainly to prohibit trespassing and poaching. As time went on, scientific – or at least natural history – observations were incorporated into legislation. An Act of 1533 banned the taking of eggs of wildfowl between 1 March and 20 June each year, and the slaughter of adult birds between 31 May and 31 August; this was because there were signs of a serious decline in the numbers of 'dukkes mallardes wygeons teales wyldgeese and diverse other kyndes of wildfowle'. The Act noted how some people were taking large numbers of birds 'in the somer season at such tyme as the seid olds fowle be mowted and not replenysshed with fethers to flye nor the yonge fowle fully fetherede perfectlye to flye'.

Pollution was a problem even earlier. Horace mentions the blackening of buildings in Rome. Seneca was repeatedly advised to leave Rome for his health; he wrote to one Lucillus around AD 61 that no sooner did he leave Rome's oppressive fumes and cooking smells than he felt better (*Epistolae Morales* 104). The earliest recorded smoke pollution incident in Britain was in 1257 when Henry III's wife (Eleanor of Provence) moved from Nottingham to Tutbury Castle because of the stench of sea-coal in the town (Brimblecombe, 1987). Ironically, Mary, Queen of Scots, complained about the stink of the privies when she stayed at Tutbury in 1585. In 1306, the Knights Templar as owners of a mill at the mouth of the River Fleet (off Fleet Street) were prosecuted for blocking the river and preventing offensive waste and offal from the butchers and leather workers of Smithfield market escaping into the Thames.

In 1662 John Graunt, a draper, published a pioneering work of demography, *Natural and Political Observations ... Made upon the Bills of Mortality*, using the weekly records kept by parish clerks. He showed the death rate in London was much higher than in rural areas, and argued that this was due to the smoke-polluted air producing 'suffocations which many could not endure'. The diarist, John Evelyn (1620–1706) who had written a tract on coal smoke *Fumifugium* or *The Inconvenience of the Aer and the Smoke of London Dissipated* seized upon this and in an oft-quoted passage described London as shrouded in

> such a cloud of sea-coale, as if there be a resemblance of hell upon earth,
> it is in this volcano in a foggy day: this pestilent smoak, which corrodes the
> very yron, and spoils all the moveables, leaving a soot on all things that it
> lights: and so fatally seizing on the lungs of the inhabitants, that cough
> and consumption spare no man. (Evelyn, 1661)

He laid the blame for this squarely on the owners of a 'few Funnels and Issues, belonging to only Brewers, Diers, Lime-burners, Salt and Sope-boylers'.

Evelyn saw no excuse for the air of London being so bad. The city had been built on 'a sweet and agreeable eminency of the ground' with a gently sloping aspect that allowed the sun to clear the fumes from the waters and lower grounds to the south. Notwithstanding, it was another three centuries and many more pea-soup fogs before Parliament passed a comprehensive Clean Air Act (1956), and then only because of extreme – and in some ways irrelevant – political pressures.[4]

Environmental problems arise through unmanageable stresses being placed upon the systems that deal with insults. Natural organic pollutants are quickly broken down into harmless and usually helpful components. Thus an apple core thrown into a hedge rapidly disappears, although an orange or banana skin remains because it has no common bacterial or other detrifers in a temperate country like Britain. Running water will oxidise sewage into valuable nutrients *unless* the amount of sewage overwhelms the oxidising capacity of the stream or river. These exceptions are important: 'nature' can be overwhelmed more easily in some situations than others. Whereas small settlements can dispose of their rubbish by dumping it locally, larger towns and cities need to have special arrangements for dealing with their refuse. The sewage outlets of villages become wholly inadequate when the villages grow into towns. Notwithstanding, most environmental problems are generated locally and dealt with locally.

The General Inclosure Act of 1845 is sometimes described as the first conservation legislation in Britain, because at a time when urbanisation was proceeding rapidly and fortunes could be made by enclosing and then selling urban plots for building, it acknowledged that enclosure was the concern of all the local inhabitants, and not merely of the lord of the manor and a privileged group of commoners; and that the health, comfort, convenience, exercise and recreation of all local inhabitants should be taken into account before any enclosure was sanctioned. In 1865, the Commons, Open Spaces and Footpaths Preservation Society was formed to resist the continuing enclosure of common land; it was the forerunner of the host of pressure groups which now exist to protect or conserve nature.

Two points are worth making about the subsequent development of modern attitudes. First, the simple Christian idea of personal responsibility has been replaced increasingly by that of state control: Locke's principle of a person's unfettered rights over property has moved towards a situation of statutory responsibility, with the state intervening ever more in the economic and social life of the citizen. Today, the Western world has reached a position almost diametrically opposed to Locke's, but there has been a radical reassessment of attitudes that goes much further than rights in physical property alone. The area of responsibility of the Church has shrunk, and matters of economic and commercial significance have reverted to individuals or the state. The state is acknowledged as the ultimate authority to which the individual owes a duty for the management of the natural resources 'entrusted' to its care. These changes have, naturally enough, proceeded at different rates in different countries, and have gone much further in some (for instance the Netherlands or Great Britain) than in others (such as the United States), depending on different attitudes to centralised government and, ultimately, on different population–resource balances. Ironically, the new approach to the ownership of resources and the responsibility attendant upon it, sometimes referred to as 'fiduciary ownership', is not so far removed from the traditional Christian attitude as might appear at first sight, despite the complete secularisation of responsibility, and the substitution of the state for God.

Secondly, the British perception of the environment has matured for particular geographical and biological reasons. In many developing countries, the natural world is still seen as a resource to be exploited – trees to be sold for timber, forest to be cleared for agriculture, plant and animal compounds to be patented for pharmaceuticals, wildlife and scenery to be managed for tourism, and so on. Even in continental areas of the First World, natural 'goods' are often treated as utilitarian possessions for human use and management. For example, the Rhine is 1,320 km long, the longest river in Europe. Between its glacial source in Switzerland and its mouth at Rotterdam it receives each year 3,000 tonnes of zinc, 1,100 tonnes of arsenic, and most damaging in some ways, 19 million tonnes of salt (sodium chloride). All these pollutants have to be monitored and controlled for the sake of those who live along the course of the river and who use it for irrigation, industry or drinking, quite apart from its significance as a transport artery (Bennett, 1992: 54–91).

In Britain, the whole of the land surface has been modified by human activity. Although we have significant proportions of some species within our bounds (e.g. grey seals, great skuas), most species that are rare in Britain (such as the osprey or natterjack toad) are not threatened over their international range. We have some habitats (particular estuaries, maritime heath, sea bird colonies) which are very special in the global context, but are not important in the financial sense. For these reasons, the Nature Conservancy Council (whose function but not purpose has now been divided between separate organisations for England, Scotland and Wales) declared in 1984 that the rationale for nature conservation in Britain 'is primarily cultural, that is the conservation of wild flora and fauna, geological and physiographic features of Britain for their scientific, educational, recreational, aesthetic and inspirational value'. The NCC statement then made an interesting clarification:

> The term cultural should not be misconstrued: it is used here in the broadest sense as referring to the whole mental life of a nation. This cultural purpose shades imperceptibly into that which is clearly economic, that is dealing with aspects of resource utilisation providing the commodities for material existence and regulated by commercial factors. [Indeed] it is perhaps undesirable to distinguish sharply between the two, for both are necessary to the quality of life, and many nature conservation activities serve both purposes ... Science has an important place within this range of cultural purpose, as an end in itself and also as a means of supporting the technical practice of nature conservation. (Nature Conservancy Council, 1984:75)

We are thus faced with two trends: from individual to corporate responsibility, and from simplistic reaction to a considered, multifactorial, and, in a dangerous term, 'holistic' approach. But a third difficulty intrudes: the environment is not divided by national or political boundaries, but is a global entity. And that is beyond personal perception and realistically foreseeable political will.

From Local to Global

We are aware of problems in our own 'backyard': noise, smell, litter, erosion, species loss, air quality, urban dereliction, loss of countryside, traffic jams, and so on. These are the goads that spur people to take an interest in the environment. But increasingly there has come a recognition that some hazards are truly global. Perhaps the first inkling of this was the discovery that the derivatives of the chlorinated hydrocarbon insecticides (i.e. the DDT family) which had been so effective in mosquito (and hence malarial) control in the 1950s were becoming concentrated in food chains and affecting the fertility of predatory birds (owls, hawks and the like), and were also turning up far from the source of their application – in the fat of Antarctic penguins and the milk of Inuit women. No one knew if they had any detrimental effects on human health but a warning bell was sounding.

Then in 1986, radioactive fallout from the nuclear disaster at Chernobyl affected reindeer in Lapland, deer in Scotland, sheep in Wales, far from the site of the explosion. Long-term transport of radioactive particles was well known and well monitored since nuclear weapon testing in the 1950s, but was generally perceived to have only a marginal, chronic affect. Chernobyl showed that the assumption was radically incorrect.

However, the clearest example of human-induced damage to the global environment was the discovery in 1984–5 of severe ozone depletion in the atmosphere 20–30 km above Antarctica. Ozone is formed naturally by the addition of a third oxygen atom to the normal biatomic molecule of oxygen (O_2), under the influence of ultraviolet (UV) radiation from the sun. The ozone layer acts as an absorber of UV, reducing the latter's impact at the earth's surface, where it can be a powerful carcinogen. Every 1 per cent decrease in atmospheric ozone increases UV irradiation of the earth's surface by around 2 per cent, and this leads to an estimated 8 per cent increase in skin cancer in white-skinned people. At the same time it was shown that the chloro-fluoro-carbons (CFCs) widely used in refrigerators and as spray-can propellants (for deodorants, etc) had increased significantly in the atmosphere, and then soon afterwards that CFCs were active in breaking down ozone.

Banning CFCs was clearly sensible and should have been simple. It involved a single group of chemicals made by a small number of firms with little doubt about their effects. Nevertheless considerable international bargaining was required before an agreement was signed in 1987, and even this remains imperfect: the phasing out of CFCs has been slower than it should be, there are stories of massive imports of CFCs into developing countries from countries where their manufacture is still legal, and there are concerns that the vast numbers of fridges which will be sold in countries like India and China will use CFCs because they will be cheaper than more 'environmentally friendly' chemicals. Notwithstanding, control of CFCs is the best example so far of international action for environmental causes, and is repeatedly lauded by politicians as an example of what can be achieved. Unfortunately, other global problems – deforestation, disposal of toxic wastes and particularly the spectre of climate change are scientifically and politically far more complicated (Brenton, 1994).

Climate change or the greenhouse effect is undoubtedly the most serious threat facing life on earth as we know it, short of all-out nuclear war. As long ago as 1827, the French mathematician Jean Baptiste Fourier suggested that the earth's atmosphere traps the heat of the sun in the same way as glass captures heat in a green-house. It was then shown that the amount of heat trapped depends upon the presence in the atmosphere of certain 'greenhouse gases', of which carbon dioxide, methane and the CFCs are the most potent. Crudely speaking, the higher the proportion of greenhouse gases in the atmosphere the warmer the planet will become. If there were no greenhouse gases, the earth would be 33°C colder than it is, and life might never have got started. Then in 1896 the Swedish scientist Arrhenius pointed out the possibility that the coming of the industrial revolution and the large-scale burning of fossil fuels could raise the surface temperature of the earth, with possible sea-level rises and disruption to weather patterns (Christianson, 1999).

This hypothesis attracted little scientific interest over the next three-quarters of a century and only began to get serious attention with increased international scientific cooperation on meteoro-logical and atmospheric questions following the International Geophysical Year of 1957–8. Little notice was taken of it, for under-standable if pusillanimous reasons. The earth's climate is a highly complex physical system, involving not only the entire atmosphere but also the ocean circulations, and is in any case subject to wide natural fluctuations, the best known being the Ice Ages. However, interest quickened in the late 1980s. The years 1987 and 1988 were among the hottest of the century and followed two years (1981 and 1983) with above-average temperatures. The end of 1987 had seen a swathe of destruction in the Channel Islands and southern England by a gale, and a chunk of ice 40 km wide by 155 km long broke off the coast of Antarctica. The following year (1988) brought hurricane Gilbert to the Caribbean and a catastrophic drought in the American mid-west. James Hansen, a NASA scientist, testified to a US Senate sub-committee that it was 'time to stop waffling so much and say the evidence is pretty strong that the greenhouse effect is here'.

Concern was not confined to the developed world. The South Pacific Forum, speaking for the small Pacific island states, many of them low-lying and therefore seriously threatened by any sea-level rise, drew attention to the '500,000 environmental refugees' who might be one of the early results of global warming. This was a highly significant contribution, because it came from a group of 'devel-oping' countries prepared to join the industrial–scientific complex of the North in a subject where arguments were too often polarised between North and South.

In 1990, the UN General Assembly woke up to the problem, and a Framework Convention on Climate Change was drafted and then agreed at the Rio Summit (the United Nations Conference on

Environment and Development [UNCED]) in 1992. The framework included a statement that action on climate change could not wait for the resolution of scientific uncertainties, that developed countries should take the lead and compensate developing countries for any additional costs incurred in taking action under the convention, and that signatories should meet regularly and amend their commitments to reduce greenhouse gas emissions as necessary.

Following Rio, the Scientific Group of the Inter-Governmental Panel on Climate Change cautiously stated:

> Our ability to quantify the human influence on global climate is currently limited because the expected signal is still emerging from the noise of natural variability, and because there are uncertainties in key factors. These include the magnitude and patterns of long-term natural variability and the time-evolving pattern of forcing by, and response to, changes in concentrations of greenhouse gases and aerosols, and land surface changes. Nevertheless, the balance of evidence suggests that there is a discernible human influence on global climate.

Even this careful statement was too much for some (e.g. Lomborg, 2001), but there is certainly a massive majority consensus that drastic action to restrict carbon dioxide producing activities will have to be taken as soon as possible.

The amount of carbon dioxide in the atmosphere has increased by over a quarter since the industrial revolution, and is rising at an increasingly rapid rate. This means that the blanketing effect of the atmosphere is growing. The current estimate is that sea level will rise by about half a metre by the year 2100 – not too serious for the UK, but calamitous for Bangladesh, Egypt, large parts of China, and many islands. Serious impacts are expected on water supplies, especially in the more vulnerable parts of the world. Droughts and floods are likely to become more frequent and more intense.

In the summary of its White Paper on the Environment, which formed the official UK input to UNCED, the government began:

> Mankind long believed that, whatever we did, the Earth would remain much the same. We now know that is untrue. The ways we produce energy and the rate at which we multiply, use natural resources and produce waste, threaten to make fundamental changes in the world environment. Nature is under threat.

Not only are we running out of world, we are so ill-treating the world that we have that we are reducing its carrying capacity. Can this bad behaviour be reversed? How should we view the world?

Values and Valuations

'Ethics is about how we ought to live. What makes an action the right, rather than the wrong thing to do? What should our goals be?' (Singer, 1994:3). Although ethics is conventionally treated as a branch of philosophy, it is really a cross- (or perhaps an extra-) disciplinary problem, occupying the no man's land where philosophy, psychology, politics, economics, human biology and management techniques meet. These all contribute to the values we place on certain actions or objects. Some things we value highly and care for; other things are less valuable to us and their protection is of less interest to us. There have been centuries of debate about the source and subjectivity of values and valuation. My concern here is to recognise that there are differences in the values we attribute to things or processes, and therefore of the commitment in time, money or effort that we are prepared to contribute towards them.

'Value' is a key concept, not least because it is a trait which strongly influences decision-making. It is important to ethicists because the nature of the 'good life' is:

> based on conceptions of what is of intrinsic or ultimate value in a life ... The first reason [for examining ideas about what kind of life is really worth living] is the need to challenge the dominance of the assumption that the good life requires ever-rising standards of material affluence. This assumption is in opposition to the overwhelming majority of serious thinkers, past and present, from a wide variety of cultures. That does not show that the assumption is mistaken, but it gives us grounds to reflect and reconsider, especially since there is no evidence that – once we have provided for our basic needs – our increasing affluence makes us happier. The need for such reflection is greatly reinforced by the second reason for needing to revive discussion of this topic. We are running up against the limits of our planet's capacity to absorb the wastes produced by our affluent lifestyle. If we wish to avoid drastic change in the global climate, we may need to find a new ideal of the good life which is less reliant on a high level of material consumption. (Singer, 1994:179)

The difficulty is rescuing the notion of environmental 'value' from the arrogance of economists, obfuscation by philosophers, and rhetoric from politicians (Ashby, 1978). Mary Midgley has commented that:

> G. E. Moore and other moral theorists, have used the word 'value' as a central weapon in the campaign to assert the self-sufficiency of man and to defend him against seeming to have any need of religion. They have

observed that serious attitudes to the whole cosmos tend to be religious, and because institutionalised religions have often been harmful, they have wanted to resist that trend ... [Sadly, the idea of 'value'] is somewhat polluted by its constant use in economic contexts and other cost–benefit calculations, where it reverts to its literal meaning of 'price.' Moore, solemnly discussing the comparative 'values' of various large-scale states of affairs (in *Principia Ethica*, 1903, chapter 6) managed to give an uncomfortably condescending impression of a distinguished connoisseur pricing pictures in an exhibition. He wrote as if he stood in a secure, neutral, outside position, evaluating these things as an expert. But that is not a human situation at all. (Midgley, 1997:97–8)

A further complication is that value has at least four different meanings: cost in the market-place, quantified as cash; usefulness, for persons or society; what Locke called 'intrinsic natural worth', which is the objective quality of the thing itself, in contrast to the market-place cost (which is its value only in relation to the value of other things which can be acquired in its stead); and the meaning attached to symbols or concepts, such as a national flag or liberty. The same object can carry all these values. Thus, a piece of land has a market value; it has value-as-use for a farmer or developer; it may have intrinsic value for its beauty; and it can be valuable as the symbol of homeland, to be defended against enemies. Even worse, these four meanings may change independently for the same thing. For example, water in a river in highland Scotland or in lowland England will be valued by an economist in terms of its usefulness – whether it is drunk, fished or treated as an amenity; it may be an object of beauty or a stinking sewer; it may represent a boundary between counties or countries; or a barrier to the spread of pests; and so on.

The link between environmental values, ethics and action was highlighted by the Cow Green Reservoir saga. In 1964, the Tees Valley and Cleveland Water Board wanted to build a reservoir at Cow Green in a remote valley in upper Teesdale so as to provide an adequate water supply to the industrial area of Teesside. The reservoir was to meet the needs of expanding industry, and in particular to enable the chemicals company ICI to build the largest ammonia plant in the world. There was no problem of rehousing people or dispossessing farmers; no one lived around Cow Green, and the place was useless for agriculture. But the site overlapped the sole remaining one in England for a rather dull little plant called the Teesdale Sandwort (*Minuartia stricta*), along with some other rare plants believed to the survivors of the Ice Age in Britain (Clapham, 1978).

It seemed likely that the Teesdale Sandwort and its fellow relics would be imperilled if the reservoir were built. A Teesdale Defence Committee was set up. Letters were written to *The Times* expressing grave anxiety about the fate of the flora. The issue became a conflict of values: on the one hand an important industry needing water (with a hint that there might be unemployment if the ammonia plant could not be built); on the other hand the 'integrity' (that was one of the emotive words used) of a few patches of natural vegetation in a high and unfrequented stretch of moorland. In past years there would have been no discussion: the Teesdale Sandwort would have stood no chance against the ammonia plant. But in the 1960s a botanical David going into battle with an industrial Goliath aroused massive public support. The affair went to Parliament. A Select Committee of the House of Commons recommended that the reservoir be approved, but when its report came back to the full House an amendment was moved, 'That this House declines to consider a Bill which would involve irreparable harm to a unique area of international importance.' The amendment was defeated – but only by 112 votes to 82. The matter then went to the House of Lords, where it was remitted to another Select Committee. That Committee met 19 times and even visited the site. During the debate on the Bill, which lasted eight hours, it became clear that the reservoir could be built without destroying the botanical interest of the area, if care were taken. After all this, the reservoir was built; but it occupies only some 6 per cent of the limestone outcrop where the rare plants grow, and the Teesdale Sandwort still flourishes there. The importance of the episode was that Parliament concerned itself with the value of a particular natural environment, and acted from what may be termed altruism. The Teesdale Sandwort did not directly affect the well-being of electors, but both Houses of Parliament spent time and energy considering its value.

The Teesdale debate shows the difficulty of thinking wholly in terms of the financial or even the utilitarian worth of an environmental feature. This point is important. It is obviously necessary to 'cost' values as objectively as possible, but this can lead to ridiculous results. This was gloriously highlighted by the approach of the Roskill Commission appointed by the British government in 1968 to recommend the best site for a new London airport. It was important that possible sites should be compared as rigorously – which meant quantitatively – as possible. The assumption was that while local opposition to the siting of an airport would be understandable, it would be more easily overruled if it could be 'objectively' demonstrated that the benefit to the majority should not be thwarted by the selfish interests of a few.

The main task of the Commission was to compare costs and benefits of four possible sites (Cublington, Foulness, Nuthampstead and Thurleigh). The largest single element of cost for an airport is 'airspace movement' (*c.*42 per cent of the total). This was similar for all four sites. The next largest amount is 'passenger user' costs (*c.*38 per cent). This allocates passengers to airports in proportion to the distance to be travelled. The calculation used by the Roskill Commission depended heavily on the assumed capacities of the four airports, and the assumption that the relationship between accessibility and traffic would remain constant (i.e. that there would be no change in the methods of getting to the airport); the first assumption is arbitrary, and the second is dubious. But the most questionable part of the Roskill costings was the attempt to put a monetary value on amenity losses. For example, some ancient churches would have had to be destroyed at three of the four sites. Their 'loss' was calculated on the insurance value of the buildings concerned. It was recognised that this method 'did not fully take into account historic benefits'. The problem was that insurance values must be related to either market values or replacement costs; since there is no market for the sale of old churches, their market value is rather low.

Adams (1970) repeated the Roskill calculation for an airport centred on Westminster. Such an airport would cut journey time by at least an hour as compared to an airport outside London. Updating the average cost per journey in the year 2000 for people in central London to be £2 per journey, the annual savings would be £400 million a year or £12,000 million over an assumed thirty-year life for the airport. There would be a large property cost because of the value of houses in central London, but it seemed reasonable to assume that a 12 kilometre square central London site could be purchased for around £2,500 million and another 18 square kilometres could be insulated against sound and depreciated property values for a further £1,000 million. Westminster Abbey was in the centre of the area, but it could be insulated or moved; in any event, it was unlikely to be 'worth' much more than its insured value of £1.5 million. The loss of central London parks would be a major amenity loss but this was taken into account by Adams's costing and anyway the airport itself would be a major recreational amenity. The safety of those on the ground would not cost too much: Roskill anticipated an average of one third party accident over thirty years, and the costs assumed were only £9,300 for each fatality and £625 for each injury. So all in all, there seems to be as good an 'objective' case for building the next London Airport in Hyde Park as anywhere.

Economists argue that their role in contributing to policy is legitimate because they are neutral and hence unbiased about competing values. The problem is that any economic analysis necessarily depends on weighing all the respective merits of costs and benefits, and this in turn is based on the utilitarian assumption that an action or development is legitimate if it makes more people better off than those who lose. In fairness to economists, they now mostly recognise that they have to incorporate into their calculations factors which formerly would have been omitted. For example, a manufacturing process may produce waste products which have to be disposed of as pollution into air or water. Such 'externalities' are part of the manufacturing 'cost', which a manufacturer would once have sought to ignore in the interest of minimising costs and the price of the product, but which should properly be charged to the manufacturer rather than the 'environment' which otherwise bears it.

In recent years 'contingent valuation' has emerged as an additional technique for assessing the costs and benefits of environmental projects and decisions which fall outside existing markets; it builds in what people would pay *if* there were a market. This in turn has led to a recognition of the need for 'deliberate judgements' rather than automatic computation. 'Value' can be construed as the fruit of judgement, involving both subjective and objective criteria (Holland, 1995).

Clearly, there is a continuing need to:

i.   improve valuation techniques, including valuing future costs and benefits more carefully;
ii. integrate environmental considerations into all economic decisions;
iii. incorporate a sustainability constraint in the appraisal of environmental programmes (Pearce *et al.*, 1989:151–2).

However, another challenge for policy makers is how to assimilate – and budget for – the vast sums involved in providing 'environmental services', that is the 'goods and life-support functions provided by natural ecosystems and their species that sustain and fulfil human life' (Daly, 1997). In a crude and almost certainly underestimated calculation, Costanza *et al.* (1997) calculated that the world's ecosystems contribute $33 million million a year to the world's sustenance (by such processes as photosynthesis), a sum twice the annual gross national product of all the nations of the globe (see also Abramovitz, 1997). Damage to services of this magnitude would be extremely expensive – if not catastrophic.

One way of looking afresh at environmental accounting is the idea of the 'ecological footprint', which is 'the land (and water) area that would be required to support a defined human population and material standard indefinitely' (Wackernagel and Rees, 1996). Traditional communities depend on and draw their needs from a finite area around their territory. As cities have grown and consumption has risen, the size of their ecological footprint has increased. All 'developed' countries are overconsuming on this model, effectively plundering the natural capital of the earth for food, housing, transport, consumer goods and services (p. 159, note 2). For example, the UK has an 'ecological footprint' three times the area of the country (the eighth worst of the countries surveyed by the World Economic Forum in 1991). Every person is drawing on 4.6 hectares of land, but the 'eco productivity' of the UK is only 1.5 hectares per person. If this capital were being replaced in some way, this might be justifiable, but there is no evidence that it is. Globally, we currently use 40 per cent of the total annual plant growth, 60 per cent of available freshwater, and 35 per cent of the continental shelf productivity (Pimm, 2001). We are living unsustainable lives and – here is the nub – the market is failing through undercharging us despite our overuse. An acute example of this is overexploitation of fish stocks. It is 'more efficient' for the fishing industry to catch as many fish as can be sold in as short a time as possible than merely to remove surplus stock and maintain long-term stability of the populations of cod, herring, and so on. Conventional economics requires supplementing with some sort of constraint to stop us running out of world.

Money, Quality of Life and the Environment

There is an automatic assumption that quality of life depends on an ability to purchase it. There is obviously an element of truth in this, but there is no direct correlation between the two. Although the quality of life on the streets of Calcutta or in the *barriadas* of Peru is manifestly virtually non-existent, with short life-span, rampant disease and effectively no opportunities for escape, there are paradoxically considerable interpersonal relationships which are absent and mourned in the anonymity of modern cities by those displaced in 'urban regeneration' projects or regretted when they look back to stable rural settlements. It is this loss of community which is a major stimulus for moving from town to country – which, of course, requires a degree of affluence to make it possible.

Unfortunately, rural idylls are too often not the expected Arcadia for incomers. Diana Forsythe (1982) has described the poignant impact of 'incomers' on one of the Orkney islands, which she calls Stormay. In 1981 the island had a population of 186, of which 77 (41 per cent) were incomers, all except nine of them from outside Orkney. These immigrants produced discord:

> Despite the incomers' expressed desire to preserve the Stormay way of life, their very presence is helping to destroy it. Although individually the incomers are generally pleasant and well meaning additions to the island's community, they are also contributing to a cultural evolution in which ethnic, regional and national differences are being eroded away, to be replaced by a more standardised and homogeneous way of life. In 1981, incomers were still a minority on Stormay, albeit a vocal and powerful minority. But the receiving population on Stormay is relatively old, whilst continuing in-migration from Scotland and England brings in a steady stream of young adults in their prime childbearing years. In the face of this in-migration, its influence augmented by national radio, television and standardised education, the number of people who actually use and identify with Stormay speech and customs will inevitably diminish. There is tragedy in this situation for both islanders and incomers. The Stormay folk have welcomed the migrants as bringing new life and new ideas to their depopulated and ageing community, but they already have reason to regret their generosity. The energy the incomers bring to the island is committed to a vision of the future in which local people have no active part. They have sought to attain this vision by moving to a remote island to partake of the mystique of country life. But these migrants are not countrymen, nor do they really wish to become so; instead they seek a stage on which to act out an urban conception of what rural life should be like. The coming of urban refugees may revitalise the community in a demographic sense, but it will also transform it beyond recognition, for most incomers have little understanding of the distinctiveness and value of Orkney's cultural heritage as different from their own. In the long run, the conflicts that have accompanied the incomers' move to the island probably will be resolved through the submergence of the way of life of the receiving community – a high price to pay for the personal fulfilment of a few. (Forsythe, 1982:89, 94)

Of course, this example is not typical: incomers to Orkney are rarely poverty-stricken slum dwellers; a small island community will probably never be a stable nirvana for affluent urbanites. But it indicates some of the factors involved in the search for a 'good life'.

Goulet (1995) has identified three goals sought by all individuals and societies. He regards them as truly universal (p. 133). They are:

1. *Life sustenance* (or death control). Wherever there is a dearth of life-sustaining goods (food, medicine, adequate shelter and protection), absolute underdevelopment exists.
2. *Esteem* (i.e. the sense that one is respected as a being and not as a mere tool for others). Because of the status attached to material success in developed countries, esteem is nowadays equated with those who possess material wealth or technological power. Notwithstanding, in the dominant world view of most traditional societies, the fullness of *good* (some ideal image of society and the worthwhile human life) is distinct from the abundance of *goods*.
3. *Freedom* (i.e. a range of choices for individuals or societies, or the reduction of constraints in the pursuit of a perceived good). Economic growth does not lead automatically to freedom, or provide a proof for its existence (Arendt, 1963:218), and the avail- ability of choice is complicated by a paradoxical desire in developed societies to 'escape from freedom', which usually means a search for security. Another way of referring to freedom in this universal sense is as a transcendental need, i.e. relating to goods which cannot be measured or priced, although no less real. They include religion and friendship (Goulet, 1990). Such transcendental goods are part of that which distinguishes us from non-human animals (p. 75).

The fundamental importance of Goulet's three universal goals has been documented in many diverse societies – Asian, South and Central American, European (Goulet 1995 and references therein). This is not the place to pursue the subject of development ethics in detail, but merely to repeat the distinction between the quality of life and the quantity of possession, and recall the responses of men and women down the centuries that there is 'something more' to life than mere biological existence. René Dubos (1973:83) asserts that 'the measure of man is his ability to overcome the constraints of determinism so that he can select or create his persona instead of passively accepting his biological individuality'. He argues that the most searching criterion of humanness is the definition of Paul Tillich, that 'Man becomes truly human only at the time of decision.' Environmental awareness is a moral issue as well as a historical one.

Constraints and Attitudes: Two Examples

Most of the Scottish Highlands is a wet desert forged through human activity, although whether the main damage was done in early medieval times by wood cutting or by overgrazing cattle and then sheep in the early modern age is disputed (Smout, 1991).[5] By the eighteenth century, the population was inflated by the need of the clan chiefs to maintain their private fighting forces and was certainly exceeding its sustainable ecological footprint (Richards, 2000). Then the Jacobite rebellions led to the introduction of a money economy, resulting in increased rents and other economic measures by the lairds to support their standard of living and to maintain the labour force required for working the land and long-line fishing around the coast.

In this situation, some of the more compassionate landowners sought to provide for their people by helping them to emigrate, one of the better documented cases of an environmental refugee movement (e.g. McLean, 1991). But – and this is its relevance here – hundreds of people were displaced from their traditional homes and relocated to marginal land along the coast. A few ended up in model towns like Wick and Ullapool, but the suffering and bitterness of the 'clearances' have left a deeply festering sore in the Highlands (Grimble, 1962; Prebble, 1963). Hunter (1995) argues that it is a Highland *angst* resulting from an abiding passion of place that has shaped the inhabitants of the land over fifteen hundred years; in contrast, Smout (1991), identifies it as a folk memory exaggerating traditional attitudes (including the well-nurtured antipathy of crofters and small farmers to landowners) coupled with a post-Romantic glow melding Victorian ingenuity to an alert tourist industry.

Hunter has sought to establish his interpretation by calling on witnesses from warriors and poets of old. He describes the way the Highlands have been treated as equivalent to the assaults of imperialism and colonialism in countries round the world. He cites Duncan Ban MacIntyre's magnificent poem 'In Praise of Ben Dorain' as 'indicating MacIntyre's detailed understanding of the natural environment', which is certainly true, though whether love for one's native place translates into a permanent upset when one is removed from it is another question. John Veitch (1887), one time Professor of Logic at Glasgow University, anticipated the same point as Hunter in a systematic teasing out of the 'feeling for nature in Scottish poetry' from the thirteenth century onwards. He believes that in Scotland 'we have a specially typical feeling for nature ... love for free, wild nature and the objects that fill up the landscape ... and an imaginative sympathy for the grand and powerful in nature'.

The role of religion in this passion for place is equivocal. For Hunter the

> adversarial approach to nature was ... reinforced by Christianity. The Bible, as a result of stressing humanity's God-given right of dominion over the rest of the divine creation, encourages a dim view to be taken of any components of the natural world which manage, as it were, to maintain their independence. (Hunter, 1995:45)

This is an oversimplification, and is very different from the early Christianity of Ireland and Scotland described by Esther de Waal:

> Elsewhere in Europe the Christian Church was fulminating against the natural world, imposing its strictures on the landscape, cutting down sacred trees, despoiling sacred wells, and denying the natural rhythm that depended on the slow turning of the sun and moon and planets ... In the Celtic approach to God ... the world was brought into being in order that through its study the character of the creator might be learnt ... Creation reveals God. (de Waal, 1991:68)

Ian Bradley (1993:54) reckons that 'Celtic Christians derived their sense of the goodness of creation from living so close to nature and having the time and the temperament to study and contemplate its variety and beauty.'

How do theses facts add up? We tend to translate both our past and our hopes into some sort of physical context. Our past may be an ideal to which we want to return or a hell which we want to avoid; our future may be an actual place or an imaginary nirvana shaped by advertising or envy. Whatever that future's relationship with reality, place and people are major anchors to our perceptions. Islam, Judaism, Christianity, Buddhism all centre on historical events. The history of the Hebrews in the Old Testament is an extended story of land, its treatment and its misuse. Walter Brueggemann puts it thus:

> In the Old Testament there is no timeless space but there also is no spaceless time. There is rather *storied place*, that is a place which has meaning because of the history lodged there. There are stories, which have authority because they are located in a place. This means the biblical faith cannot be presented simply as an historical movement indifferent to place which could have happened in one setting as well as another, because it is undeniably fixed in this place with this meaning. And for all its apparent 'spiritualising,' the New Testament does not escape this rootage. The Christian tradition has been very clear in locating the story in Bethlehem, Nazareth, Jerusalem, and Galilee. (Brueggemann, 1977: 185)

The folk memory of the Highlanders is dominated by the clearances; it can be regarded as a microcosm of the commodification of land. But we can too easily over-simplify the clearances by ignoring their precipitating factors. Agricultural revolution and its associated suffering in England was acute in Napoleonic times. In Scotland

> Gaelic society and clanship were in decay long before the later eighteenth century ... in the 1760s and 1770s there was a marked acceleration in the rate of social change and in subsequent decades, material, cultural and demographic forces combined to produce a dramatic revolution in the Highland way of life. In simple terms traditional society was destroyed in this period and a new order based on quite different values, principles and relationships emerged to take its place ... Most clearances before 1815 were not designed to expel the people .., That the occupiers of the soil adhered tenaciously to the traditionalist concept of *duthchas* [*i.e.* the area settled by each clan as its collective heritage, protected but not dominated by the gentry] long after clanship had been abrogated by the conduct of the chiefs and leading gentry is testimony more to cultural disorientation rather than cultural alienation occasioned by the first phase of Clearance. (Devine, 1994:32–41)

The scenic splendours of the Scottish Highlands are the product of millennia of climatic and economic pressures. To many Scots they are the legacy of inhuman greed, attitudes forged by calamities hallowed by folk memory rather than a long-continued and often uphill battle for survival in a harsh environment. For James Hunter (1995:13) the crucial factor was the continued and 'developing relationship between people and place in Scotland' since the arrival of the first folk known as Scots, while Christopher Smout (1991) dates the key elements as emerging through romanticism etched by suffering over the past couple of centuries. They are, of course, both right: our attitudes to the environment have deep roots, but they also have more recent and luxuriant growths which can mask and obscure the real trunk.[6] Our practical task is to tease out the factors underlying and determining such attitudes.

My second example of the interaction between environmental attitudes and constraints is concerned wholly with human artefacts: the proper way to dispose of the redundant Brent Spar oil storage platform, a 14,500-tonne structure anchored in the North Sea 190 km north-east of Shetland, where the sea depth was 140 m. The formal position agreed in the Geneva Convention on the Continental Shelf (1958) was that 'Any installations which are abandoned or disused must be entirely removed', although a later guideline from the UN's International Maritime Organisation stated that (oil) platforms in water deeper that 100 m need only be partially removed, so long as there are '55m of clear water above any submerged remains'.

The Brent Spar was established as an oil reservoir by its owners Shell in 1978, and was an important element in the export of North Sea oil from the large Brent Field. However, it became redundant in 1991 and was costly to maintain. Shell's original intention had been to return it to land and break it up there, but the structure was damaged during its construction and might not have survived towing to the coast. Moreover the only inshore water deep enough for the Brent Spar was around Norway, and the Norwegian authorities were unwilling to accept the rig.

Shell commissioned a group of independent experts to advise on the best practicable environmental option for disposal. They examined thirteen possible methods of abandoning or reusing the structure. They concluded that the most appropriate one, involving the least risk of anything going wrong, the minimum danger to both environment and workers, and the relatively low cost, was to sink it in deep water. This advice was accepted by both Shell and the British government, and towing to a deep-water disposal site started.

Everybody had acted as responsibly as they knew how. But at this point, the environmental group Greenpeace began a programme of 'direct action' and propaganda against Shell, with calls for an international boycott of Shell products. Shell petrol stations in Germany were fire-bombed; Shell's behaviour was targeted in Germany as an environmental crime, and an official complaint was made to the British Prime Minister by German Chancellor Kohl. In the face of this, Shell changed its strategy, and Brent Spar was towed into a sheltered site off Norway (the Norwegians having changed their attitude) for further thought about its future.

There were many unsavoury details in this saga, Greenpeace claimed that the Brent Spar contained '14,500 tonnes of toxic rubbish' and 'over 100 tonnes of toxic sludge', whereas 14,500 tonnes was the total weight of the structure, and most of the sludge was inert sand. The scientific concern was of possible contamination of the shallow waters of the North Sea (or worse, of land) which was why deep sea disposal was selected; in the deep-sea, natural hydrothermal vents expel heavy metals in quantities that rival the entire output of the world's mining industry (German and Angel, 1995). Greenpeace established a broadcasting studio on the Brent Spar while it was under tow. Both BBC and ITV news organisations later confessed to being manipulated by Greenpeace.

It is difficult not to react against the tactics used by Greenpeace, but they succeeded in influencing environmental attitudes and changing the policy of a major transnational corporation. The Greenpeace defence was that the end justified the means, and that transnationals have too often flouted both public opinion and environmental rectitude. In the case of Brent Spar, Shell took all reasonable steps to minimise the environmental impact of its disposal, and were wrongly pilloried. Their conclusion from the episode was 'that emotions and beliefs can ultimately have as much influence on our "licence to operate" as hard facts and demonstrated performance; and that we need to consult more, earlier, with external stakeholders in order to find the best way forward'.

This enshrines the dilemma of 'running out of world'. Decision makers call for advice, but are quick to avoid its implications. Politicians, adept as some of them are at making evasive pronouncements, dislike receiving ambiguous evidence; but it is inevitable that scientific evidence on complex issues, such as global warming, should be hedged with reservations and blurred by words like 'probably' and 'possibly'. 'Certainty' is not a word scientists like to use. They wince when they hear a minister, after taking the best scientific advice, announce that some food can be regarded as *absolutely* safe to eat. US Senator Muskie spoke for many politicians when he called for 'one-armed' scientists; advisers who will not say, 'On the one hand the evidence is such and such, but on the other hand ...'

The way forward is not to distort evidence. Too many environmentalists have cried wolf too often, and then found themselves ignored. What we have to do is to learn how to combine the grim reality of 'running out of world' with the love and wonder of our surroundings so that our decisions, however irrational or emotive they may appear, are those which are right for us and our fellows, never mind our grandchildren and all the other creatures which make our life possible.

I end this section with another story about caring for creation. Morton Boyd, former director of the Nature Conservancy in Scotland, has described his conversion from dedicated technocrat to fervent environmentalist:

> As a young engineer working on the construction of Loch Sloy pipelines (a major hydroelectric scheme), I admired greatly the big-hearted spirit of my engineering mentors in overcoming the forces of nature. I saw an intrinsic beauty in the precision of their technology and in their works in concrete and steel. To the technical eye, the scheme was an epic in the harnessing and unleashing of the might of nature. There was no conflict in the engineers' minds about the probity of their actions against the

serene backdrop of Loch Lomondside. Their work was professional, honest and even patriotic.

I had greater difficulty in reconciling that probity. Although I did not know it at the time, the benign influence of wilderness which so gripped John Muir in the high Sierra of California, had touched me in my own way in my own place. From the human vulgarity of the workers' camp to the blasting open of the mountain, I saw a gigantic offence on nature which would endure for all time, graven on the face of the mountain.

To escape from the harsher realities of life on the job, I took a tent to the lochside where the call of sandpipers and the balm of lapping waters replaced the racket of the camp. Weekends and holidays I spent in the hills with deer and ptarmigan, far from pneumatic drills and rivet guns. Was mountaineering simply a thirst for adventure following my flying days in the RAF, or was I running away from my destiny? I came from a line of stonemasons and blacksmiths of which I was proud. Engineering was bred into me, but I was possessed by a new and compelling idea, as much mystical as it was rational: a burning desire to research nature in order to communicate its beauty to my peers, and to care for it had become an imperative in my life. Although I did not know it at the time, the personal dilemma from which I emerged in 1948 to follow a career in conservation instead of engineering, was to become in later years, one of global proportions. Today, it is enshrined in the concept of 'sustainable development,' which has become a slogan in world conservation, a centre piece of international congresses on the environment, and a plank in the policies of national governments. (Boyd, 1993:152)

Morton Boyd's reaction against the intrusions of hydroelectric pipelines above Loch Lomond has the same root as Greenpeace's activism against Brent Spar and James Hunter's pining for repeopled Highland glens. We are 'running out of world'; the problem is how we treat the world we have – the only one we have.

NOTES

1 In 1909, the US Bureau of Soils claimed: 'the soil is the one indestructible, immutable asset that the nation possesses. It is the one resource that cannot be exhausted, that cannot be used up'. In May 1934, a storm picked up 350 million tonnes of topsoil and re-deposited it over the eastern United States (an estimated 12 million tonnes fell on Chicago alone). In March 1935, over a million hectares of wheat were destroyed by dust storms. By 1938, 7 million hectares of land had lost the top 12 cms of soil and another 3½ million hectares the top 6 cms.

2 The Royal Society of London and the US National Academy of Sciences joined together for the first time ever in 1992 in issuing a statement, 'Population growth, resource consumption and a sustainable world'. They followed this in 1997 with a declaration on 'Towards sustainable consumption'. The latter begins: 'What matters is not only the present and

future number of people in the world, but also how poor or affluent they are, how much natural resource they utilise, and how much pollution and waste they generate. We must tackle population and consumption together ... we are concerned with the long-term quality of life of all peoples ... the consumption patterns of the richer countries may have to change; and for global patterns of consumption to be sustainable, they must change.'

3   The Royal Commission on Environmental Pollution is the only standing Royal Commission in Britain with a largely science-based remit. It was set up in 1970, partially as a response to growing perception of environmental hazards including the manifold effects of persistent pesticides and of oil pollution from the new generation of super-tankers. (The *Torrey Canyon* wrecked off the Scilly Isles in 1967 was a sharp stimulus to public concern.) It thus predates the surge of environmental awareness in 1972 marked by the publication of *The Limits of Growth* and *The Blueprint for Survival* and the United Nations Conference on the Human Environment in Stockholm.

4   During the nineteenth century there were repeated attempts to pass clean air legislation in the UK Parliament, but it was not until the London smog of 1952 led to the abandonment of *La Traviata* at Sadlers Wells and the collapse of prize cattle at the Smithfield Show that a comprehensive law was approved. An excellent account of the political equivocation involved in this saga has been given by Eric Ashby and Mary Anderson (1981).

5   Only 4 per cent of Scotland was wooded in 1600 compared with a 50–60 per cent cover in the Mesolithic period. The replacement of cattle by sheep led to further deterioration, and less possibility for recovery.

6   The 'clearances' are merely one example of emotions provoked by the ownership of 'native' lands: Australia, the Balkans, Indonesia, Ireland, North America, New Zealand, Palestine, Sri Lanka – the list is apparently endless. My Scottish example is merely one where digging below the rhetoric reveals possible resolutions unacceptable to those involved (Johnston and Walker, 2000).

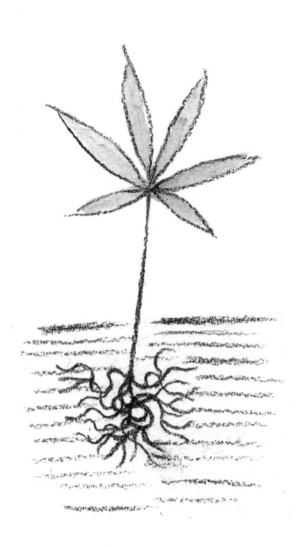

8
Governments and Greens

Environmental awareness is not merely a scientific issue, nor one of interest only to those intellectually fascinated by the boundary between science and ethics; at root, it is the battle for our survival and quality of life. This has emerged from our gradual but increasing consciousness that the exploitation of the Earth, a planet marked by misuse of land, air and water, has limits; that we can too easily harvest living resources too heavily; and that increasing human numbers cannot be ignored.

This consciousness has led to a wide variety of responses at local, national and international levels. In Britain, some of these came together in 1963 in conferences on 'What sort of countryside do we all want to see in 1970?' organised by the newly established statutory Nature Conservancy supported by the Council for Nature, an umbrella body for voluntary societies, and the Royal Society of Arts which had recently surveyed the relationships between industry and the countryside. They were chaired by the Duke of Edinburgh and involved the whole environmental spectrum – academics, planners, farmers, leaders of the forestry, mining, water and power industries and landowners.

A major theme was that the industrialisation of agriculture and the increasing pressures on the countryside for recreation and building meant that measures to preserve wildlife and scenery could no longer be confined to nature reserves. Max Nicholson, Director General of the Nature Conservancy wrote of the 'environmental revolution' that was occurring

> Near the heart of this revolution is a new sense that a 'good' or 'high-quality' or 'healthy' environment is not only more pleasant but may be essential to a sound and viable civilisation. Closely linked with that sense is a *new awareness* that we now have it in our power to conserve or to damage and destroy the countryside on a vast scale ... Part of the significance of the 'Countryside in 1970' conferences comes from the ... making of a loose triple alliance between the nature conservationists, the

amenity and rural preservation movement, and the outdoor recreational
interests which have almost simultaneously felt the supply of their fundamental requirements threatened by explosive processes of development
and of population expansion. (Nicholson, 1966:128)

Environmental Pessimism

During the early 1970s conservation concern and predictions of
environmental doom peaked. In 1962, Rachel Carson's *Silent Spring*
provoked attention about the insidious dangers of persistent pesticides in the United States (research in the UK was probably more
advanced than in North America at that time; Monk's Wood
Experimental Station was opened in 1961 with a remit to investigate
the ecological effects of pesticides); and in 1967 the wreck of the
Liberian oil tanker *Torrey Canyon* off Land's End alerted the British
public to the ever-present risks of oil pollution.

But the genteel environmental calculations were rendered
redundant within a few years by the Arab–Israeli wars and a massive
increase in the price of fossil fuels. Lord Ashby (who had been the
first Chairman of the Royal Commission on Environmental
Pollution) took a 'Second Look at Doom', pointing out the ominous
instability of human systems (Ashby, 1975). He argued:

> if we experience a shift in the balance of economic power between nations
> which own resources and nations which need those resources to keep
> their economies going, one sure consequence would be an increase in the
> tension with social systems on both sides ... The tempting way to resolve
> these tensions is by autocracy and force.

Environmental problems did not go away with the destruction of the
pre-1970 consensus. A human population growing by 180 people a
minute with increasing expectations of its needs had to face uncom-
fortable choices about its future. In 1980, the United Nations
Environmental Programme (UNEP), the International Union for
the Conservation of Nature (IUCN, now the World Conservation
Union), and the World Wildlife Fund (now the Worldwide Fund for
Nature) issued a 'World Conservation Strategy' (WCS, 1980), linking
successful development with sound conservation.

The threefold aim of the WCS was:

1. to maintain essential ecological processes and life-support
   systems;

2. to preserve genetic diversity;
3. to ensure the sustainable utilisation of species and ecosystems.

Its purpose was to underline the indivisibility of development and conservation. A people that destroys its neighbourhood as it 'develops' has no long-term future. In a phrase which has entered common parlance, 'sustainable development' must be the strategy for all nations.

The achievement of this aim was assumed to be inevitable, once the problem and possible solutions were defined. This was a major fallacy; right decisions do not automatically spring from accurate knowledge, as Ernest Schumacher argued (p. 103) and as we have seen from the prolonged saga of smoke pollution legislation in Britain (pp. 139–40). This was belatedly recognised when the reception of the WCS was reviewed in 1986 (Jacobs and Munro, 1987) and led to a commitment to include a section on ethics in any revision of the WCS. (This formed ch. 2 of the revised Strategy, published as *Caring for the Earth* [1991]).[1] However, the UK had already acted. Because the Strategy was in part a United Nations document, it required responses from member nations of UNEP. The UK response (*The Conservation and Development Programme for the UK* [1983]) was composed of reports from seven groups, dealing with industry, urban, countryside, marine and coastal issues, international policy, education and ethics. The oddity was the group on ethics, included at the urging of Max Nicholson. The group dealing with education called its report 'Education for Commitment', but – in Schumacher's phrase – metaphysical reconstruction was also needed. I was commissioned to produce an Ethics Report, guided by a Review Group chaired by Lord Ashby and appointed by a national coordinating committee.

The Review Group met only once. It mirrored environmentalism as a whole, being split, apparently irrevocably, between managers and those who regarded our environmental plight as wholly the fault of human greed and incompetence. At the time it seemed pointless to pursue the debate within the group. I developed an aphorism that 'we are both part of nature and apart from nature'.[2] This formed part of our report, which was written by me with considerable help from Lord Ashby and individual discussion with other members of the group. It would be good to think that this aphorism (or rather, the truth on which it is based) helped to defuse the polarisation in environmental attitudes, at least in the UK where environmental debates have been much more rational and non-confrontational than over the building of high dams in Turkey or China, burial of radioactive material in the USA, or logging in Canada.

Environmental Ethics and the Rights of Nature

What are the necessary components of environmental ethics? Certainly important are the factors that determine attitudes. This is where ethics comes in; not as a branch of academic philosophy, but in the fundamental sense as an expression of moral understanding 'usually in the form of guide-lines or rules of conduct, involving evaluations of value or worth'.

Concentrating on value rather than 'rights' immediately introduces controversy, because most environmental debates and action are based on the assertion of environmental rights. Is this proper – or, for that matter, sensible? The logic and development of the 'rights of nature' have been set out lucidly by Roderick Nash (1989). It is an interpretation which takes us back once again to John Locke and his *Two Treatises of Government* (1690). Locke's starting point was that all people are equal and free before God and each other. Locke saw this as an absolute and unchanging 'natural' law and derived from it a list of the 'natural rights' of humans: life, liberty, health and goods.

Locke did not go as far as his contemporary Thomas Hobbes (1588–1679) in characterising life in a state of nature as 'solitary, poor, nasty, brutish and short', but he did argue that insecurity in nature meant that rational people need to organise a society and a government. He called this process a 'social contract'. Through it individuals surrender some of the freedom characteristic of the unconstrained 'natural state', but retains the pre-social or God-given rights to life, liberty and property. Indeed the whole point of social and political organisation is to safeguard these fundamental values.

In some respects, Locke's argument can be traced back to the philosophers of the ancient world, who had a clear conception of natural, as opposed to humanly instituted, law. Although they did not speak about 'rights', they understood that people pre-existed government or indeed any civil order. The state of raw nature depended on the biological principles of existence and survival. In Latin these principles were called *jus naturae* or *jus naturale*. In contrast, the ideas of justice that humankind added to this basic order were thought of as the *jus commune*, the common law applied to the people and embodied in the laws of states.

The Romans also invoked another body of moral precepts: the *jus animalium*, which implied what were later called inherent or natural rights independent of human civilisation and government. As the third-century Roman jurist Ulpian understood it, the *jus animalium* was part of the *jus naturale* because the latter includes 'that which nature has taught all animals; this law indeed is not peculiar to the human race, but belongs to all animals'. In other words, nature as a whole constitutes an order that humankind should respect.

After the decline of Greece and Rome and the advent of Christianity, care for the natural world fared poorly in Western ethics (p. 41). Increasingly people assumed that nature (including animals) had no rights; non-humans existed solely to serve humans. The relationship of people to nature was driven by expediency and utility, defined in terms of human needs. The Christian version of this argument used Genesis for evidence that God gave human-kind dominion over nature and the right to exploit it without restraint.

As medical science emerged in the seventeenth century, it relied on vivisection to study the workings of the body. This practice drew the wrath of early humanitarians, and the vivisectors turned to René Descartes (1596–1650) to justify their research methods. For Descartes, animals were insensible and irrational machines. Lacking minds, they could not be harmed. They were, in Descartes' sense of the term, unconscious. Humans, on the other hand, had souls and minds. Rationality, in fact, defined the human organism: 'I think, therefore I am.' This dualism of humans and nature was seen as permitting vivisection and indeed any human action towards the environment. Descartes left no doubt that people were the 'masters and possessors of nature'. The non-human world was a 'thing'. Descartes understood this objectification of nature as an important prerequisite to the progress of science and civilisation.

The treatment of animals was not a major concern for John Locke, but property was, and the fact that animals could be owned resulted in their acquiring some rights in his philosophy. For Locke's contem-porary John Ray, this was more than mere utilitarianism. In his *The Wisdom of God Manifested in the Works of Creation* (1691) he summarised his creed in a single sentence: 'It is a generally received opinion that all this visible world was created for Man; that Man is the end of the Creation, as if there were no other end of any creature but some way or other to be serviceable to man ... yet', Ray continued, 'wise men nowadays think otherwise.' Ray believed that animals and plants exist to glorify God or, as his Cambridge friend Henry More put it, 'to enjoy themselves'. This way of thinking neatly dethroned humans from the dominant status accorded them by traditional Christianity and Cartesian science.

Interestingly enough, another (slightly later) contemporary, Alexander Pope (1688–1744) expressed his faith in the organic unity which green religion nowadays claims for its own underpinning. In his *Essay on Man* (1733), he wrote that living things

> All are but parts of one stupendous whole,
> Whose body Nature is, and God the soul.

Drawing the implications of this for human–animal relationships, he continued:

> Has God, thou fool!, work'd solely for thy good,
> Thy joy, thy pastime, thy attire, thy food? ...
> Know, Nature's children all divide her care;
> The fur that warms a monarch, warm'd a bear.

With 'Nature's children' defined as everything alive, Pope laid the intellectual foundation for an expanded ethic depending on relationships rather than rights.

This leads us to Henry Thoreau (1817–62) and John Muir (1838–1914). Thoreau believed in an 'oversoul' or godlike moral force that permeated everything in nature. His understanding was that 'the earth I tread on is not a dead, inert mass; it is a body, has a spirit, is organic and fluid to the influence of its spirit' (Thoreau, 1906, 3:165). This organicism or holism was reinforced for Thoreau by both science and religion, leading him to refer to nature and its creatures as 'his society', extending the usual human meaning of that term. 'I do not', he wrote in his journal for 1857, 'consider the other animals brutes in the common sense'.

For Muir, as for Thoreau, the basis of respect for nature was to recognise it as part of the created community to which humans also belonged. Not only animals, but plants and even rocks and water were 'sparks of the Divine Soul'. But civilisation, and particularly Christianity with its dualistic exposition of people and nature, obscured this truth for him. He called alligators, commonly regarded as ugly and hateful vermin, 'fellow mortals', filling the 'place assigned them by the greater Creator of us all' and 'beautiful in the eyes of God'. The moral implication follows: 'How narrow we selfish, conceited creatures are in our sympathies! How blind to the *rights* of all the rest of creation!' (my italics). This entry in Muir's 1867 journal seems to be the first association of rights with what a later generation would call 'environment.' Its basis lay in Muir's perception of humans as members of the natural community.

For Muir the notion of the rights of nature was effectively an expression of humility. This is not the same as modern usage, in which a moral right tends to be treated as an end in itself. In this sense, a right may either imply a responsibility or provide the basis of a claim. 'Nature's rights' received their fullest examination in a 1972 US Supreme Court case *Sierra* v. *Morton.*

In 1969, the US Forest Service granted Walt Disney Enterprises permission to build a leisure complex in the Sierra Nevada of California. The Sierra Club appealed against this, but lost on the grounds that they were not the plaintiff in the case and therefore had no legal right to be heard. The Supreme Court decided against them by a four to one majority, but the dissenting judge commented that:

> The critical question of 'standing' would be simplified and also put neatly in focus if we ... allowed environmental issues to be litigated ... in the name of the inanimate object about to be despoiled, defaced, or invaded ... Contemporary public concern for protecting nature's ecological equilibrium should lead to the conferral of standing upon environmental objects to sue for their own preservation.

The judge cited a review by a Californian lawyer, Christopher Stone (1972), titled 'Should trees have standing?' in which Stone reasoned that *something* was in danger of injury by the development, and the courts should be sensitive to its need for protection. Stone believed that society should 'give legal rights to forests, oceans, rivers and other so-called "natural objects" in the environment – indeed to the natural environment as a whole'. He recognised that trees and rivers could not institute proceedings on their own behalf, but suggested that extending the idea of trusteeship could give them 'standing' in the legal sense. He contended that natural objects had definite needs, the denial of which resulted in perceptible deterioration. For example, polluted air or water caused damage. Stone suggested that such damage could be quantified and recompense collected by human guardians on the behalf of the affected air or water. Stone's argument was that it is only when we perceive nature as like us that we will be able to generate love and empathy towards it, and hence attribute rights to it; when it has rights, it can have full protection. (Although the Sierra Club lost its appeal, it won its war: discouraged by long delays, Walt Disney Enterprises did not pursue its planning permission and in 1978 the US Congress added the disputed territory to Sequoia National Park.)

Lawyers and philosophers saw the case as opening a conceptual door to the rights of nature. John Rawls's *A Theory of Justice* (1971) began to be applied to environmental issues. Although Rawls himself had specifically restricted his argument to human interests, others contended that Rawls could be understood as supporting a moral obligation to resist environmental degradation in the interests of future human generations (e.g. Manning, 1981). Some were even more radical. For example, Tribe (1974) proposed adding nature to the contractual arrangements between people that Rawls presumed occurred at the beginning of any society. In an approach reminiscent of Darwin, Tribe wrote about a 'spirit of moral evolution' that had recently spread to include native peoples and women and was beginning to incorporate animals and plants, and might in the distant future include 'canyons ... a mountain or a seashore'.

Not all agreed. Mark Sagoff ridiculed the idea that 'all of nature marches forward in legal equality, with rights for all, without regard to race, creed, colour, sex, leaf structure, or atomic number'. How, Sagoff wondered, did Stone purport to know what inarticulate natural objects wanted? It seemed reasonable to him that wildness might simply be the preference of creatures struggling for survival in a tooth-and-claw world. For Sagoff the way out of the dilemma was unapologetically to accept anthropocentric morality. He preferred to argue that people 'have a right to wild mountain valleys for their cultural, spiritual, and aesthetic value – to people' (Sagoff, 1974).

Stone's response was to argue for 'moral pluralism', that is that ethical activities may be presumed to exist on several different logical planes. He used an analogy with maps that display different information about the same area and meet different needs: 'There is no one map that is right for all the things we want to do with maps, nor is one map more right than another.' In the same way, he argued, different ethical systems could direct human behaviour toward other people, the environment, and also embryos, clones, robots, and other unconventional entities (Stone 1987).

At this point, warning bells begin to sound, because 'rights language' is most commonly used as an expression of dissent from political or social restriction by (or on behalf of) those who are oppressed or underprivileged. Rights are asserted in an adversarial and assumedly non-negotiable sense, whereas our relationships with the environment are dynamic. Although the idea of a 'right' in nature was originally employed by Muir as support for the weak, in modern use it has become an expression of aggressive defence. The only way that rights ethics per se can properly provide a coherent basis for individuals living together in moral – or indeed ecological – communities is to emphasise that each claim of rights must be linked to a reciprocal and irrevocable acknowledgement of an obligation (MacIntyre, 1981: 64–7; Northcott, 1996:102). The rights–obligation partnership is an essential part of social membership: 'Morality consists of virtues which there is an obligation to practice, principles upon which there is an obligation to act, and rules which there is an obligation to follow, these being the expression of shared moral convictions, i.e. convictions about human life and conduct' (Milne, 1986:16).

Debates about rights have been important in the greening of philosophy, but they have spilt over into confrontationalism and 'ecowarfare' (Manes, 1990). Despite their ubiquity, it would be better to avoid rights language and rights claims when dealing with the environment. They are almost always divorced from the obligations that ought to be logically and morally linked to them, and deflect attention from responsible care and protection, which has a prior moral claim.

Environmental Stakeholders

There are four interests which must be taken into account in seeking any environmental ethic: self-interest, public or community interest, intergenerational or posterity's interest, and nature's own interest.

1. *Self-interest.* As individuals we are a mixture of selfishness and altruism. Selfishness is well described by Hardin's (1968) 'tragedy of the commons'. Imagine a common which can support forty beasts with twenty herdsmen entitled to graze their animals. This means two beasts per farmer. But any of the twenty may reason that there would be a negligible effect overall if they acquired a third animal; for the individual there would be a spectacular 50 per cent increase in personal output and wealth at the expense of only one extra animal on the common. The problem is that all twenty are likely to think in the same way, and sixty animals will appear on land capable of feeding only forty. Result: deterioration of pasture and animals. Hardin originally applied this parable to the number of children each couple agrees to have, but later extended it to the way we treat the environment. For example, waste (sewage, chemicals or radionuclides) costs less if a manufacturer releases it into a common stream, air or sea, and then pays his 'share' of purifying the common. In such a case, voluntary cooperation for the group good would be largely fictitious.

   Self-interest gives us three options for our environmental concern. First, let everyone cooperate in cleaning up litter, observing the speed limit, giving up using aerosols containing fluorocarbons, except me; in other words, pure selfishness. Secondly, let me involve myself in these activities, even if no one else does: pure altruism. And thirdly, cooperation, on the condition that everyone contributes fairly. But human nature usually needs intervention by authority to reach a consensus. This is where the public interest comes in.

2. *Public interest.* The public interest is not a simple extension of individual self-interest: trawlers largely destroyed the Newfoundland cod and North Sea herring stocks by pursuing their self-interest, although if the fishing industry had disciplined itself, a sustainable catch rate might have been achieved; if everyone visits nature reserves, the reserves become degraded and largely valueless; if everyone moves out of the city, the suburbs lose the qualities that attracted people in the first place; and so on. Unfortunately there is no easy way to deduce the real public interest when faced with the discordant preferences of individuals. A dispute as to what is the public interest about (say) energy policy, or water pollution, or the preservation of wilderness has to be resolved by bargaining and compromise between adversaries arguing from their own perceptions. Decision makers are forced to balance objective fact with public perception of the problem.

3. *Posterity's interest.* Environmental decisions differ from techno-logical ones in that they are more likely to have long-term or even permanent effects. Once a species is extinct, no wishful thinking can resurrect it; once a hill is quarried away, cosmetic landscaping can produce only a shadow of the original; once the tropical rain forest is cleared, the ground is an eroding disaster, not a fertile prairie. In taking decisions, we can rarely do more than consider that they may affect many future generations (although economists have a complex system of 'discount accounting', which gives the impression that present decisions may have negligible costs if properly spread over time). John Ruskin wrote:

> God has lent us the earth for our life; it is a great entail. It belongs as much to those who come after us and whose names are already written in the book of creation, as to us; and we have no right by anything we do or neglect to do to involve them in unnecessary penalties, or deprive them of benefits which was in our power to bequeath ... (cited by Patten, 1990)

This quotation frequently resurfaces. A variant was attributed to Mrs Thatcher in the UK government's White Paper, *This Common Inheritance* (1990:10): 'We do not hold a freehold on our world, but only a full repairing lease. We have a moral duty to look after our planet and hand it on in good order to future generations.' It is a concept which has developed as 'sustainability' or 'sustainable development'.

4. *Nature's interest.* Finally, we come to the most difficult consideration, the interests of nature itself: to protect birds and bees seems to contribute little to helping the homeless, the hungry, the underprivileged. Yet it is here that we come full circle in our insistence that we are both apart from nature and a part of it, and that these two aspects of our relationship to the world are logically or operationally separated only at the risk of degrading the whole. And it is here that we come back to the World Conservation Strategy, with its emphasis that sustainable human existence depends on a responsible concern for conservation, the management of the natural world.

Nature's worth is difficult to justify from a human point of view. One way is to invoke some sort of mystical sacramentalism; that is the way of the New Age (p. 92). But the commonest rationalisation is explicitly utilitarian: that we should preserve as many species as possible in case they are useful to us (e.g. as a source of anti-cancer drugs, or the elusive elixir of eternal youth). This is really self-interest. As an alternative, Ashby has argued that we should learn to value a landscape or a biological mechanism in the same way that we are prepared to protect and pay for human artefacts like buildings or paintings (Ashby, 1978). Bryan Norton has developed a variant of this, which he calls a 'weakly anthropocentric' approach, based on the premise that we are continually being transformed by our contact with the world around us, which is therefore an integral part of our human development (Norton, 1987).

In his examination of ways to protect nature's interest, Ashby suggested that we should seek to value ecological and evolutionary *processes* as distinct from the *ends* of these processes. The emphasis on nature's 'services' (photosynthesis, soil stability, detoxification, etc.) is an expression of this. Ashby's starting point is that we are well aware that nature is in increasingly short supply, and will have to be rationed unless we are careful. But:

> man uses the environment not only to satisfy his material needs; he depends upon it for aesthetic satisfaction. Thoreau wanted to preserve the wilderness so that he could have wilderness and tranquillity, not for the sake of the wilderness but for himself ... [However] any man-centred approach puts the environment at risk, for it is essentially a utilitarian approach ... The argument that to over-exploit the environment is to kill the goose that lays the golden eggs is a sound argument, and in practical politics it is often an effective one to use. But it is not an argument which supports the interests of nature against those of man. And it's a shaky

argument for conservationists to use, for they profess to be interested in nature for nature's sake, not for the sake of man; in the goose for its own sake, not just for its gold eggs. (Ashby, 1980:28)

In his search for a non-human-centred ethic of nature, Ashby compares the process of evolution to the playing of a Beethoven sonata:

You don't play it toward any goal. What matters, what is intrinsically valuable, is the experience of playing it. Its intrinsic worth does not reside in the printed marks on the page. The printed marks could (as Einstein said) be transformed into a diagram of air pressure curves. This would be a rationally faithful way to express them, but it wouldn't convey what Beethoven intended to convey. Only the process of playing the music can do that ... [For nature] one practicable rule of thumb would be to apply to the treatment of natural objects criteria similar to those we apply to the treatment of objects created by man. To permit a river to be damaged by pollution would be the same kind of negligence as to permit a Renaissance mural to fall into disrepair. In the course of evolution some species will anyway become extinct; to hasten their extinction by wanton hunting or by unnecessarily depriving them of their natural habitats (as happens when wetlands are drained) would be the same kind of insensitivity as to pull down, without good reason, a mediaeval church. This argument does not rest on such concepts as beauty (that is a man-centred value), nor does it imply a divine immanence pervading nature (that would be a resort to pantheism); though both of these concepts are useful adjuncts to an environmental ethic. In other words, in our examination of the man/nature link, we ought to make sure we respect the 'nature' end of it as much as the 'man' end of it.

Our Common Future

The World Conservation Strategy catalysed a process of analysis and concern which has significantly affected the way we view our world. Richard Mabey commented that it was

the first major international policy statement to affirm the *human* importance of conservation ... On the surface the problems of conservation present themselves as practical ones: how to manage woods so that they produce timber at the same time as sustaining wildlife, which areas of countryside are best used as farmland and which as nature reserves. Yet underneath there are more fundamental and less easily resolved conflicts of values – about who can legitimately be said to 'own' natural resources, about the rights of humans and animals, about the relative importance of present livelihoods and past traditions – conflicts which involve deeply held personal beliefs and meanings. (Mabey, 1980:27)

The WCS began to mould the attitudes of decision makers around the world and to break down the formidable barrier between the advocates of development and those of conservation. It was followed by a document which had a more obvious impact, the UN-inspired Brundtland Report, *Our Common Future* (World Commission on Environmental Development, 1987).

In her Foreword, Gro Harlem Brundtland was clear about the issues that had to be faced:

> The environment does not exist as a sphere separate from human actions, ambitions, and needs, and attempts to defend it in isolation from human concerns have given the very word 'environment' a connotation of naivety in some political circles. The word 'development' has also been narrowed by some into a very limited focus, along the lines of 'what poor nations should do to become richer', and thus again is automatically dismissed by many in the international arena as being a concern of specialists, of those involved in questions of 'development assistance'. But the 'environment' is where we all live; and 'development' is what we all do in attempting to improve our lot within that abode. The two are inseparable.

The Report made many detailed recommendations, but its lasting achievement has been to insert the phrase 'sustainable development' into the political agenda.

The idea of sustainable development is not new. It is generally dated from the United Nations Conference on the Human Environment held in Stockholm in 1972.[3] In the background book written for the Conference, *Only One Earth: The Care and Maintenance of a Small Planet*, Barbara Ward and René Dubos (1972) defined the fundamental task of humankind as 'to devise patterns of collective behaviour compatible with the continued flowering of civilisations'. This became the concept of 'development without destruction' in the Stockholm statements and was explicit in the World Conservation Strategy of 1980, whose first chapter was called 'Living resource conservation for sustainable development'.

But it was the Brundtland Commission that brought sustainable development into wide circulation and acceptance by politicians. The Commission's definition of sustainable development was 'Development that meets the needs of the present without compromising the ability of future generations to meet their own needs' (WCED, 1987:43).[4]

The revised version of the WCS *Caring for the Earth* (1991) redefined sustainable development as 'improving the quality of human life while living within the carrying capacity of supporting ecosystems'. From this it follows that a 'sustainable economy' can be recognised as the product of sustainable development, as one which 'maintains its natural resource base' and one able to support continuing development 'by adapting and through improvements in knowledge, organisation, technical efficiency, and wisdom'.

Acknowledging the failure of the 1980 Strategy to command greater response, the revised Strategy emphasises that:

> an ethic is important because what people do depends on what they believe. Widely shared beliefs are often more powerful than government edicts. The transition to sustainable societies will require changes in how people perceive each other, other life and the Earth; how they evaluate their needs and priorities; and how they behave. For example, individual security is important, but people need to understand that it will not be attained solely (or even largely) through indefinite growth in their personal level of consumption.
>
> Establishment of the ethic needs the support of the world's religions because they have spoken for centuries about the individual's duty of care for fellow humans and of reverence for divine creation. It also needs the backing of secular groups concerned with the principles that should govern relationships among people, and with nature. Such alliances will be timely and right even if the first purposes of religions and humanist groups are not the same as those of this Strategy.

The Strategy contained in *Caring for the Earth* was a major element in the preparations for the United Nations Conference on Environment and Development at Rio de Janeiro in 1992 (the Earth Summit) (Holdgate, 1996).

It is clear that the ethic called for by *Caring for the Earth* and the one argued ten years earlier in the UK response to the World Conservation Strategy have much in common: a belief that we will care for and protect what we value, an acceptance that community, future generations and nature itself have an interest in any determinations of value, a recognition that rights are inseparable from obligations, an assumption that attitudes must change if we are to develop a truly sustainable ethic, a perception that human action (and not inaction) is a necessary component of effective conservation (as well as of sustainable development), and an acknowledgement that all sectors of society need to be involved if the ethic has any chance of effectiveness.

The ethic in *Caring for the Earth* is explicitly global. Ron Engel, Chairman of the group which developed it, has described how this must mean finding a middle way between a universalism which is culturally imperialistic and a relativism which denies any universally shared values and principles:

> Over the course of the past several decades there have been many calls for a world ethic that will bring into one common discourse and practice our duties to one another and to the earth. Some call it a 'global ethic,' others an 'earth ethic,' others an 'ethic for survival,' others an 'ethic of living together world-wide,' and others an 'ethic of global solidarity.'
>
> Ethics is not something imposed by one group, class or profession on others. In fact, it is precisely the opposite. It is the one activity that most self-evidently makes us equals. Most simply put, ethics is the ability to distinguish good and evil, right and wrong, in our relationships to one another, and in our relationships to all of life. Thus we are all ethicists ...'
>
> But ethics is not only our inherent birthright: it is also embedded in culture; indeed it is primarily by means of culture that moral values are transmitted, criticised and transformed. Ethics are taught, thought about, practised, reformed by means of religions, by means of national and local traditions, by means of family life and educational institutions, by means of art, ritual and sacred places, by means of law, philosophy, politics and also, as many would hold, by the sciences. (quoted by Holdgate, 1996:122)

Commenting on this, Martin Holdgate, former Director General of IUCN (and also a former Chief Scientist to the UK Department of the Environment), underlines the need for an acceptable environmental ethic to tackle the linked themes of unity and diversity. We are global citizens.

> We inhabit a shared Earth, and an increasingly interdependent world civilisation, and if it is to survive, that civilisation must be guided by shared values. Moreover, there are no global values that are not local values: the foundation for global agreements and the basis for their implementation lie alike in attitudes and ethical approaches in many places and cultures. Each person's ethic will be guided by each person's deeper beliefs. (Holdgate, 1996:124)

But the ethic must be diverse as well as universal: 'It must draw on various faiths, principles and forms of expression in a mutually creative way. It is not that "anything goes" – but that the diverse inputs should come together to build a whole that is greater and richer than the sum of the parts.' Virtually all the major world faiths recognise a spiritual being who stands above and beyond the world (and is usually seen as its creator),[5] and affirm the spiritual nature of people and their importance to the creator being, with a strong emphasis on our responsibility to care for one another and for the world. In contrast to modern secular statements which emphasise human 'rights', religions emphasise duties – to worship, to help others, to be of service to all living beings, to pursue peace. Most recognise the need for change in a world where self-seeking has become dominant, but many also insist that change is possible – if it is led by the creator's spirit.

A Global Ethic

Parallel to and contemporaneous with the concerns of environmentalists in the Stockholm and Rio Conferences, the Brundtland Report and the two World Conservation Strategies, world religious leaders have also been groping towards a global ethic, driven on the one hand by the Justice, Peace and Integrity of Creation Programme (JPIC) of the World Council of Churches[6] and on the other by the Tübingen theologian, Hans Küng (1990, 1995).[7]

There have been other statements, other declarations from both religious and scientific bodies (Callewaert, 1994; Bakken, Engel and Engel, 1995). Two points emerge:

First, environmental concern is now truly global. Although the 'not in my back yard' syndrome is with us and will certainly persist because there is a proper place for self-interest as long as it is balanced by other interests (pp. 172–3),[8] people in all countries are aware that pollution, overpopulation, climatic change and land degradation do not respect political or economic boundaries. One of the unexpected but most important results of the Earth Summit in Rio was not contained in official statements and agreements, but was the recognition by many developing countries that the 'environment' is not a First World plot to impose burdens and brakes on the developing world, but that the environment is common to all.[9]

And secondly, the constituents of a global ethic are becoming clearer. We will examine these in the next chapter.

NOTES

1   The only reference to ethics in the original WCS is without elaboration or justification: 'A new ethic, embracing plants and animals as well as people, is required for human societies to live in harmony with the natural world on which they depend for survival and well-being' (Section 13.1).
2   Joseph Sittler (1954:371–2) made much the same point thirty years earlier: 'There are two ways by which man has sought to do justice to the realm of meaning in the natural world; two forms of relationship by which he has

sought to come to terms with what he cannot silence. First, nature can be subsumed under man ... [Secondly] Man is subsumed under nature ... Neither of these ways is adequate, and man knows it. For neither does justice either to the amplitude and glory of man's spirit or to the felt meaning-fulness of the world of nature. Christian theology, obedient to the biblical account of nature, has asserted a third possibility: that man ought properly stand alongside nature as her cherished brother, for she too is God's creation ...' Commenting on this statement, Douglas Hall (1986:162) noted that its weakness lies in the lack of evidence for the assumption that 'man knows'.

3   It had earlier roots in the World Council of Churches' call for a 'sustainable and just society', which emerged from consultations in 1970 and 1973 which in turn had arisen from concerns about the 'problem of technology, environment and the future of society' (*Faith, Science and the Future*, 1978:3).

4   Pearce *et al.* (1989:173–85) list more than two dozen definitions used by different authors.

5   The Christian, Judaic and Islamic view is that the world of nature and all living things, including humanity, are created beings: the works of God. In contrast, Buddhists believe that the world is the consequence of fundamental laws, in whose unfolding human beings originated as spiritual entities that came down to the world, were attracted by it, and became a part of it. As such, their conduct can significantly affect the course of nature. When people are righteous, nature itself runs aright; when people are greedy and destructive, whether through ignorance or deliberate choice, things go wrong.

6   The JPIC process was initiated by the German theologian, Jürgen Moltmann, who convinced the 1983 Assembly of the WCC that the traditional Christian call for 'peace with justice' was meaningless unless it took place within a *whole* creation, a creation 'with integrity'. The idea of 'Justice, Peace and the Integrity of Creation' (JPIC) evolved from and replaced the notion of a 'Just, Participatory and Sustainable Society' which had dominated WCC thinking through the previous decade. Developing countries had associated 'sustainability' with the maintenance of colonial injustice, and welcomed JPIC as the implicit rejection of global society in favour of regional associations. Conversely, it was obviously important that environmental concern be seen as much more than a luxury for rich nations. The phrase 'the integrity of creation' was intended to convey the dependence of creation on its creator and also the worth and dignity of creation in its own right (i.e. its intrinsic value). The JPIC process progressed with different emphases and hopes in different parts of the world and culminated in a global consultation in Seoul in 1990 (Gosling, 1992; Niles, 1992). The Seoul conference revealed discord rather than harmony, with a significant proportion of participants seeing meaning in creation through mysticism or traditional religions rather than Christian unity, and a more general unease about the theological pluralism exhibited by some of the speakers (Thomas, 1993).

7   The Küng initiative has been a specifically multi-faith exercise culminating in a 'Declaration Toward a Global Ethic' from the 'Parliament of the

World's Religions', which met in 1993 in Chicago. It proclaimed: 'We are convinced of the fundamental unity of the human family on Earth. We recall the 1948 Universal Declaration of Human Rights of the United Nations. What is formally proclaimed on the level of rights we wish to confirm and deepen here from the perspective of an ethic: the full realisation of the intrinsic dignity of the human person, the inalienable freedom and equality in principle of all humans, and the necessary solidarity and interdependence of all humans with each other.

By a global ethic we do not mean a global ideology or a single unified religion beyond all existing religions, and certainly not the domination of one religion over all others. By a global ethic we mean a fundamental consensus on binding values, irrevocable standards, and personal attitudes. Without such a fundamental consensus on an ethic, sooner or later every community will be threatened by chaos or dictatorship, and individuals will despair ...

Earth cannot be changed for the better unless the consciousness of individuals is changed. We pledge to work for such transformation in individual and collective consciousness, for the awakening of our spiritual powers through reflection, meditation, prayer, or positive thinking, for a conversion of the heart. Therefore we commit ourselves to a common global ethic, to better mutual understanding, as well as to socially-beneficial, peace-fostering, and Earth-friendly ways of life' (Küng and Kuschel, 1993).

8   The Prince of Wales summed up the way towards a 'sustainable earth' in his 2000 Reith Lecture as 'enlightened self-interest'. This is certainly an important element, although other commentators emphasised that the situation was more complicated (Patten, *et al.*, 2000).

9   The realisation that we all share one world is sadly confused by the fears about 'globalisation', whether well-founded and spurious (French, 2000).

9
Convergence and Stewardship

The UK government White Paper *This Common Inheritance* (1990) begins with a chapter called 'First Principles'. It contains a reflection on economic growth and the quality of life, and then sounds a warning:

> Ever since the Age of Enlightenment, we have had an almost boundless faith in our own intelligence and in the benign consequences of our actions. Whatever the discoveries of science, whatever the advances of commerce and industry, whatever the rate at which we multiplied as a species, whatever the rate at which we destroyed other species, whatever the changes we made to our seas and landscape, we have believed that the world would stay much the same in all its fundamentals. We now know that this is no longer true. This perception could have consequences for national action and international diplomacy as far-reaching as those which resulted from the splitting of the atom. (para. 1.8)

Stewardship

The document then goes on to assert that 'the starting point for this government [to determine policies and priorities for environmental care] is the ethical imperative of stewardship, which must underlie all environmental policies' (para. 1.14; see also pp. 193f.). Stewardship is defined as the 'duty to look after our world prudently and conscientiously'. This would seem unexceptionable, but in fact environmental stewardship is highly contentious to some people. They argue that we cannot manage our world, either because we do not know how to do it, or because stewardship implies an improper dominion over a system of which we are a part, a pretentious attempt to improve an imperfect world. Stephen Jay Gould puts this second criticism firmly:

> The views that we live on a fragile planet now subject to permanent derailment and disruption by human intervention [and] that humans

must learn to act as stewards for this threatened world ... however well intentioned, are rooted in the old sin of pride and exaggerated self-importance. We are one among millions of species, stewards of nothing. By what argument could we, arising just a geological micro-second ago, become responsible for the affairs of a world 4.5 billion years old, teeming with life that has been evolving and diversifying for at least three-quarters of that immense span? Nature does not exist for us, had no idea we were coming, and doesn't give a damn about us ... We are virtually powerless over the earth at our planet's own geological time scale ... On geological scales, our planet will take good care of itself and let time clear the impact of any human malfeasance. (Gould, 1990:30)

There are two answers to the statement that 'our planet will take good care of itself'. The first is that in past aeons 'the planet did not take care of itself' but was upheld and indwelt by God, and the Anthropic Principle is evidence for this (p. 12). This argument will obviously appeal only to strongly religious people. The second is that before humans existed on earth, nature could be regarded as procreating, diversifying and developing, through 'natural processes'. But, like it or not, we are here with enormous potential for good or ill. Unless we behave as good stewards, greed and misuse will lead to a non-sustainable future. We see all too much evidence for this (Chapter 7). Theologically we are called to 'glorify God and enjoy him forever'; secularly, we have a responsibility to ourselves, our community, our children and nature itself to care for our environment, whether we call our activity stewardship, trusteeship, guardianship, curatorship or tenancy. The key is a conscious understanding and duty of care for our world. This is very different from treating stewardship as 'an easy retreat to a comfortable concept which avoids coming to terms with deeper philosophical and theological issues inextricably interwoven with the environmental crisis' (Palmer, 1992:68), or as a flail where it is 'reduced to a reasonable way of managing time, talent and treasure ...' (Jegen, 1987:102).

Another set of criticisms has come from the Australian philosopher John Passmore in his seminal book *Man's Responsibility for Nature* (1974, revised 1980), in which he asserted that there has never been a strong stewardship tradition in the Western world and that it is arrogant to attempt to develop an environmental ethic based on it. He allows that:

important changes in moral outlook can occur, have occurred; in producing some of these changes, individual reformers, whether statesmen or prophets, have played an important part. But the degree to which their reforms have been in the long run successful depends on the degree to which they have been able to appeal to and further develop an existing tradition. (Passmore, 1980:40)

Passmore's belief was that we do not need a new ethic or tradition, but merely an enlightened form of dominion.

This conclusion has been strongly contested by Robin Attfield (1983, revised 1991), on the ground that there has been a much stronger stewardship strand in history than Passmore allows. Passmore denies that stewardship is 'peculiarly Christian', claiming that it is 'a Western and modern concept, dating back [only] to Kant' (Passmore, 1980:185). Attfield joins Glacken (1967:168) in arguing that we are specifically commissioned as 'stewards of God', and 'in any case the Old Testament cannot be reconciled with either the anthropocentric view that everything was made for mankind or the despotic view that people are free to treat nature and nonhuman creatures as they please' (Attfield, 1991:28).

Bruce Reichenbach and Elving Anderson (1995) have explored the biblical implications of stewardship in detail. They identify three functions: to fill, rule and care for creation as 'stand-ins' for God. 'We have obligations to God and to the persons and things over whom we are stewards, not only to profit the Landlord but also to benefit and do justice to other stewards and the creation itself' (1995:56). They then face the 'seemingly contradictory obligations' of a steward – to promote the good of the owner through both conservation and change. They quote the parable of the talents (Matthew 25.14–30):

> One servant takes seriously the stewards' preservative role. He knows that his master is a hard man, and, not willing to risk what was entrusted to him, he hides [his talent] in the ground, so that when the master returns nothing that he was given charge over will be lost. The steward expects praise for his preservation of the owner's resources. But to his shock and dismay, the mere preserver receives condemnation, not praise. Why has he not invested the capital, expanded the owner's possessions, and enriched his master? He has failed as a steward and is immediately relieved of his position. What the owner had entrusted to him is turned over to one of the two stewards who achieved a profitable return on their investments of the owner's property. One point of the story, then, is that stewards who never risk the trust but merely preserve, fail in their office. They have an obligation to both preserve and profit (or change).

This raises five questions for Reichenbach and Anderson:

1. *As stewards engaged in improving the world, what should we change?*
   Though the universe is ordered, the order is not always beneficial

either to humans or non-humans. The environment that makes agriculture possible can also threaten it: the earth-watering rain may cause floods; the life-giving sun bakes the crops and may create conditions for devouring insects. Happiness and pain, gain and discord are mixed. Should we try to tame the world for our benefit – or change ourselves for the benefit of the world? Whatever way, change is required.

2. *Whilst we may agree that change could be beneficial, is it mandatory?* Moreover, is it the world or ourselves that should change? The stewards in Jesus' parable were not *advised* to invest their trust, but were commanded to do so; the preservationist was subsequently condemned for disobedience. As stewards, we are required to invest in change; we have a moral injunction to improve the world. But more: our normal response to an obligation to improve something is one which will fit our own needs, wants and behaviour, but this may give us a conflict; to change what we rule whilst benefiting ourselves may betray the trust placed in us.

3. The obligation for positive action leads to asking: *why should we change the world?* As stewards, we hold a trust for the landlord, but what is the profit to God for any change we make? The classical assumption is that God is perfect, lacking nothing; he created out of his goodness, not any need. On this view, God as the landlord gets from his creation nothing that he needs; nothing can contribute to him and his existence. He receives praise or glory, but the praise, as it were, only adds to an already overflowing cup. One cannot add meaningfully to the infinite. God does not benefit from changing the creation.

But the classical picture is closer to Neoplatonism than biblical understanding, and in fact the landlord gains a great deal from his creation. The creation contributes to God's ongoing life by and through the goods realised in the universe – moral and spiritual goods, realised through the proper actions, motives, and virtues of his created stewards; goods of self-realisation, where the creation and the stewards realise the potentialities that fulfil them; and aesthetic goods – order, harmony, and beauty. In other words, we should change what detracts from meaningful existence and overall goodness and beauty, as well as that which has been damaged by our own acts.

4. *If we are to be involved in change, what are the limits of the change?* Are there things that must be preserved, left unchanged? In the first Genesis creation story, we are told six times that God declared his creation was good. The standard understanding of this is that 'natural evil' is a punishment for human disobedience, resulting

in pain in childbearing, difficulties in farming recalcitrant land, and mortality. Goodness, according to this view, was there in the beginning; it is a reflection of the goodness of God. Not even with the creation of finite creatures was evil introduced, only its possibility. Only when humans act in defiance of God does evil actually begin.

There is a real and very important sense in which 'the true knowledge of God – the Being, Nature and Attributes of the Infinite' for which we are searching on behalf of Adam Gifford – should be seen in the intelligibility of nature. If the world was an indeterminate chaos, it would be impenetrable to human reason. In other words, the signs of God in nature are not in the contrivance and adaptation beloved by the arch-deist, Archdeacon Paley, but in the accessibility of nature to study – and in the disorder when we fail to fulfil our stewardship function(s).

5. *Is there a sense in which God 'takes risks'?* The parable of the talents implied that those entrusted with the talents were required to take risks. But the landowner (and the providers of talents) also faced risks. For Polkinghorne (1994:85) both moral and natural evil are the result of God's 'risk-taking'. It is not the case that the physical universe is a mere backdrop to the human drama with its accompanying moral evil. Natural and moral evil cannot be disentangled. 'We are characters who have emerged from the scenery; its nature is the ground of the possibility of our nature. Perhaps only a world endowed with both its own spontaneity and its own reliability could have given rise to beings able to exercise choice' (Polkinghorne, 1994:87).

Polkinghorne goes on to recognise that the Christian answer to evil centres on the cross of Christ; we return to this later (p. 247). In the present context, the point is that evil is not a sign of God's incapacity or indifference, but that he has given us everything within our reach to affect for good or ill. We have the power to create or destroy, to benefit or despoil. The mark of a theology of nature is best seen as God-given freedom, not extraneous clues to the existence of God.

Environmental Philosophy

We have already looked at environmental ethics (p. 171). What about the wider philosophical scene? There have been some notable attempts by philosophers to communicate environmental issues to the wider public, particularly Andrew Brennan's *Thinking About*

Nature (1988), Holmes Rolston's *Environmental Ethics* (1988) and Stephen Clark's *How to Think About the Earth* (1993), but most philosophical writing has been directed to (or against) other philosophers: 'to ask how systematic thinking about environmental matters might mesh with a whole philosophical theory is naturally to refer to a philosophical theory which includes not just ethics, but also metaphysics, epistemology, aesthetics, philosophy of mind, philosophy of science, history of philosophy, and so on' (Chappell, 1997:2). John Haldane implies similarly:

> The bulk of work in [environmental philosophy] has been concerned with formulating and making sense of a theory of ethics that captures widely held views about value in nature. Although everyone would agree that non-human natural things are of immense instrumental value to us, there is disagreement about whether such value is purely instrumental or not ... The task is associated with the analysis of the idea of intrinsic value, with the question of moral standing and thus also with a critical attitude to the scope of traditional moral theory. (Haldane, 1990)

Another complication is that environmental philosophy has tended to iron out environmental realities in searching for a 'Grand Theory', and has therefore diminished its applicability in practice (Paden, 1994).

In the light of all this, have philosophers contributed significantly to our understanding of the environment? Arne Naess, with his proposals for a 'deep ecology', has certainly influenced many people outside the philosophical community (p. 216), and A. N. Whitehead's ideas of 'process' underlie the interpretations of a significant number of environmental theologians (p. 93). Bryan Norton's (1987) espousal of the transforming effect of nature on human attitudes is a helpful bridge between anthropocentric and biocentric values (p. 173), and he has been a mediating influence in attempting to bring together warring academics (Norton, 1991). Mark Sagoff (1988) has introduced a healthy scepticism about the use and value of law in and for environmental ethics. However, the efforts of the philosophers *sensu stricto* do not seem to have produced major advances in understanding and caring for the environment, despite the explicit efforts of some (e.g. Elliot and Gare, 1983; VanDeVeer and Pierce, 1986). Andrew Light and Eric Katz (1996) seem to recognise this, when they complain that environmental ethics has 'failed to develop its practical task' because it is beholden to a 'methodological and theoretical dogmatism'. On these grounds, they call for 'a new strategy for approaching environmental philosophy and environmental strategy ... [which] more accurately refers to a cluster of related and overlapping concepts, rather than to a single view'. Perhaps the compilers of the *Cambridge Dictionary of Philosophy* (1995) were of a like mind, because they do not include 'Environmental ethics' as an entry in their 882-page volume nor is there any mention of the environment in Anthony Kenny's *Oxford History of Western Philosophy* (although the *Oxford Dictionary of Philosophy* has 21 lines on the subject in its 418 pages).

   On this ground, and from a general survey of the factors which have *apparently* (it would be presumptuous to be more definite) influenced attitudes, I believe that nature writers have been much more significant then the philosophers. People like John Ray, Gilbert White, Richard Jefferies, Henry Thoreau, John Muir, and more recently Rachel Carson, Richard Mabey, Norman Moore and television presenters such as Jacques Cousteau, Peter Scott and David Attenborough have had a massive impact. But perhaps even more important have been the historians and scientists – telling us what has and is happening, and the processes at work which need encouragement or control: historians like Charles Raven, Robert McIntosh, Donald Worster, Colin Russell, John Sheail; scientists like John Black, the Ehrlichs, Jim Lovelock and Daniel Botkin; and even theologians like Hugh Montefiore, John Cobb, Rowland Moss, Michael Northcott and Sally McFague. But the key actors have been those who have consciously and unashamedly found key pieces in the jigsaw from different disci- plines. Some of the above have recognised this, but many have tended to be selective in their syntheses, sometimes unconsciously or from ignorance, sometimes from positively doctrinaire reasons (see Berry, 1993*a*). And how do the Enlightenment fallacy and the need for Schumacher's and Oeschlaeger's 'metaphysical reconstruction' (p. 103) fit into all this?

Convergence

Emboldened by the apparent failure of 'professional' ethicists, I want consciously to step outside conventional subject boundaries. This is neither innovative nor iconoclastic as far as the environment is concerned. As we shall see in the next chapter, many if not most of those who have written or worked on environmental problems have come to them from a sense of wonder or awe; and in addition, natural scientists who seek to understand environmental processes have found themselves faced with questions normally regarded as the province of social science (Nicholson, 1987). Pioneer conservationist

Peter Scott used to speak of the four pillars of conservation (Huxley 1993:255):

1. *ethical*: we have no justification for wiping out other species which share the planet with us; they have as much right to live as we have;
2. *aesthetic*: if it is wrong to destroy great paintings, great buildings and other works of art, it is no less wrong to destroy nature's equally beautiful creations which, once gone, are gone forever. This pillar has a buttress: with increasing leisure, people increasingly seek refreshment in nature's wilder places and among her wild creatures; to destroy them is to impoverish humanity by denying it the spiritual renewal that it needs;
3. *scientific*: many species are still unknown to science; some might – almost certainly would – have uses for humankind; to exterminate a plant or animal before it even has a scientific name is an act of vandalism;
4. *economic*: people of richer countries flock to see the wildlife of poorer ones to create tourist industries which keep many of the latter afloat.

The World Conservation Strategies, the Brundtland Commission Report and the UK White Paper quoted in the last chapter all called upon and tried to integrate a range of disciplines. I believe this was neither desperation nor convention, but a true convergence of ideas towards an underlying reality. When I was commissioned to write the Ethics Section of the UK Response to the World Conservation Strategy (p. 165), Max Nicholson envisaged a statement about human nature and human biology. He was an unapologetic humanist, and contributed a chapter on 'the place of conservation' to the manifesto *The Humanist Frame*, edited by Julian Huxley (1961). Nicholson introduced his thesis from an explicitly naturalistic viewpoint:

> Man, like other animals, began life in a natural habitat. Unlike other animals – except a few which have become dependent on him – he has outgrown and almost forgotten it. This basic fact has much to do with many present-day human problems, economic, social and psychological. Unfortunately, most of those who have been most aware of it have been heavily influenced by sentiment and nostalgia towards the Yeomen of England, or even the Noble Savage ... On the other hand those able to grasp the historical, economic, social and technological evolution of mankind have often been illiterate in terms of the life and earth sciences: at best they have expressed strong aesthetic misgivings. The problem, therefore, has slipped through one of the cracks in our education. (in Huxley, 1961:387)

A full environmental ethic must take full account of our nature and limitations as *Homo sapiens*, but if we are not careful, we will fall into the same trap as Lynn White (and also Max Nicholson, q.v. p. 84), in believing that our actions are determined solely by self-interest, and ignore the evidence that we are 'more than' naked apes in a moral and religious sense.

The 1980s saw a convergence of environmental thinking at all levels. The decade began with the World Conservation Strategy and the development of environmental ethics in the light of it ('pragmatic ethics' *sensu* Light and Katz, see p. 188). It continued with the work of the Brundtland Commission which reported in 1987. It closed in 1989 with a Conference on Environmental Ethics in Brussels under the auspices of the Economic Summit Nations (the G7) (Bourdeau, Fasella and Teller, 1990).

A Code of Environmental Practice

In his charge to the Brussels Conference, European Commission President Jacques Delors began with the problems which he believed must modify our approach and behaviour to the environment, since

> none of these can be approached separately: they mesh together and transcend our traditional frameworks of thought and action ... [They] highlight man's dependence on his environment, hitherto ill-perceived. They underscore the sudden fragility of man's relationship with nature, which has traditionally been one of mastery based on use and exploitation. It is in the broadest sense *the very conditions of humanity which current problems compel us to rethink and rebuild, insofar as continuing our traditional modes of life* on earth would lead to ever-increasing damage and before long *threaten to destroy us.* (Delors, 1990; my italics; these are the words of a sombre banker, not an excitable green activist)

Based on this diagnosis, Delors called for an ethical approach to cope with the problems, that is, an approach that

> concerns the values which govern social behaviour. It is the bedrock of law and therefore determines the various codes by which we act, codes hallowed by tradition and whose real cruxes must now be re-established. The continuous degradation of the setting for life which man has received from his forebears will of necessity prompt him to adopt an approach to that legacy in terms of duties and responsibilities.

He called for 'a code of environmental ethics' (Delors, 1990:20) and this was subsequently prepared by a small working group.[1]

The code set out a series of responsibilities and obligations, but its core was a deceptively simple statement of the basis for an acceptable environmental ethic: *Stewardship of the living and non-living systems of the earth in order to maintain their sustainability for present and future, allowing development with forbearance and equity.* Health and quality of life for humankind are ultimately dependent on this.

The code was formally received by the G7 and the EC heads of state, and was one of the source documents for the Earth Charter planned for the Earth Summit but which fell by the political wayside during the pre-conference negotiations. The Earth Summit finally agreed a rather general Rio Declaration on Environment and Development (Thomson, 1993). The code also formed the meat of a document *Christians and the Environment* (1991), prepared at the request of the General Synod of the Church of England (p. 196).

The International Covenant on Environment and Development

In his 1990 report, the UN Secretary General called for a Covenant on Environment and Development: 'The Charter of the United Nations governs relations between States. The Universal Declaration of Human Rights pertains to relations between the State and the individual. The time has come to devise a covenant regulating relations between humankind and nature.' The International Environmental Law Commission responded to this call, producing a document which codified environmental 'soft law' contained in a range of agreements and treaties such as the Stockholm Declaration of 1982, the World Charter for Nature, and various enactments at the Earth Summit, into proposed binding 'hard law' – thus laying a basis for global environmental protection.

The details of this lengthy legal document are not relevant here. My reason for introducing it is to present the contents of the 'fundamental principles' of the Covenant which contains 'the most widely accepted and established concepts and principles of inter-national environmental law'. It is possible to restate these as a set of Ten Premises (or following a well-known precedent, as Ten Commandments, albeit in the sense of descriptive rules [or 'creation ordinances'] rather than arbitrary laws handed down from on high in the Mosaic manner [Berry, 1999a]) (Box 1). They are all positive statements without discriminatory clauses, and hence accord with equity for all. The significance of this restatement is that it contains the key elements of all the major international pronouncements – the Stockholm Declaration [S], the Charter for Nature [C] and the

Rio Declaration [R] (the letters in Box 1 on p. 194 refer to the articles in these three major statements). Considered together, they seem to provide the necessary components for a 'world ethic for sustainable living', as called for in the revised World Conservation Strategy, *Caring for the Earth* (1991). This does not imply global control or global uniformity, but it does signify agreement on the basis from which local or regional decisions have to be made.

The original reason for re-stating the Fundamental Principles of the Covenant was to identify the assumptions which require response at the individual, corporate, national and international levels. A practical aim was to distinguish moral commitments from the legal obligations of the Covenant. Many international agreements nowadays involve a two-stage process: a Charter with a set of principles and a clause by which 'all signatories undertake to place the commitments contained in the Charter on a secure and binding international legal basis', and a consequent Treaty with detailed specific obligations. If the Covenant had been presented in this way, states might have been readier to accept the ethical principles contained in the Charter, and thence to negotiate over the obligations as a signatory. However the Law Commission preferred to retain the Covenant as a unitary document.

The re-stating exercise highlighted the commonality on the environment which has grown within the international community over the past two decades. There seems to be a desire for an ethical underpinning which would support the empirical requirements for sustainable development of the lawyers and the authors of *Caring for the Earth* (as well as the Brundtland Commission Report, *Our Common Future*, and the UK policy statement, *Our Common Environment*). If there is a relatively simple way of expressing our attitude towards the environment, there is hope that it could be widely accepted by individuals and leaders from both developed and developing nations. What is important is that the ten premises *represent a convergence of ideas describing the whole nature, properties and management of the earth.* I believe that, properly constructed, they could provide as cohesive a focus for sustainable development and international conservation as does Darwinian theory for biology. Religion is one of the inputs into the premises; law and economics are outputs.

Lawyers, politicians, even conservationists have to look upon the world and its life as humans. High-minded biocentrism (or deep ecology) cannot avoid this. We are a part of nature; but equally certainly we are apart from nature.

Finally, the premises are concerned with responsibilities rather than rights. We have already seen some of the problems of basing

Box 1

Ten Premises for Sustainable Living

1. Environmental conservation and sustainable development are essential for human health and well-being on a planet with finite resources and carrying capacity (S 13; C 2; R 1, 4).
2. Nature as a whole warrants respect; every form of life is unique and is to be safeguarded independently of its worth to humanity (C Preamble, 1).
3. The global environment both within and beyond the limits of national jurisdictions is a common concern of humanity, held in trust for future generations by the present generation. All persons have a duty to protect and conserve the environment; each generation has a responsibility to recognise limits to its freedom of action and to act with appropriate restraint, so that future generations inherit a world that meets their needs (S 2, 4; C 3; R 4).
4. To achieve sustainable development, environmental protection and management must be an integral part of all development efforts. States have in accordance with the Charter of the United Nations and the principles of international law, not only the sovereign right to their own resources, but the responsibility:
    a. to protect and preserve the environment within their own jurisdiction or control;
    b. to ensure that activities within their jurisdiction or control do not cause serious damage to the environment of other states or to areas beyond the limits of national jurisdiction;
    c. to work with and collaborate in good faith with other states and competent intergovernmental and non-governmental organisations in the implementation of the Covenant;
    d. to minimise waste in the use of all natural resources and ensure that renewable natural resources are maintained sustainably, and to develop and adopt the most efficient and environmentally safe technologies for the harnessing and use of energy (S 7, 14, 21; C 4, 7; R 4, 12).
5. All states and all people shall cooperate in promoting health, social well-being and environmental quality by striving to eradicate poverty; this is an indispensable requirement for both sustainable development and distributive justice, and can be achieved only by eliminating unsustainable patterns of production and consumption and by promoting appropriate demographic policies (R 5, 7, 8).

6. States have a responsibility to anticipate, prevent and minimise significant adverse effects of human activities on the environment; lack of full scientific certainty must not be used as a reason to postpone action to avoid potential harm to the environment (C 11; R 15, 18, 19).
7. States shall take all necessary measures to ensure that the full costs of prevention or compensation for environmental damage, as well as the costs of restoration of the environment, are borne by the person or organisation whose activities give rise to such damage or the threat thereof, unless such obligations to bear costs or restore the environment are otherwise allocated by national or international law. States have the right to be protected against or compensated for significant environmental harm caused by activities outside their own jurisdiction (S 22; C 12; R 13).
8. States shall require environmental impact assessments for all proposed activities likely to have a significant environmental effect and shall include the full social and environmental costs of all environmental impacts within the calculation of those effects (C 11; R 17).
9. States shall establish and maintain a legal, administrative, research and monitoring framework for environment conservation, giving full and equal consideration to environmental, economic, social and cultural factors. In particular, states shall:
    a. regularly review their policies on the integration of planning and development activities and publish their findings;
    b. develop or improve mechanisms to facilitate the involvement of concerned individuals, groups, organisations, indigenous peoples and local communities in environmental decision making at all levels, and provide effective access to judicial and administrative proceedings affecting the environment;
    c. make clear the full social and economic costs of using natural resources and ensure the equitable distribution of income generated (S 18, 20; R 9, 10, 22).
10. Justice, peace, development, and environmental protection and management are interdependent and indivisible, and vital to the integrity of creation (S 1; R 25). States have a responsibility to work towards an environmentally aware citizenry that has the knowledge, skills and moral values to protect and preserve the environment and to achieve sustainable development.

environmental decisions on the assumption of rights (p. 166). It is unlikely that we can purge rights from our environmental discussions, but it is important to be aware of their limitations: the more things and people that have rights accorded to them, the more licence can they claim and the more regulations are needed to restrain them. Rights ought to be anathema to any environmentalist concerned with *responsible* care and protection of the natural world.

Religion and the Environment

Most of this chapter has been concerned with a progressive convergence of attitudes to the environment at 'official' and global levels. But this convergence has also been taking place between religious and secular viewpoints.

In 1990, the General Synod of the Church of England requested 'a statement of Christian Stewardship in relation to the whole of creation to challenge Government, Church and people to engage in a critical review of human responsibility to the living environment'. A statement was prepared[2] and accepted by the Synod (*Christians and the Environment* [1991]). The statement began with the Christian understanding that we all share and depend on the same world, with its finite and often non-renewable resources; the Christian belief that this world belongs to God by creation, redemption and sustenance; that he has entrusted it to humankind, made in his image and responsible to him; and hence that we are in the position of stewards, tenants, curators, trustees or guardians, whether or not we acknowledge this responsibility. It then defined stewardship as caring management, not selfish exploitation, involving a concern for both present and future as well as self, and a recognition that the world we manage has an interest in its own survival and well-being independent of its value to us.

In words taken from the introduction to the Brussels Code, the General Synod paper acknowledged that we depend for survival, health and psychological well-being on the physical integrity of the biosphere and the cultural continuity of our own local environment. It went on:

> We have a common interest in shaping an attitude to the world that encourages a more responsible use of natural resources and gives thought to the complex question of the well-being of the whole creation. This is a religious imperative, but also implies an ethic common to all human-kind, and one which demands response from individuals, communities, corporations and nations. Christ's demands go beyond the simple claims

of justice; they require that any sacrifices ought to be distributed according to capacity. This means that the main burden of responsible action will fall on those in the more highly developed countries whatever their historical or present role in causing environmental degradation; this does not absolve the less developed or poorer countries from accepting a proper share of the necessary cost.

'It's wonderful what the hand of man can do to a piece of earth, with the aid of Divine Providence, Wilks.'

'You should have seen this piece, Sir, when Divine Providence 'ad it all to itself.'

Punch cartoon of 7 Feb. 1934 by George Belcher, reprinted from *The Reverend Mr Punch*, Mowbray, 1956.

In other words, Christians have a particular responsibility to the environment because of their acknowledgement and worship of God as creator, redeemer and sustainer.

> Abuse of the natural world is disobedience to God, not merely an error of judgement. We must examine our life-style and work out our attitudes to the world around us as part of our service and stewardship, recognising that there are differences of opinion between Christians (for example, over the proper treatment of animals) but affirming that we are responsible and accountable to God for our behaviour. Notwithstanding, we have a duty individually and corporately to discover and express our care for creation in both spiritual worship and practical works.

The Church of England represents a small part of Christendom, albeit a significant one because of its Catholic and Reformed doctrine and its reliance on Scripture for its ultimate court of appeal. But the Anglican Communion worldwide joined with the Church of England and sent a message to the Earth Summit in Rio (Berry, 1993*b*:263–4):

> Our common belief is (in the words of a policy statement from the Episcopal Church of the USA) that all creation is of God and as part of creation we are given the specific tasks of responsible and faithful stewardship of all that is.
> This involves:
> 1. The clear understanding from both scripture and enduring tradition that:
>   a. Responsible stewardship means that we are representative caretakers, managers or trustees, accountable for our actions;
>   b. The Christian gospel of reconciliation extends from 'a change from a level of human existence that is less than that envisaged by our Creator, to one in which humanity is fully human and free to move to a state of wholeness in harmony with God, with fellow human beings and with every aspect of his environment' (Statement of Sixth Meeting of the Anglican Consultative Council, 1987);
> 2. The misuse or misappropriation of the finite resources of the earth by ever increasing numbers of people is unsustainable, unjust and morally reprehensible;
> 3. Human dignity cannot be achieved or maintained in a degrading environment with a declining resource base. The traditional Christian aims of peace and justice must be supplemented by informed environmental care;
> 4. Environmental stewardship depends on the attitudes of individuals, corporations and governments. Because it involves maintaining the

earth's sustainability for present and future allowing forbearance and fairness for all, current attitudes may have to change radically, particularly to manage actions with effects distant in time or place from their origin;

5. There is an encouraging convergence between the churches and secular bodies that stewardship is the basic ingredient for human survival and development, in the finite world in which we dwell.

The Thirteenth Lambeth Conference of Anglican Bishops (1998) recognised:

> A great challenge and opportunity lies before the Church ... The gravity of the present challenge to the global ecosystem arises from the techno-logically enhanced impact of human intervention on our planet. Scripture was inspired in a different world, but biblical insights into the nature of the God–human–world relation provides a firm foundation for a contem-porary ecological theology. (Anglican Consultative Council, 1999:24)

David Hallman (1994) has brought together comments on the emerging environmental consensus from Christian communities round the globe. He identified two sources of hope:

1. *The commonalities emerging across all disciplines.* The conceptual revolution in physics and the insights of biology, astronomy and chaos theory have their parallels in a blossoming of ecotheology. Around the edges, thinkers and practitioners are exploring more sustainable and just approaches to organising the economic life of societies. The hopefulness is the presence of God's Spirit throughout different realms of human endeavour, illuminating common themes of the inter-relatedness of all creation.
2. *The hope from communities at all levels.* We do not function as individuals but as members of sustaining and energising communities. We need to identify allies from whom we can learn and in conjunction with whom our efforts will be more effective.

A parallel but very different experience is expressed in *Friday Morning Reflections* written by four senior members of the World Bank staff from Washington: David Beckmann (a US Christian), Ramgopal Agarwala (a Hindu from India), Sven Burmester (a Danish secular humanist) and Ismail Serageldin (a Muslim from Egypt). Their experience was that 'Spiritual values have been dangerously slighted in shaping the world's development and that humanity's survival may be at stake' (Beckmann *et al.*, 1991:xi). Even more eclectically Jonathan Porritt and David Winner have reviewed the development of the 'green movement' throughout the world and found that 'salvation lies in opening our spirit to the presence of the divine in the world, acknowledging joyfully a sense of wonder and humility before the miracle of creation, and *then* going out and taking action to put things right, inspired by that vision' (Porritt and Winner, 1988:253).

Martin Holdgate (1996:145) distilling his experiences at both national and global levels concludes that 'some guiding values' are emerging which

> link what strikes at the mind and heart as ethically sound principles, with the mind's fears of what may happen otherwise, and with our calculations of personal and group advantage. The universal themes are a recognition that long-term sustainability must be an object of policy now, that equity between peoples and nations in their use of, and impact on, the finite resources and vulnerable systems of the planet must be improved, and that personal obligations to other people and to the world of nature need to be codified and communicated.

The question that we have to face is what are the limits to these universal themes? How can we refine them so that they can be incorporated into the policies of governments around the world? How can we build upon the convergence and consensus that is developing about 'creation care'? Are all religions equal from this point of view? Do we have to seek a lowest common denominator of religious expression, or can we recognise truth beyond 'nature spirituality'? Only when we have some answers to these questions can we expect to go forward confidently beyond the restrictions of our own political, racial or religious boundaries.

NOTES

1   The group comprised R. J. Berry (UK)(Chair), D. Birnbacher (Germany), Ph. Bourdeau (Belgium and Commission of the European Communities), Abbyann Lynch (Canada) and A. Morishima (Japan). The code was first published by Berry and Bourdeau in the Proceedings of a Conference on 'Sustainable Development, Science and Policy' held in Bergen in May 1990; it is more easily available in Berry (1993*b*:253–62).

2   The statement was drawn up by a working party of the Church of England Board for Social Responsibility. Its members were the Bishop of Gloucester (John Yates), Rowland Moss, Ruth Page and myself.

10
Awe and Wonders

The psalmist was afraid when he looked up at the hills. The high lands were refuges for robbers and the source of a variety of natural hazards. 'Where shall I find help?' he asked (Psalm 121.1). And he speaks for a vast range of people down the centuries who have found fear, wonder or discomfort in wild nature. But we are not consistent: thirteen centuries after the psalmist, Fraser Darling (1970:85) wrote, 'The wilderness does not exist for our re-creation or delectation. This is something we gain from its great function of being, with the oceans part of the guardianship of the world in which we have so recently become denizens.' This recalls Bryan Norton's idea of being imperceptibly but continually 'transformed' by our contacts with the natural world (p. 173).

Such 'transformation' surfaces in all sorts of testimonies. Arne Naess, the prophet of 'deep ecology', traces his lifetime preoccupation with what he calls 'practical philosophy' to years in childhood:

> inspecting and marvelling at the overwhelming diversity and riches of life in the sea ... [Then] when fifteen years old I managed to travel alone to the highest mountain region in Norway – Jotunheimen ... The effect of this week established my conviction of an inner relation between mountains and mountain people, a certain greatness, cleanness, a concentration upon what is essential, a self-sufficiency; and consequently a disregard of luxury, of complicated means of all kinds. (Naess, 1989:2–3)

John Muir came across two orchids in a bed of moss when he was trying to escape enlistment during the American Civil War. He wrote:

> They were alone ... I never saw a plant so full of life; so perfectly spiritual, it seemed pure enough for the throne of its Creator. I felt as if I were in the presence of superior beings who loved me and beckoned me to come. I sat down besides them and wept for joy.

He treasured that moment as one of the supreme moments of his life (Austin, 1987:7).

Max Nicholson has described how he was 'captivated and carried away' at the age of seven by the displays in the Natural History Museum in London. Following this,

> wherever I went birds were my first interest, but plants, mammals, butterflies and other creatures shared part of the attraction. Scenery too, such as woods, hills, stream-sides and above all the sea-coast excited wonder and eagerness for more ... In those early days there was a special magic in visible change – a sudden fall of snow, a swirl of mist, an overnight sheet of white hoar-frost on the grass, the shapes of great clouds passing across with their shadows, the buds and catkins and new foliage of spring and the eagerly awaited but ever surprising return of the swallow and the cuckoo. Such signs of the dynamic and dramatic workings of nature were an unfailing counterpoise to taking it for granted, or looking on it as a picture gallery or museum. (Nicholson, 1970:18)

Harvard biologist and pioneer sociobiologist Ed Wilson has re-called the summer his parents divorced. He was sent away for the summer.

> Each morning after breakfast I left the small shorefront house to wander alone along the strand. I waded in and out of the dependably warm surf and scrounged for anything I could find in the drift. Sometimes I just sat on a rise to scan the open water. Back in time for lunch, out again, back for dinner, out once again, and, finally, off to bed to relive my continuing adventure briefly before falling asleep.
>
> I have no remembrance of the names of the family I stayed with, what they looked like, their ages, or even how many there were. Most likely they were a married couple and, I am willing to suppose, caring and warm-hearted people. They have passed out of my memory, and I have no need to learn their identity. It was the animals of that place that cast a lasting spell. I was seven years old, and every species, large and small, was a wonder to be examined, thought about, and, if possible, captured and examined again. (Wilson, 1994:8)

Julian Huxley also began a fascination with the natural world at an early age. His

> first conscious memory dated from when I was four. I was being taken for a walk by the nursemaid ... and out of the hawthorn hedge there hopped a fat toad. What a creature, with its warty skin, its big eyes bulging up, and its awkward movements! That comic toad helped to determine my career as a scientific naturalist.

He never lost his excitement for nature. Over forty years later he stayed on the small Welsh island of Skokholm:

> Here I felt, perhaps even more than in Africa, the power and the independence of nature – nature that helps things make themselves, as Charles Kingsley wrote in *The Water Babies*. The swarms of puffins flying down from the cliffs and resting on the sea, the screeching of guillemots, the great black-backed gulls screaming and devouring the plump young shearwaters as they stumbled to the cliff-edge before attempting their first flight, yet (if they survived the predatory gull's attack) immediately at home and knowing what to do when they reached the water; the occasional gannets soaring on their wide white wings: all these manifestations of the vast interrelated web of life never ceased to provoke my interest and wonder. (Huxley, 1970:27, 218)

Composer Peter Maxwell Davies has written of his first visit to the Antarctic:

> The cliff faces are alive with the crack of ice, the whoosh of tumbling snowdrift, the rustle and clatter of falling scree. Occasionally there is a really startling boom, reminiscent of the one o'clock cannon above Edinburgh's Princes Street, or an even more spine-tingling deep, deep gong stroke, as a small geological event changes the landscape one iota, in the course of its eternal metamorphosis. There is almost no wind, but occasionally an astonishing sound whistles from the peaks to the south, almost subliminal at first, but growing into an alto-flutish lament that resonates somewhere between your ears, then reveals its true origin when a high and complex counterpoint, suggesting ghostly oriental flutes, pulses across the whole ice shelf ... I suddenly realise that Antarctica reminds me more than anything of the hidden artwork in medieval cathedrals created by sculptors and painters to the greater glory of God. One is unaccustomedly hypersensitive here to the act of Creation. Elsewhere on earth, man is the most successful mammal: in Antarctica, wonderfully, he has only a precarious toehold. (Davies 2001:35, 48)

It is not only the great and the good, the articulate and professional who have an empathy with nature. William Beach Thomas described the visit of a Lakeland farmer to his brother in Liverpool:

> The place to him was a Tower of Babel. He disliked its alleged amusements, though he saw one film that he liked. He disliked the scenes of daily life, the feeling of imprisonment, the houses in between; but above all he disliked the continuous presence of talking people. At the end of a long description of their interference with his natural thoughts, he said with a gasp 'Oh I did feel lonely!' and he had no wish to be in any sense paradoxical or epigrammatic ... 'Now,' he said, 'on the fells I never feel

lonely, and, what's more, it leaves something behind' ... That is pure Wordsworth from a man who had never read a word of Wordsworth.

What is it that solitary, but never lonely, hours on the fells leaves behind? ... Most people perhaps who have spent long hours in lonely and lovely places, and have enjoyed them, have at intervals become conscious of a sense of communion such as both Hudson and Jefferies confessed in sober prose. It may be said to compare with what certain religious sects call conversion ... The influence of an unexplained mood or inspiration or sense or what you will, even though itself momentary, persists and the world is never quite the same again. You are henceforth at home in it; and to feel lonely in beautiful surroundings is to deny the companionship of nature. (Beach Thomas, 1946:12, 14)

Examples of such experiences could be continued indefinitely, each slightly different, but all describing something lastingly significant for the person concerned. Sometimes such experiences may be near-hallucination. Ernest Shackleton, after an 800-mile crossing of the Antarctic Ocean in an open boat, landed on the barren south shore of South Georgia. He and his companions had to cross the unexplored high interior of the island to reach human settlement. He later described this:

'I know that during that long and racking march of thirty-six hours over the unnamed mountains and glaciers of South Georgia it seemed to me often that there were four, not three. I said nothing to my companions on the point, but afterwards Worsley said to me, 'Boss, I had a curious feeling on the march that there was another person with us.' Crean confessed to the same idea. (Shackleton, 1919:211)

Frank Smythe (1937:187) had a not dissimilar experience at over 28,000 ft on Mount Everest: 'All the time I was climbing alone I had the strong feeling that I was accompanied by a second person. This feeling was so strong that it eliminated all loneliness that I might otherwise have felt.' He even divided his mint-cake, and 'it was almost a shock to find no-one to give it to'.

Whence Awe?

Where do we get our feelings of awe and wonderment? Are they merely the 'noise' around our sensory perceptions of the outside world, or is there 'something more'? Are these feelings an indication of an inner reality – a sort of biological or psychological equivalent of the Anthropic Principle? For Jim Crumley (2000:101) they are 'a collaboration of landscape forces, of light, of weather, of space, the mingled chemistry of which creates a tangible presence of nature that demands a response in those who encounter it'.

Alister Hardy believed they were almost tangible in their authenticity and set out to collect and analyse 'religious experiences' in an effort to develop a scientific natural theology. He included in his definition of religious experience, 'the numinous, the love of nature and the inspiration of art' (ch. 5 of his second volume of Gifford Lectures, Hardy, 1966). I am not wholly persuaded of the value of his enterprise, because 'experience' comes from a set of interactions, and study of the outcome in a complex process like this is an inefficient way to learn more about the interacting elements. Notwithstanding, it can give important clues and has been used in the early stages of many scientific disciplines – not least the study of behaviour. What is intuitively obvious and confirmed by the Religious Experience Research Unit set up by Hardy is the commonness of wonder and awe (Hay, 1982; Hardy, 1984). It is not worth debating whether or not such responses are universal. Like virtually any behaviours they can presumably be suppressed consciously; more important is the frequency with which they are elicited.

Anthropologists have put considerable effort into recording the ways different cultures and different ethnic groups perceive and treat their environment. Gene Anderson (1996) calls such ways 'ecologies of the heart'. Lynn White's (1967) description of the technological control of nature beginning with the invention of the ploughshare and its embracing by Christian apologists can be regarded as the origin of a particular 'ecology of the heart'. Clarence Glacken's *Traces on the Rhodian Shore* (1967) is a systematic survey of the 'ecology of the heart' in Western culture. Max Oeschlaeger (1991) has traced the development of the North American idea of wilderness (see also Golley, 1993*b*) and James Hunter (1976, 1995) has done the same for the crofting communities of the Scottish Highlands.

Can one generalise? Donald Worster (1993) has warned of distortion in analysing attitudes to the environment, because historians are rarely natural historians; their understanding tends to be incomplete, an outworking of the distortion induced by the split between the 'two cultures'. However, differences between different traditions are trivial compared to their common features. Marvin Harris (1968) calls this variety 'a transcultural residuum in the human experience'. His argument is that from the earliest hunters on the African savannah to the atomic era, the dominant drive has been to discover the most rational and efficient way to feed oneself.

Fraser Darling (1951) was cynical about this, 'The human ecologist will never neglect the belly of the people.' On this interpretation every culture is based on simple biology; at bottom it is simply an attempt to answer the eternal calorie problem – how to get the most nutrition out of a situation, what the best cost–benefit answer to the problem is.

How does this relate to feelings of awe? For Gene Anderson they are connected:

> The common theme of all traditional resource management ethics is not spiritual harmony with some disembodied and abstracted Nature, but actual personal and emotional involvement with the actual landscape and its non-human inhabitants. People interact with their surroundings. In all cultures, these surroundings become meaningful – not just as sources of food and shelter, but as sources of beauty, power, excitement, and other human values. In those cultures that endure and do not collapse, the meanings of nature are bound up in systems of respect and protection. Often, mutual obligations exist between people and the beings or forces they believe to exist in the wild. (Anderson, 1996:174)

This plea for pragmatic realism is supported by the comprehensive exploration of the nexus of nature, history and myth undertaken by Simon Schama (1995). His argument is that our experience of nature is necessarily channelled through history; for him awe is historically constituted emotion, largely created by the Romantic cult of the sublime. For example, Rousseau and Thoreau are conventionally seen as sending us back to the wild to recover spontaneity, but their own motives were more a reaction against convention than a search for Arcadia. Thoreau pondered whether to become 'a mail carrier in Peru – or a South American planter – or a Greenland whaler, or a settler on the Columbia river – or a Canton merchant – or a soldier in Florida – or a mackerel fisher off Cape Sable – or a Robinson Crusoe in the Pacific' but decided against, 'for our limbs indeed have room enough, but it is our souls that rust in the corner. Let us migrate interiorly without intermission, and pitch our tent each day nearer the western horizon' (Thoreau, *Journal* for 21 March 1840). He practised what he preached: his 'wilderness hut' by Walden Pond was 100 metres from a commuter rail line and within a thirty-minute walk of the local inn, kept by his aunt.

Notwithstanding, however much our attitude to nature is explicable as a Romantic abstraction, there seems to be something more. There are too many examples in literature of wonder, fear and respect in the observation of the natural world that are not dependent on history. Some call it spirituality – sometimes 'ecological spirituality' – and seek it as an end in itself (Skolimowski, 1993); for others, it is a sign of an underlying property or relationship. Job responded to Yahweh when challenged to look at the wonders of nature, 'I know that you can do all things and that no purpose is beyond you ... I have spoken of things which I have not understood, things too wonderful for me to know ...' (Job 42.2–3). The psalmist writes,

> The word of the Lord created the heavens;
> all the host of heaven was formed at his command.
> He gathered into a heap the waters of the sea,
> he laid up the deeps in his store-chambers.
> Let the whole world fear the Lord, and all the earth's
> inhabitants stand in awe of him.
> For he spoke and it was;
> he commanded and there it stood.   (Psalm 33.6–9)

For native peoples, closeness to the natural world often seems to manifest as a profound love–hate relationship. This is typified by the Celtic Christianity of Scotland and Ireland. Ian Bradley (1993) has described the poetry and artwork of the Celts as an 'exuberant celebration of creation' derived from knowledge of the Bible and their pre-Christian inheritance, and arising

> from living so close to nature and having the time and the temperament to study and contemplate its variety and beauty. They tended to establish their monastic settlements in wild and remote places, having a particular penchant for islands and often retreating to caves and cells for seclusion. It was hardly surprising that they grew to love the cry of sea birds, the barking of seals and even the buzzing of the insects who were sometimes their only companions (Bradley 1993:54).

Environmental Filters

We see nature through a series of filters. However much we claim to be objective, the way we perceive the world is conditioned by the cultural, social, economic and political milieu in which we grew up. Gender, religion, race, socio-economic position and physical appearance all affect the kinds of experiences we have and therefore the way we think.

David Suzuki calls these perceptual filters. He has illustrated them by a conversation with a newly appointed Canadian Minister of the Environment. Suzuki asked him what he felt was his most serious challenge.

> He answered immediately 'global warming.' Impressed, I asked how serious it was. 'We're talking about the survival of the species. If we don't

act now, we face catastrophe,' he said. I was ecstatic and went on: 'So does this mean your government will cancel all mega-projects to develop oil and gas and concentrate on conservation and energy alternatives?' His response was a shock: 'We can't annihilate the past. We made political promises that we have to carry out.' Here was an intelligent, well-meaning person who articulated an understanding that global warming threatened our very survival, yet failed to integrate that crisis into his political priorities. (Suzuki, 1995:5)

Such experiences led Suzuki to set out a number of 'sacred beliefs' which act as filters:

1. Human beings are superior to other life forms; we are insulated from the natural world because our intelligence enables us to understand and control our surroundings.
2. Science provides us with the rationale upon which our control is based.
3. We can manage new technologies so their hazards can be minimised.
4. Through environmental assessments, we can avoid environmental problems from new developments such as dams, clear-cut logging, factories, etc.
5. The economy is the major priority that must occupy us, and all other areas make up a part of the economy.
6. Growth is the criterion of 'progress'.
7. In a democracy, we elect people to represent us and lead us into the future.

There is truth in all these propositions. They are an expanded and updated version of Lynn White's 'our science and our present technology are tinctured with orthodox Christian arrogance towards nature'. It is not my purpose to comment on them in detail. Notwithstanding, they add up to the composite filter which shapes our attitudes to the external world and strengthen Simon Schama's thesis that 'landscape is memory: there is no unmediated perception of nature. Every landscape comes framed.'

Wilderness

It is worth digressing at this point to ponder on wilderness, both because wilderness tends to be a touchstone for 'naturalness' and also because a major part of 'green' rhetoric is that the global commons (atmosphere, oceans and Antarctica) must be preserved against 'the pox called man';[1] for environmentalists, wilderness represents both a history and a symbol of human journeying towards a 'Promised Land'.

The cult of wilderness is strongest in the United States, where its development has been mapped by Max Oeschlaeger (1991) and Frank Golley (1993*b*). Traditionally, wilderness was a hazardous place, where wild beasts and robbers preyed on the unwary, and where tracks were sparse (and therefore travelling difficult). In the United States, this has been replaced by a romantic arena within which humans are supposedly subservient to nature (despite 4-wheel-drive vehicles, etc.). Enthusiasm for such a myth would have been anathema to the Puritans who saw the 'Promised Land' to which they had come as a 'hideous and desolate wilderness' that had to be tamed and transformed, and the wild animals eliminated (among whom they counted the native Indians, who were to be treated as Amalekites and put to death, as Samuel commanded Saul when the Israelites were fighting for the biblical Promised Land [1 Samuel 15.3: 'Go now, fall upon the Amalekites ... Spare no one; put them all to death, men and women, children and babes in arms, herds and flocks, camels and donkeys'.] Carroll, 1969).

It was axiomatic to the neo-classicists of the late seventeenth century that order was intrinsically more beautiful than irregularity. Keith Thomas has collected contemporary comments:

> William Cobbett detested the 'rascally heaths' near Marlborough. 'I have', he wrote, 'no idea of picturesque beauty separate from fertility of soil.' The gardener Samuel Collins spoke for many contemporaries when he said in 1717 that the best of all flowers was a cauliflower; and the affectations of the landscape-gardeners received short shrift from Dr Johnson, who hated talk about prospects and views. 'That was the best garden (he said) which produced most roots and fruits; and that water was most to be prized which contained most fish.' 'The generality of people,' observed William Gilpin in 1791, found wild country in its natural state totally unpleasing: 'there are few who do not prefer the busy scenes of cultivation to the greatest of nature's rough productions.' In general indeed, when we meet with a description of a pleasing country, we hear of haycocks, or waving cornfields or labourers at their plough. (Thomas, 1983:257)

This changed in the eighteenth century in Britain and nineteenth century in North America; the wild came to be regarded not as a resource or an obstacle but as an end in its own right, requiring protection.

How should we respond? In what sense or ways should we protect wilderness in a world where productive land is precious and where we are called to be stewards and manage the world on behalf of the creator? Roderick Nash (1982:20) condemns Judeo-Christianity as 'arousing and nurturing apathy' towards wilderness and anything not under human control, echoing the Lynn White–John Passmore arguments. Against this, Susan Bratton (1993) points out that a great many events of importance to Christianity occurred in a wilderness: the wilderness journeys of the patriarchs; the Exodus as a formative time for the emerging nation of Israel; David hiding from Saul in the caves above the Dead Sea and then defeating his rebellious son, battling on heavily forested slopes. The psalmists and prophets repeatedly use wilderness and the wild as part of their imagery to instruct the faithful in the contrasting graces of the coming kingdom. Both Christ and John the Baptist prepared for ministry in the wilderness of Judea, and the fathers of the early Church culti-vated ascetic lifestyles in the isolated deserts of Palestine and Egypt.

In later centuries, there developed a strong association between wild places and a spiritual quest. Solitariness and asceticism were the context for overcoming the demonic. But wilderness was not always about conflict; peace followed war. The Celts were very positive about their experiences with nature, and saintliness often involved kindness and protection of both animals and landscape. Francis of Assisi encouraged retreating into wild places for spiritual exercise; he himself often walked through fields praising God. However, such withdrawals were temporary and a preparation for evangelism and serving the poor, unlike those of later monastics who often retreated from society for years at a time.

Wilderness experience for spiritual enlightenment has retained its place in the contemplative traditions, although it was condemned by both Luther and Calvin. In the *Institutes*, Calvin wrote:

> It is a beautiful thing to philosophise in retirement, far from intercourse with men. But it is not the part of Christian meekness to flee to the desert and the wilderness and at the same time to forsake those duties which the Lord especially commanded. Though we grant there was nothing else evil in that profession [of flight], it was surely no slight evil that it brought a useless and dangerous example into the church. (III.20–IV.20)

The Reformers tended to interpret Bible passages about nature as allegories or metaphors. While the early desert fathers treated literally the animals in Isaiah 11.6–9 ('The wolf shall lie down with the lamb', etc.), for Luther the wolf is a false teacher, the lambs are Christians, the leopards are persecuting tyrants, the goats are martyrs, and the lions the rich (*Lectures on Isaiah 1–39*). And on John the Baptist 'crying in the wilderness', Calvin wrote:

> The word *wilderness* is here used metaphorically for *desolation* or the frightful ruin of the nation, such as existed in the time of captivity. It was so dismally shattered, that it might well be compared to a *wilderness* ... When John began to preach, Jerusalem was in a sense a *wilderness*: for all had been reduced to a wild and frightful condition. (*Commentary on a Harmony of the Evangelists,* cited by Bratton, 1993:236)

The attitude of the Reformers to wilderness did not mean that they lacked a creation theology. Calvin wrote an extensive commentary on Psalm 104 and the *Institutes* included a chapter on 'the knowledge of God [that] shineth forth in the fashioning of the universe and the continuing government of it'. The Reformers' problem was that withdrawal into the wilderness and a lifelong celibate asceticism detracted from salvation through faith alone, and diverted personal life away from family and service, which they saw as Christ's purpose for his Church.

Is wilderness spiritually necessary? Psychologists have addressed this question without to my knowledge producing any definitive advice. Bratton (1993:17) quotes the authors of the US Wilderness Act as believing that a wilderness experience involves 'spiritual, aesthetic and mystical dimensions' and notes that the US Forest Service text on *Wilderness Management* claims that 'In today's bustling world [wilderness] offers a place where a simpler, less complicated life exists, at least momentarily; it offers a chance to be re-humanised.'

Thor Heyerdahl sought peace on what he believed was an unspoiled tropical island, occupied only by natives uncontaminated by the greed and distortions of Western society. He and his wife found misery instead. They developed boils. Their feet swelled up like balloons when they got wet – and damp could not be avoided. In the rainy season, the sores spread, and the pain forced them to stay in bed. The soil in the forest around them turned to mud, and their hut and bedding became mouldy. Mosquitoes settled on their mosquito nets in enormous numbers. Pygmy ants arrived to feed on the mosquitoes and the Heyerdahls were enveloped in bamboo dust, which covered everything and even made breathing difficult. Their hut was a disaster. The locals had swindled them, building it of green rather than ripe bamboo, aware that the wood would be eaten by beetles and reasoning that they would be well paid for building a replacement. Food became short; the Heyerdahls found the natives were stripping the fruit and vegetables from the area where they were living, forcing them to buy food. One of the local boys planned to release a box full of baby scorpions in the Heyerdahl's hut. They were thrust back upon their inner resources and found them wanting; they were relieved to escape back to Europe. On his return to his native Norway, Heyerdahl wrote:

> There is no Paradise to be found on earth today. There are people living in great cities who are far happier than the majority of people in the South Seas. Happiness comes from within, we realise that now ... It is in his mind and way of life that man may find his Paradise – the ability to perceive the true values of life, which are far removed from property and riches, or from power and renown. (Jacoby 1968:69)

Henry Thoreau came to the same conclusion: 'It is vain to dream of a wildness distant from ourselves. There is none such. It is the bog in our brain and bowels, the primitive vigour of Nature in us, that inspires that dream' (quoted by Schama, 1995:578).

Notwithstanding, Bratton (1993:272) lists seven reasons for finding and spending time in our own personal wilderness:

1. to develop an appreciation of creation and the creator – although understanding the creator presupposes both faith and knowledge (Hebrews 11.3, 6 ['By faith we understand that the universe was formed by God's command, so that the visible came from the invisible ... But without faith, it is impossible to please him, for whoever comes to God must believe that he exists and rewards those who seek him']);
2. rest and refreshment;
3. spiritual exercise, and communication with God;
4. to seek change in oneself;
5. preparation for a difficult situation;
6. putting culture and society into perspective;
7. developing a sense of the importance of community.

Bratton concentrates on the first of these, pointing out that all the others can be practised anywhere. She acknowledges that:

> the common pattern among Christians today is to suppose that there is not any general need for contact with wild nature, but to treat it as an option for the few believers interested in monastic spirituality or environmental questions. This approach confuses the responsibilities of those with specialised Christian callings with those of the entire church. In the end, nothing is necessary to salvation except the acceptance of Christ's person and work on the cross ... There is no reason every Christian

should spend forty days in the wilderness with the wild beasts or that every Christian should travel in Horeb, since these journeys prepared for prophetic ministry. On the other hand, every Christian needs to comprehend God's role as Creator as well as God's role as Saviour (and the two are integrally related). All Christians, therefore, should have some exposure to creation, free from human tinkering and modification, as the work of a loving and caring God. (Bratton, 1993:274–5)

René Dubos comes to the same conclusion from the starting point of a microbiologist, not a theologian. He has written:

> Our separation from the rest of the natural world leaves us with a subconscious feeling that we must retain some contact with wilderness and with as wide a range of living things as possible. National parks contribute a value that transcends economic considerations and may play a role similar to that of Stonehenge, the Pyramids, Greek temples, Roman ruins, Gothic cathedrals ... Correcting the damage done to nature by industrialisation is probably well within our powers, but to formulate new positive values for modern life will be much more difficult ... The futures we invent are viable only if they are compatible with the constraints imposed by the evolutionary past. This does not mean that the more desirable future is one which would take us back to the pre-technological womb. But nature and external nature must be kept in mind whenever plans are made to change the conditions of life. (Dubos, 1973:166, 280)[2]

Heyerdahl and Dubos are describing their own personal reactions to wilderness, much as the anecdotes I included at the beginning of the chapter are individual experiences of nature. But we can all link with wilderness through the biblical narrative traditionally interpreted as a description of the human pilgrimage, which afflicts or inspires us today just as much as in Old Testament times, albeit in different forms. In this we can share also in the large number of journeys in literature – in ancient Hebrew, Greek and Latin; Chaucer's pilgrims, More's *Utopia*, Bunyan's *Pilgrim's Progress*; Swift's *Gulliver's Travels*; the Viking sagas and the myths of Melanesia. We are all familiar with many of them, from the Odyssey to Jules Verne and Arthur Clarke, and on to the explorations of the New Age. The abundance of these descriptions encourages one to believe that 'journeying' is a universal requirement of the human condition.[3]

Things happen when one leaves home in ways which they do not if we stay in the same place. At times it may be true that it is better to travel hopefully than to arrive. Is this a justifiable aim in life? Put crudely, is there a green pasture prepared for us by Adam Gifford's 'First and only Cause'? Is there a purpose to existence or is life no more than a gigantic game of snakes and ladders? Can we discern meaning from studying the world or is natural theology merely intellectual aerobics? Are we fooling ourselves to believe that there is more to existence than Henry Thoreau's 'bog in our brain and bowels'?

Re-divinisation

The move from being part of nature to separation from it followed by virtual sanctification of wilderness, took place in the eighteenth century when ideas from ancient Greece and Rome came together with biblical tradition into a recognisably modern form:

> [with] cataclysmic ecological consequences; they would drive us relentlessly to create the man-made landscape we inhabit today and in the process nearly wipe out that wilder America. They would also leave us, for many intricate reasons, feeling guilty about what we have done and would encourage that peculiar search for national atonement we have called environmentalism. (Worster, 1993:9)

This last can conveniently be discussed as 'ecosophy,' or 'deep ecology' as it is more commonly known. Its origin in its modern form was an article by the Norwegian philosopher, Arne Naess, 'The shallow and the deep, long-range ecology movement' (Naess 1973). For Arne Naess and the exponents of deep ecology whom he inspired, notably George Sessions and Bill Devall in North America and Warwick Fox in Australia, scientific ecology involved philosophical and religious principles that completely undermine traditional ways of understanding the human–environment relationship, or what deep ecologists call the 'dominant paradigm' of Western thought regarding nature (Fox, 1996). A new paradigm was needed, the most radical component of which is what Naess calls 'ecological egalitarianism'. Other deep ecologists commonly use 'biocentrism' or 'anti-anthropocentrism' to refer to it and related ideas; Naess himself spoke of 'a core democracy in the biosphere'. The central notion is, in Naess's words, 'the equal right [of every form of life] to live and flourish'; Bookchin (1994) calls this 'palaeolithic spirituality', pouring scorn on Naess's characterisation.

Naess (1989:28) defined shallow ecology as 'the fight against pollution and resource depletion', with its chief objective 'the health and affluence of people in the developed countries'. He defines deep ecology as:

1. rejection of the human-in-environment image in favour of 'a relational, total-field image'; together with

2. biospheric egalitarianism – in principle. The 'in principle' clause 'is inserted because any realistic praxis necessitates some killing, exploitation and suppression'.

Naess acknowledges that his deep ecology did not – and does not – emerge from ecological science, but that ecology 'suggested, inspired, and fortified a set of views that had a source elsewhere, beyond scientific logic, beyond facts, beyond induction' (Worster, 1985:x). He claims that the crux of the deep ecology position 'reflects the insights and experience of the field ecologist'; he calls this 'self-realisation', which is of course a key aspect of the so-called New Age approach (Golley, 1987). This has not stopped Naess criticising science. He has set out eight differences between deep and shallow ecology, to the disparagement of the latter (1984). Brennan (1988:141–2) has set out Naess's contrasts (Box 2).

Two things are immediately clear from the distinctions in Box 2: they involve confrontations and a metaphysical position based on rights together with the sort of reductionism indulged in by Capra and his followers. I have already criticised these interpretations (pp. 171, 90 respectively) and need not return to them here.

A different approach to intrinsic value has been developed by Holmes Rolston (Edinburgh Gifford Lecturer, 1997–8). In an argument dangerously close to the evolutionary ethics of the Huxleys, Simpson and Waddington, he suggests that nature itself is a 'source of values, including our own. Nature is a generative process to which we want to relate ourselves and by this to find relationships to other creatures. Values include far more than a simplistic human-interest satisfaction. Value is a multifaceted idea with structures that root in natural sources' (Rolston, 1986:121). In other words, Rolston includes history (including evolution) and contingency in his understanding (and, incidentally, also strong criticisms of the readiness of sociobiologists to ascribe many human behaviours to preconceived models) (Rolston, 1999). This leads him to the notion of 'systemic value', in which he joins Aldo Leopold, who told us to:

> quit thinking about decent land use as solely an economic problem. Examine each question in terms of what is ethically and aesthetically right, as well as what is economically expedient. A thing is right when it tends to preserve the integrity, stability and beauty of the biotic community. It is wrong when it tends otherwise. (Leopold, 1949:242–5)

The step from individual to systemic values is potentially important. Leopold called his idea a 'land ethic'. It involves acknowledging that

Box 2: Shallow and Deep Ecology Compared

Shallow Ecology	Deep Ecology
Natural diversity is valuable as a resource for us.	Natural diversity has its own (intrinsic) value.
It is nonsense to talk about value except as value for humankind.	Equating value with value for humans reveals a racial prejudice.
Plant species should be saved because of their value as genetic reserves for human agriculture and medicine.	Plant species should be saved because of their intrinsic value.
Pollution should be decreased if it threatens economic growth.	Decrease of pollution has priority over economic growth.
Third World population growth threatens ecological equilibrium.	World population at the present level threatens ecosystems, the major threat being posed by the population and behaviour of industrial states more than by those of any others. Human population today is excessive.
'Resource' means resource for humans.	'Resource' means resource for living beings.
People will not tolerate a broad decrease in their standard of living.	People should not tolerate a broad decrease in the quality of life but should be ready to accept a reduction in the standard of living in over-developed countries.
Nature is cruel and necessarily so.	Humankind is cruel but not necessarily so.

we belong to the land as much as it belongs to us, and in this has resonances with Naess's 'biotic equalitarianism'. But Leopold (and Rolston) are clear that the values and ethics they espouse involve obligations.[4] The danger is that a land ethic can easily carry overtones of ecological linkages in an attempt to strengthen the argument, and may imply that some systems are biologically closer than others. Rolston, for example, frequently refers to ecosystems and the 'liberating effect of evolution', although he does not build these into the concept of systemic value. He needs to tread carefully in this area.

Bible Wisdom

At this point, 'wisdom' in the Bible becomes relevant, both because the wisdom writings frequently refer to creation ('nature' is not a biblical word) and also because they put the issues of awe and the divinisation of creation into a wide perspective (Murphy, 1996). The Bible claims that the world is not silent, but proclaims a message for all to hear (Psalms 19.2; 145; 148). 'The creation doctrine of wisdom does not speak directly to the ecological concerns that have agitated recent discussions. But it does contribute to forming a basic human attitude that can have an ecological 'fallout,' so to speak' (Murphy, 1996:121; see also Anderson, 1984:152–71).

This is nowhere clearer that in Ecclesiastes, which picks up the challenge not infrequently issued by positivists of one sort or another, that religious claims should be tested in the same way as scientific hypotheses. There are a number of responses to this challenge (Jeeves and Berry, 1998), not least Christ's own response that 'Whoever chooses to do the will of God *will know* whether my teaching comes from him or is merely my own' (John 7.17), but one of the most detailed examinations involving experimental testing was by Qoheleth, the spokesman in Ecclesiastes.

Ecclesiastes describes a series of experiments carried out by the narrator on different facets of human existence – sex, asceticism, hedonism, despotism, among others: the author is portrayed as one with the resources to carry out these experiments on his own desires and aspirations, and one who is ruthless in analysing his data ('I hated life', 2.17, cf. 5.13–17). Where a mathematician writes 'QED' at the end of a proof, Qoheleth wrote 'futility' or 'vanity' (the word occurs thirty-eight times in the book).

Theologians have argued interminably about the meaning, sources, dating, authorship, and so on of Qoheleth. Michael Fox (1989:80) sums up crisply, 'Qoheleth has an essentially empirical methodology: he seeks both to derive knowledge from experience and to validate ideas experientially.' The book includes cosmology (1.4–11), anthropology (1.12–3.15), and social criticism (3.16–6.10), and incorporates critiques of religion (4.17–5.6) and ideology (6.11–9.6), and ethics (9.7–12.7). The conventional critics' complaint that there is no structure to the book as a whole, increases its credibility for an experimentalist, because scientific experimentation is essentially pragmatic, with new tests implied by the results of previous ones. Read from the standpoint of a scientist, the book shows a clear development of understanding. Qoheleth makes an important preliminary judgement, 'He [God] has made everything to suit its time; moreover he has given mankind a sense of past and future, but no comprehension of God's work from beginning to end' (3.11), and a more definitive pronouncement at the end of his experimental programme, 'Fear God and obey his commandments; this sums up the duty of mankind. For God will bring everything we do to judgement, every secret, whether good or bad' (12.13–14).

Although 'vanity' is the commonest word in Ecclesiastes, it would be wrong to assume that the whole argument is dominated by negativity and frustration. Perhaps more than any other book in the Bible, the text is dominated by a few repeated words, which can be regarded as the author's reaction to the different examinations carried out. Such words are 'profit' (in the sense of 'surplus', e.g. 1.3; it is a word not found elsewhere in the Old Testament), 'portion' or 'lot', 'toil', 'joy', 'wisdom' (which occurs fifty-two times), the 'fear of God' (which flows from the mystery and incomprehensibility of God; if one cannot understand what God is doing, reverential fear is a proper response, and one which provides the context but not the motive for obedience, 12.13), 'retribution in this life' (not in the sense of punishment or reward, but in the sense of the Old Testament assumption that God is involved in all that occurs), and 'death' (as the antithesis of the fulfilled life).

Wisdom is clearly central to Qoheleth's enterprise, and this causes problems to traditionally minded theologians, because of the apparently missing link between behaviour and rewards or retribution as found in both secular literature and in Deuteronomy, Psalms, Proverbs, Ecclesiasticus, and so on (Deane-Drummond, 2000). This almost mechanical consequentialism is not present in Job and in Ecclesiastes. In Job, the correspondence is defeated by a theology of transcendence: Job demands to see the justice of God, who is above and free of any 'order' of things. The Israelite belief in the justice and fidelity of a personal God triumphs. For Qoheleth there is more to religion than salvation (Murphy, 1992:lxix):

> God is utterly present and at the same time utterly absent. God is 'present' in each event and yet no event is a 'place of encounter' with God, since humans do not understand what his will is ... Events do not speak any longer the language of a saving God. They are there, simply. (Gorssen, 1970:314–15)

This is the same judgement that Aubrey Moore made about the effect of Darwinism on the inadequate deistic idea of God (p. 10).

In *Letters and Papers from Prison* (1971), Dietrich Bonhoeffer comments, 'It is only when one loves life and the world so much that without them everything would be gone, that one can believe in the resurrection and a new world.' Roland Murphy extends this:

> Qoheleth loved life: 'Whatever task lies to your hand, do it with might; because in Sheol, for which you are bound, there is neither doing nor thinking, neither understanding, nor wisdom' (9:10). It was because of his appreciation of life and wisdom that he perceived the awfulness of death and the vanity of life itself ... The work of Qoheleth can be seen as a veritable purification of the ongoing wisdom movement, a blow in favour of divine freedom. It can also serve to purify the faith and convictions of the modern reader, whose eschatological hopes can sometimes distort the proper relationships of human being to God. (Murphy, 1992:1xix)

Awe and Stewardship

This brings us back to stewardship. If our proper approach to the environment is that of stewardship (Chapter 9), what relationship does the encounter with the world described in the wisdom literature have to the response expected from a steward? We have already noted that the idea of stewardship as a model for creation care is doubted by some because it seems to require belief in transcendent Lord who can exercise discipline; this may be acceptable to those who already have such a belief, but it is worthless to those who are agnostic or opposed to such divine action. It is here that 'wisdom encounters' become important, because they can pave the way for accepting a lord who expects his followers to be stewards.[5]

For Richard Bauckham (2000) the significant change in the understanding of the human dominion over nature occurred with the Italian humanist writers of the Renaissance, who were preoccupied with the theme of the supreme dignity of humanity, set out in their understanding of Genesis 1.26. In Renaissance humanism the vertical relationship of humanity to nature – human beings as rulers over the rest of creation – was emphasised to the virtual exclusion of the horizontal relationship of humanity to nature – human beings as creatures who share with other creatures a common creaturely relationship to the creator. Humanity's place within creation was abolished in favour of humanity's exaltation above creation (Harrison, 1999).

A major corrective came from Francis Bacon (p. 33). He does not speak, like the Italian humanists, of human deification or of humanity as a kind of god over the world. He accuses traditional natural philosophy of the sin of pride in wanting to be god, because it constructs an idea of nature out of imagination. The philosopher creates the world as he would have liked it to be – thereby 'playing God' – instead of humbly observing the world that God has actually made, as Bacon's empiricist does. In this sense, Bacon sets the tone for the scientific enterprise. Bacon's scientist is not a god who can recreate the world in any way he will, but one who can subject it to the purpose of human benefit for which God created it by mastering the laws of nature. Despite the continued reference to God the creator, this is the point at which Western attitudes to nature moved from being theocentric to being almost exclusively anthropocentric. In the Baconian tradition it makes little practical difference that atheistic scientists eventually took their place alongside believing scientists.

The problem has been that in moving from dominion to involvement, scientists (and they are not alone in this) have suppressed their 'awe' of the world in their work. In other words, they have succumbed to a dualism between supposed objectivity and alleged subjectivity. The blame for this attitude is often laid on the so-called 'desacralisation' of the world: by treating it as an object, we give ourselves licence to misuse it. However, attempts to 're-sacralise' creation are usually little more than pantheism. A better way forward is to return to the lost attitudes of the wisdom tradition. In essence, this is converging on the rediscovery of natural history described by Charles Raven (p. 50). This is one of the main themes of Chapter 11.

NOTES

1   'The Earth is a beautiful place, but it has a pox called man' (Nietzsche), cited by Lyn Margulis (1995).
2   'As modern man becomes increasingly urbanised, the resulting shift away from "wilderness" has largely sequestered us from the values of nature. Those of us who live in large towns and cities have become less exposed to the natural world and unless we make a determined effort to return to such wild places for recreation, then it's unlikely we will be able to recognise, let alone take advantage of its healing qualities' (McNeish, 2001:178).
3   Jim Perrin (1997:33–4) notes that 'In the centuries between the fall of Rome and the Reformation ... the sense comes down of a restless movement of scholars, poets, princes and the wealthier of the ordinary people backwards and forwards between Loretto, Assisi, Walsingham, St. David's, Canterbury, Ynys Enlli, Santiago de Compostelo, Jerusalem, in search of – what? The simple – perhaps facile – answer is spiritual enrichment, and that in itself raises a beautiful paradox. These journeys of

a distance, harshness, discomfort and danger almost unimaginable to us cosseted dwellers of the late twentieth century were steps towards the state of Grace ... The simple paradox runs that in the comfort of material things lies temptation and sin, in the austerity of the journey whose object is reverence, lies salvation. And yet, I still get a sense from the records of mediaeval pilgrimage of something beyond all this – the unspoken reason, the passion unstated for which these hardships of the journey were to be endured ... As the great age of pilgrimage got under way, there came about in the teachings of the Church that was its chief promoter a curious disjunction between a journey's object and the actuality of the landscapes it must traverse ... [Did the pilgrims] arrive at the wisdom that it is not the journey's object but the journey itself that matters, along the course of which the incidental can be the transcendent?'

4   Religion is an essential link for Rolston in overcoming the frequent assumptions of reductionism and naturalism in biological systems. For him, religion is 'the secret that makes possible the human passage from genetic nature to transmissible culture' and is 'required for the genesis of culture' (Rolston, 1999:328); although religion serves a social function, it also embodies truth – Rolston develops a sort of biological version of the Anthropic Principle (p. 12).

5   'God as deliverer is not mentioned in the wisdom texts, nor is there any mention of any of the great saving events of Israel's history, such as the Exodus. Creation and history is the arena where God's presence is sought. Creation provides for the orderly parameters with which human existence is lived ... To know God is to discern the harmonious order for which we were created: persons to God; persons to each other; and persons to the rest of nature' (Birch and Rassmussen, 1978:102).

11
Science and the Cross

I have ranged widely in this book – from ecology to Ecclesiastes, from patristics to pollution. I have repeatedly had to resist the temptation to dig deeper into some topics, and I may have got the balance wrong and be accused of superficiality. I have been driven by two goals: the need to interpret for the current age Lord Gifford's charge to 'Advance ... the study of Natural Theology' from my stand-point as a natural scientist who believes that there is a God and that he has revealed himself to us; and even more by fear about the impli-cation of false or inadequate understandings of this God for the future of the world. I am torn between the carping cloisters of academic propriety and the dangers of rejection by espousing unorthodoxy. I am encouraged that I am on the right lines by Keith Ward (1998:14) who believes 'that the third millennium of Christian existence will bring a new integration of scientific and religious thought, the development of a more global spirituality, and a retrieval of some of the deepest insights of the Christian faith'. But how best can we bring together the multifarious strands I have explored?

John Habgood (1993) in his Centenary Gifford Lecture quotes the lady from East Barnet (an updated version of the man on the Clapham Omnibus), 'I don't actually believe in the Resurrection, but I do think that there's something going on up there.' Habgood inter-preted this to mean that 'if there is certainty at all in religion it seems to belong at this point of ineffability, at the point where philosophy and theology run out into silence'. An implicit agenda of this book is to discover if it is possible to make explicit Habgood's 'ineffability'. I do not think it is a vain hope; I am encouraged by the report that 40 per cent of randomly selected senior US scientists affirm they believe in a personal God (remarkably, an incidence unchanged in surveys carried out in 1916 and 1996; the chief difference between the two surveys was that there was a greater proportion of believing biologists and correspondingly less of believing physicists in 1996 than in 1916) (Larson and Witham, 1997).

Where does academic enquiry end and unjustified extrapolation begin? Prophecy can too easily feed on credulity and unhappiness.

Ronald Knox has wonderfully satirised the *angst* that he conceived as sweeping London with the announcement of a new sin discovered. He ends his account, 'Curiosity is the most odious of vices. But confess now, when you began to read this history of yourself, had you not a faint hope that, before reaching the end of it, you would find out what the New Sin really was?' (Knox, 1928:97).

More seriously, Peter Washington (1993) has chronicled the history, frauds, claims and ridiculousness of many of the searching groups and their charismatic leaders which lie behind the plaintive sadnesses of the New Age and other 'fringe' religious groups. His starting point is the challenges to religious authority in the mid-nineteenth century – the successes of mechanism and technology, and doubts about the Bible as God's revelation – the same questionings that fuelled the Bishop of Oxford's opposition to Darwinian evolution in his 1860 debate with Thomas Henry Huxley (p. 53). The bishop was a Canute. The waves of change have swept inexorably through society. Washington describes what happened:

> Christianity was reduced to little more than an interesting tribal story with an influential morality, more or less embodied in Christian legal and political institutions. In such a context Jesus appeared not as the unique Christ, but as one influential teacher among many, together with Buddha, Socrates, Confucius, Manu and Lao Tzu. Some of these teachers were mythical, others were historical figures wrapped in a carapace of myth which contemporary scholarship gradually stripped away – a process which suggested that Christianity itself might be a kind of fiction, a transcendent narrative that could still give meaning to each individual's own 'story', without being in any objective sense true ... No one of these developments necessarily denies the validity of Christian experience, excludes the possibility of spiritual life or militates against the existence of established churches as such – but together they do unsettle all three. Thus the religious revivals of the nineteenth century were frequently characterised by a tendency to identify 'true' spirituality with mysticism or occultism: the knowledge of ultimate reality experienced as something outside common expressive forms. This was one way of saving the spiritual from the corrupting effects of religious institutions. And while the established churches declined, interest in religion itself was never stronger. The process of unsettling beliefs aroused strong passions; as certainties became doubts, doubts gave rise to new needs. Spirituality itself was not in question, so much as a secure source of spiritual authority. It was this need for authority that made disciples so very vulnerable to charismatic teachers.
>
> The problem of the source was intimately entwined with another nineteenth-century preoccupation, the search for a single key that would solve the mysteries of the universe. A key, it was thought, might unlock the source – while, conversely, the source would provide a key ... It was

proposed, for example that all human tongues derive from one common language, all races from one mother-race, all philosophies and religions from one original doctrine.[1] Though the two greatest philosophers of the mid-century – Søren Kierkegaard and Friedrich Nietzsche – pointed out that a key and a source were the very things not to be had in a subjective age such as the nineteenth century, they went unheard. The need for belief in primal unity and ultimate authority ran too deep, even among sceptics. Though George Eliot satirises Mr Casaubon's search for a Key to All Mythologies in *Middlemarch*, it is clear that she sympathises with the attempt. It is Casaubon's methods that are at fault, not his objective. (Washington, 1993:8–11)

Washington traces a host of theosophical, anthropological and other trails sparked by the search for a 'key' to the meaning of life, from Emmanuel Swedenborg and Franz Mesmer to Aldous Huxley and his hunt for the 'perennial philosophy'. It would be hilarious if it did not reveal (and induce) so much tragedy and unhappiness. The Gnostic grail of the searchers seems to have as much reality and prospect of discovery as forty-two, which aficionados of *The Hitchhiker's Guide to the Galaxy* know is the answer to the great question of Life, the Universe and Everything (Adams, 1979:128).

Notwithstanding, there are two things upon which we can agree without difficulty: a widespread restlessness over glib assumptions about godlessness, and secondly, a turmoil in society which makes it even harder to assuage restlessness by the anaesthetic of routine (Qoheleth clearly recognised this – see Ecclesiastes 3.1–8; p. 219). Is Gifford's 'the Infinite, the All, the First and Only Cause, the one and the Sole Substance, the Sole Being, and the Sole Reality, and the Sole Existence' the 'key' sought by the Theosophists and their New Age descendants? Or is it something more? The older version of natural theology was effectively a variant of the design argument for the existence of God, and has no credibility in the Darwinian age. On the other hand, Dawkins's 'blind watchmaker' is an incomplete explanation of the world in which we live. My thesis is that a re-evaluated and re-expressed understanding of the God revealed in the Judeo-Christian scriptures (and to some extent in the Qur'ān) is a necessary and sufficient 'key' to the world, albeit one that requires completion by the specifically Christian belief in the historic Jesus as son of God.

Homo divinus

Our starting point has to be ourselves – human beings descended from and related to the apes, members of the species *Homo sapiens* and characterisable anatomically, physiologically and genetically like any other biological species. The common assumption is that we are 'nothing but' such a biological entity. If we accept we are something more (and it is an act of faith to assume that we are 'nothing but' intelligent apes), we have to ask what additional properties we possess. The Bible distinguishes us from all other animals as being made 'in God's image' (p. 75). We can perhaps be described as *Homo divinus* as well as *Homo sapiens*.

We have seen that Francisco Ayala, a geneticist, believes that the capacity for ethical behaviour has evolved like any other trait (p. 74) and that William Thorpe, an animal behaviourist, considered humans to be unique in being able to recognise 'abstract moral laws' (p. 75). Going one stage further, *imago* carries the implication of 'resemblance' or 'reflection'. C. F. D. Moule regarded it as implying 'responsibility' (p. 75), and this has been an important element in attributing to us a role as God's stewards in caring for his creation (Hall, 1986). The Bible joins these biological and spiritual traits together as indicators of the extraordinary privilege we have of being able to relate personally to God and he to us. We may suspect this possibility from 'religious experiences' (both our own and those of others) but we can only know it for certain from the Bible, God's Book of Words. God's Two Books come together as we consider the nature of humankind (p. 33).

From this understanding of *Homo divinus* made by God for relationship with him, we can make sense of the Bible's (and the Christian Church's) stories of sin and salvation. Sin is the name given to disobedience to God which led to God's alienation from us. In Genesis we are told about humans choosing their own way and specifically disobeying God.

Let me indulge in what a theologian would probably categorise as wild speculation, but which as a scientist I prefer to describe as a tentative hypothesis subject to test by the coherence of data.[2] Genesis speaks of Adam as a farmer; Pearce (1969) calls Genesis 2–4 a 'type of cultural zone fossil', telling of Adam cultivating his patch on the slopes of the Turkish plateau as climatic conditions improved following the final retreat of the Pleistocene ice-sheet. This would date him about 10,000 years ago, of a similar order of antiquity as Archbishop Ussher's dating from biblical chronology of 6,000 years ago.

It is fully consonant with Genesis that God created Adam in the body of a Near Eastern farmer, comparatively recently in archaeological terms; *Homo sapiens* became *Homo divinus*. If we accept this, the term 'man' as used by the palaeontologist or anthropologist is a much wider term than 'man' as used in the Bible (the existence of pre-Adamic humans conveniently explains such old chestnuts as where Cain got his wife from, and who were the Nephilim, Genesis 6.4). It is worth recording a comment by B. B. Warfield that 'it is to theology as such, a matter of entire indifference how long man has existed on earth'.

Continuing this line of thought, and perhaps joining Paul in arguing as a fool (2 Corinthians 11.21), can one give any credibility whatsoever to a historic Adam and Eve? (Berry, 1999*b*). No modern scholar would dream of such a claim (e.g. Primavesi, 2000, rejects the traditional story and attempts a heroic reinterpretation based on her understanding of human evolution linked to Gaia as an organising principle). The unfortunate problem is that the Bible seems to teach it. The biblical genealogies trace the human race back to Adam (Genesis 5.3ff.; 1 Chronicles 1.1ff.; Luke 3.38); Jesus himself taught that at the beginning, the creator made them male and female and then instituted marriage (Matthew 19.4ff., quoting Genesis 1.27); Paul told the Athenian philosophers that God had made every nation 'from one man' (Acts 17.26); and most notably, Paul's carefully constructed analogy between Adam and Christ depends on the equal historicity of both (Romans 5.12–19; see also 1 Corinthians 15.21–45). Paul's logic clearly rests on the fact that 'sin entered the world through one man, and death through sin'. How determinative are these texts?

Three points need to be made. First, Adam and Eve 'died' *the day* they disobeyed (Genesis 2.17), but they survived physically (and produced all their children) after their exclusion from God's presence. The death that came into the world was spiritual (separation from God), not physical death. As John Stott (1994:171) writes, 'Death in Scripture is represented more in legal than in physical terms; not so much as a state of lying motionless but as the grim though just penalty for sin.' It is human death that is referred to; When Paul speaks of death entering the world (Romans 5.12, 18–19), he qualifies it as being visited on all *people*, not on plants and animals.

Secondly, by the time Neolithic farming was beginning in the Middle East, *Homo sapiens* had already spread to many parts of the world: there were Indians in America, Aborigines in Australia, and so on. A Neolithic Adam and Eve could not be the physical ancestors of the whole human species. But we have already seen that physical relationships are irrelevant where God's human creation is concerned. Spiritual inbreathing and 'spiritual death' are not determined by or spread through Mendelian genes: they depend upon

God's distinctive (and divine) methods of transmission. As Kidner
has pointed out:

> With one possible exception,[3] the unity of mankind 'in Adam' and our
> common status as sinners through his offence, are expressed in Scripture
> not in terms of heredity (Isaiah 43:27) but simply of solidarity. We
> nowhere find applied to us any argument from physical descent such as
> that of Hebrews 7:9,10 (where Levi shares in Abraham's act though being
> 'still in the loins of his ancestor'). Rather, Adam's sin is shown to have
> implicated all men because he was the federal head of humanity,
> somewhat as in Christ's death 'one died for all, therefore all died' (2
> Corinthians 5:14) ... After the special creation of the first human pair
> clinched the fact that there is no natural bridge from animal to man, God
> may have now conferred his image on Adam's collaterals to bring them
> into the same realm of being. Adam's 'federal' headship of humanity
> extended, if that was the case, outwards to his offspring, and his disobe-
> dience disinherited both alike. (Kidner, 1967: 30)

The Bible's insistence on the spiritual unity of the human race does
not necessarily mean a genetical unity, even though this would be
the simplest interpretation. Thirdly, these points enable us to
consider the seemingly unlikely possibility of a historic 'fall'. The
New Testament passage which most explicitly refers to this is Romans
8.18–23,[4] apparently teaching that the whole creation (including
humanity) has been affected by the presence of sin in the world.
Close examination, however, shows that the fall primarily involved
disobedient humankind, although secondarily and consequentially
the rest of creation (Berry, 1999*b*).

There is a danger of trying to understand Romans 8.18–23 out of
its context. It is, in fact, part of the theme of redemption and the
Spirit's work which occupies Paul in chapters 5 to 8 of the letter to
the Romans; the passage about the fall and suffering links with
Romans 5.3–5, where suffering and hope are associated with the gift
of the Spirit. Now the fall resulted in death (Genesis 2.17; Romans
6.23), that is, separation from God. This had two consequences: the
relationship of 'love and cherishing' between Adam and Eve became
one of 'desire and domination' (Genesis 3.16; 4.7); and 'tending'
within Eden became 'toil' outside (Genesis 3.18; cf. Leviticus 26.3ff.;
Ecclesiastes 2.20–24). Romans 8.20 states that the frustration
currently experienced by creation is not innate in it, but was a consequence of 'the will of the one who subjected it'. This was presumably
an act of God, because the creation was 'subjected in hope', but the
key point is that the frustration arises because of an extrinsic event,
and can be dealt with by faith, as Paul points out in Romans 5.2.

C. F. D. Moule (1964) paraphrases Romans 8.20: 'For creation was subjected to frustration, not by its own choice but because of Adam's sin which pulled down nature with it, since God had created Adam to be in close connection with nature.' The teaching of the whole of this central section of Romans is how Christ overcame death (on the cross) and how the consequences of this are dealt with, contrasting life in the flesh with life in the Spirit (6.13). In 8.19 Paul writes about the 'sons of God' who are to be revealed; in the same passage he defines 'sons of God' as 'those who are led by the Spirit of God' (8.14). The next verse (8.20) describes the vanity and frustration which result from a failure to respond to the Spirit. The word translated 'frustration' means literally 'futility' or 'purposelessness'; in other words, the frustration of the non-human world is a consequence of the lack of the care, which we were supposed to exercise and which was ordained for it at creation, when God entrusted its dominion to us. The book of Ecclesiastes can be read as a commentary on this verse.

The message of Romans 8.18–23 is thus one of hope – not looking to the indefinite future but to the time when the redeemed accept the consequences of their reunion with God, and therefore their responsibility for nature. Paul's argument is that as long as we refuse (or are unable through sin) to play the role God created for us, the world of nature will remain dislocated and frustrated. Since humankind is God's vicegerent on earth (which is part, at least, of the meaning of being 'in God's image'), we have inevitably failed in our stewardship from the moment we first disobeyed God and dislocated the relationship. Some Christians interpret any facts which they find morally difficult as 'results of the fall' (such as 'nature red in tooth and claw', or the enormous number of human foetuses which spontaneously miscarry). We must be clear that these are no more than guesses; we are almost completely ignorant about the moral state of affairs before the fall (although we know that there were landslides and extensive floods on earth before there is any evidence of human life, and that many dinosaurs suffered from arthritis). It is highly dubious exegesis to argue from such apocalyptic passages as Isaiah 11.6–9 ('The wolf will live with the lamb ...') that particular ecological conditions were God's primary purpose. Hugh Ross comments:

> Considering how creatures convert chemical energy into kinetic energy, we can say that carnivorous activity results from the laws of thermodynamics, not from sin. Large, active, agile land animals must spend virtually all their waking hours grazing, drinking or digesting or they must consume meat ... We tend to anthropomorphise and thus distort the sufferings of animals. (Ross, 1994:63)

The most explicit curse which came as God's punishment for disobedience was death. But if death is primarily about separation from God and only secondarily about disease, decay and physical death, we are not justified in accepting the common assumption that the main effects of the fall were weeds, pathogens, earthquakes, and so on. Paul's main point is surely that as long as we refuse (or fail) to play the part assigned to us by God (that is, to act as his stewards or vicegerents here on earth), so long is the entire world of nature frustrated and dislocated; an untended garden is one which is overrun by thorns and thistles.

Charles Cranfield expresses this powerfully in expounding the Romans passage. He asks:

> What sense can there be in saying that 'the sub-human creation – the Jungfrau, for example, or the Matterhorn, or the planet Venus – suffers frustration by being prevented from properly fulfilling the purpose of its existence?' The answer must surely be that the whole magnificent theatre of the universe, together with all its splendid properties and all the varied chorus of sub-human life, created for God's glory, is cheated of its true fulfilment so long as man, the chief actor in the great drama of God's praise, *fails to contribute his rational part.* The Jungfrau and the Matterhorn and the planet Venus and all living things too, man alone excepted, do indeed glorify God in their own ways; but, since their praise is destined to be not a collection of independent offerings but part of a magnificent whole, the united praise of the whole creation, they are prevented from being fully that which they were created to be, *so long as man's part is missing,* just as all the other players in a concerto would be frustrated of their purpose if the soloist were to fail to play his part. (Cranfield, 1974:227; my italics)

Accepting Change

Our role in God's world has to change from religious pietism to political urgency. We are literally 'running out of world', and extending our influence from local despoliation (which we can see and in principle repair) to regional and global damage which can only be dealt with internationally.[5] This faces us with a difficult question: are we causing irreversible damage and approaching a threshold in our very existence? Such a threshold need not be solely the consequence of extreme physical pressure on the natural systems of the world. Václav Havel, man of both letters and political power, is persuaded that the present system is approaching its end:

> Today, many things indicate that we are going through a transitional period, when it seems that something is on the way out and something else is painfully being born. It is as if something were crumbling, decaying

and exhausting itself, while something else, still indistinct, were arising from the rubble.

Periods of history when values undergo a fundamental shift are certainly not unprecedented. This happened in the Hellenistic period, when from the ruins of the classical world the Middle Ages were gradually born. It happened during the Renaissance, which opened the way to the modern era. The distinguishing features of such transitional periods are a mixing and blending of cultures, and a plurality or parallelism of intellectual and spiritual worlds. These are periods when all consistent value systems collapse, when cultures distant in time and space are discovered or rediscovered. They are periods when there is a tendency to quote, to imitate and to amplify, rather than to state with authority or integrate. New meaning is gradually born from the encounter, or the intersection, of many different elements ... [T]he relationship to the world that modern science fostered and shaped now appears to have exhausted its potential. [But] it is increasingly clear that, strangely, the relationship is missing something. It fails to connect with the most intrinsic nature of reality, and with natural human experience. It is now more of a source of disintegration and doubt than a source of integration and meaning. It produces what amounts to a state of schizophrenia: Man as an observer is becoming completely alienated from himself as a being.

Classical modern science described only the surface of things, a single dimension of reality. And the more dogmatically science treated it as the only dimension, as the very essence of reality, the more misleading it became. Today, for instance, we may know immeasurably more about the universe than our ancestors did, and yet it increasingly seems they knew something more essential about it than we do, something that escapes us. The same thing is true of nature and of ourselves. The more thoroughly all our organs and their functions, their internal structure and the biochemical reactions that take place within them are described, the more we seem to fail to grasp the spirit, purpose and meaning of the system that they create together and that we experience as our unique 'self.' And thus today we find ourselves in a paradoxical situation. We enjoy all the achievements of modern civilisation that have made our physical existence on this earth easier in so many important ways. Yet we do not know exactly what to do with ourselves, where to turn. The world of our experiences seems chaotic, disconnected, confusing. There appear to be no integrating forces, no unified meaning, no true inner understanding of phenomena in our experience of the world. Experts can explain anything in the objective world to us, yet we understand our own lives less and less. In short, we live in the post-modern world where everything is possible and almost nothing is certain. (Havel, 1994)

Havel goes on to say that, while many assume that solutions can be accomplished through the invention of new organisational, political and diplomatic instruments, his belief is that 'such efforts are doomed to failure if they do not grow out of something deeper, out of generally held values'. In other words, doctrinaire reductionism is not only logically inadequate (p. 22), it is grossly misleading and ineffective. The same conclusion has emerged repeatedly in earlier chapters of this book, particularly out of the convergence between religious and secular viewpoints (Chapter 9) and the experiences of awe and wonder at natural phenomena which are common, and may even be universal (Chapter 10). It is tempting to generalise the wonder and respect for nature which is clearly widespread – as witness the poems and prayers of the Celtic Church – but it is easy to be idealistic and ignore the drudgery and battle for mere survival of too many on earth. My task is to draw together the relevant threads that lie behind and may quicken the latent values referred to by Havel. I am encouraged in this endeavour by Arthur Holmes (1977) who identifies four general stages in the relationship between fact and value (Plato and Aristotle; Augustine and Aquinas; Ockham and the Reformers; Kant and Hegel), and points out that only the last is *not* firmly grounded in some sort of God-concept.

The Argument – So Far

The underlying theme of everything in this book is the relation of God to his creation. In examining this relationship, I have had to assume the existence of God. If he does not exist, this obviously rules out any interaction and condemns my enterprise; natural theology (and the theology of nature) will be no more than a misleading vapour. My approach has been to explore the credibility and anticipated results (or the coherence) of the relationship in as rigorous a way as possible, and thence face the decision whether this leaves us with any firm results on which to ground a natural theology, never mind an understanding of God himself. In adopting this approach, I am following the methodology of natural science rather than theology. I am setting out to test a hypothesis. Before attempting to come to any final conclusions, it is time to rehearse the arguments so far.

In his Gifford Lectures, James Barr (1993:1) defined natural theology as the capacity for an awareness of God 'anterior to the special revelation of God made through Jesus Christ, through the Church, through the Bible'. Barr turns to Paul's sermons at Lystra (the first recorded Christian address to a pagan audience), where he appealed to such knowledge as the audience might deduce from 'natural revelation' (God ... 'has not left you without some clue to his nature, in the benefits he bestows: he sends you rain from heaven and the crops in their seasons, and gives you food in plenty and keeps you in good heart', Acts 14.17) and to the 'religious' Athenians (Acts 17.25–29); and to the important passage in Romans 1.18–20 (describing those 'who suppress the truth. For all that can be known of God lies plain before their eyes; indeed God himself has disclosed it to them. Ever since the world began his invisible attributes, that is to say his everlasting power and deity, have been visible to the eye *of reason*, in the things he has made').[6]

Barr's conclusion is that:

> theologies which in principle deny natural theology run into a deep inner contradiction. Though they aspired to provide a much deeper and more consistent base for the deployment of biblical myth through the rejection of natural theology, in effect their own principle forced them away from the realities of the Bible ... One of the most paradoxical consequences ... [is] that even if philosophical or dogmatic theology were to reject natural theology, biblical theology would have to accept it and integrate it into its own work, because natural theology is there in the Bible itself. (Barr 1993:199–200)

I have said that I do not have the competence to comment on debates within theology; my concern is to dig below them, to the relationship between God and creation (which of course includes humankind). I now return to this. It has to be kept continually in view, because our understanding of it depends on our apprehension of the world. This is not to suggest that the God–creation relationship keeps changing (in a sort of Whiteheadean way), but to acknowledge that our perception of it depends on our knowledge – or interpretation – of the world. Our forebears were clear about the transcendent God who had made the world and all that is in it, and returns to adjust (or interfere) with it as necessary. They had no problems with the idea that a creator-God could also be a God of miracles. The difficulty is that this almost wholly neglects God's immanence, and implies that God's providence is largely a consequence of the excellence of the machinery he provided in the first place. Process theology and panentheism , and the efforts of feminist theologians are attempts to amend the inadequacy of the traditional understanding of the God-creation relationship. But the old watchmaker idea of this has been reluctant to die. The vehemence of the creationists is a concern to protect God against what they see as liberalising and unbiblical heresies, and in a wider context, the furore sparked by John Robinson's *Honest to God* (1963) rested on a perception that it was an attempt to somehow emasculate God.[7]

Science helps us here. The Cartesian, pre-Darwinian world depended on mechanisms ruled by 'natural laws'. God could only operate by suspending his own laws. His sovereignty allowed him to do this, subject only to the constraints of his own nature. The notion of a God who continually upholds and interacts with his creation was completely foreign; indeed it was abhorrent, because God repeatedly declared his creation to be 'good', 'very good'. This inadequate 'God of the philosophers', as it has been called, meant that, as Don Cupitt (1984:58) recognised: 'Religion was more badly shaken when the universe went historical in the nineteenth century that it had been when the universe went mechanical in the seventeenth century.' The problem for theologians has not been to avoid the implications of an 'interacting God' but to understand and express his method(s) of interacting. Keith Ward has described his understanding:

> Rules have not been eliminated, and the rule-giver has not been pensioned off. It is God who defines the nature of things and ensures the continuity and regularity of their interactions. But now we see more clearly that God is not merely an external watchmaker, God is the sustainer of a network of dynamic inter-related energies and might well be seen as the ultimate environing non-material field which draws from material natures a range of the potentialities which lie implicit within them. (Ward, 1996:57)

What does this mean in everyday terms? The rigid structure apparently provided by rules or 'law' is a red herring. Eliminating a 'law-giver' does not result in the removal of the need for God, despite the claims of Peter Atkins (1994) and Richard Dawkins (1986, 1996), and the assumptions of many others cowed by clever words. We have to examine what is God's involvement (if there is a God) with the world at large. Is there a credible – or even a superior – way of regarding God as other than meticulous planner and craftsman? The answer is emphatically 'yes', and we explored this in Chapter 2, particularly the notion that an event may have more than one cause. This is not new (Aristotle described the different ways of analysing causation) or contentious beyond the limited but strident circle of doctrinaire materialists or obsessive reductionists, but it remains sadly hidden for most people.

The two main reasons why such ways of understanding the world are not more prevalent have complex historical and philosophical roots, which were sketched in Chapter 3: in the first place, our world – or, as we perceive it, our environment – is essentially constant (or better, irregularly variable) within our normal time frame. Consequently, 'whatever the discoveries of science, whatever the rate at which we multiplied as a species, whatever the changes we made to our seas and landscape, we have believed that the world would stay the same in all its fundamentals' (*This Common Inheritance*, 1990:1.8) – and we have been catastrophically wrong (see, for example, the Royal Commission on Environmental Pollution, Twenty-second Report, 2000). And secondly, we have acquiesced too easily to the malign influence of Plato and his followers and believed that the world and its inhabitants are imbued with unchangeable essences; change to them is impossible. These two perceptions came together in the writings of the early Church so that the world was seen as theologically constant and immutable. The existing state was the preferred or natural state, and was regarded as little more than a neutral backdrop for God's saving acts. This reification of creation was accentuated by the emphases of the Reformers and encouraged by the notion that our present existence is no more than a transient phase as we await a New Heaven and a New Earth.[8] These ideas are specifically derived from the Christian tradition, but they are ones that have conditioned Western culture and its science, and consequently have spread far beyond their source lands and the places where Christianity is (or has been) the moulding influence.

The commodification of nature and therefore of biological processes raises questions about the nature of life, and this was an issue we had to face in Chapter 4. The conclusion was clear cut: although life and reproduction can be described fairly fully in molecular and physiological terms, this does not mean that this is all there is to them. It is inadequate and inaccurate to describe us as 'nothing but' the sum of our genes or as 'nothing but' naked apes. We are obviously dependent upon our genes, but it is both behaviourally and logically inept to believe that we are determined by them. The fact that we have genes that potentiate us to be intellectual geniuses, homosexuals, kleptomaniacs or champion hurdlers may enable but does not condemn us to be any of these things. Much more important from the Judeo-Christian point of view, we are alone among living creatures in being in the 'image of God'; this implies both constraints and possibilities. Whatever else we may believe about life on Earth – both human and sub-human – we are in a privileged and responsible position; we must regard 'life' as something which has to be cared for and encouraged, not simply ring-fenced and protected at all costs.

These considerations become critical when we widen our perspective. Life is abundant and prodigal, but the Earth is finite – even though well beyond the horizons of individual perception. There are now six billion of us and our numbers are likely to double before they stop increasing. Until now, our ancestors have experienced only local shortages of space or food. These have produced significant hardship or famine, but until the last few decades there has always been somewhere to escape to, somewhere else to find food, water or land. We have now reached the situation of 'running out of world' (Chapter 7). This is not merely a lack of space in which to walk about or obtain the calories necessary for survival, but an inability to find the conditions for a quality of life beyond mere physical necessities. It is compounded by deterioration of our existing space through pollution, erosion and even more pervasive but less obvious effects like ozone depletion and the greenhouse effect. There is debate about the severity or rate of such influences. There are those who speculate about future possibilities on space stations or through new or better technologies, but we cannot ignore the reality that this world is finite and that we are misusing it in an unsustainable way. What has this to do with the interaction between Creator and creation? Just this: if this is God's world, then we are not doing a competent job looking after it, assuming that is our role.

But is that our role here on Earth? The longstanding Christian tradition is that we are stewards or trustees, mandated to care for creation. This has dissentients on both biblical and practical grounds, but the dominant understanding is that we are responsible to ourselves, our community, and our children to manage God's world on his behalf. This involves improving it, not merely maintaining it; such is the clear message of the command to 'tend the garden' and of the parable of the talents. But the way forward is far from straightforward. Perhaps the greatest complicating factor has been the persisting assumption that there is some sort of 'balance' in nature, a long tradition in biology that owes more to Platonic teachings and medieval beliefs than to empirical science. The credence given to such environmental equilibrium has fed the myth of Earth as an enormous self-regulating mechanism, often referred to nowadays as Gaia. We need to be clear that the evidence for such an integrated macrocosm is slight, but more importantly that a Gaian model for creation is closer to the mechanical God of Descartes than the personal God of the Bible. Notwithstanding, and whatever the eventual fate of the Gaian and other co-evolutionary hypotheses, their implication for theology is slight. Even if the Earth is a self-regulating system, we are not absolved from our responsibilities to look after our own interests and those of our children, never mind nature itself.

There have been many attempts to make God slot into particular environmental scenarios, all of them involving some sort of pantheism (Chapter 5). Attempts to invent a God who fits into our own perception of the world are dangerous, and almost certainly destined to fail. Honesty and reason impel us to scientific rigour. Only then can we examine the relation of the world (or its 'givenness') to the God which reason and Bible suggest (Chapter 6).

Now an interesting and encouraging development over the past two or three decades, independent of green schemes and any philosophy of science, is that public perception (variously driving or driven by governments) has been coming ever closer to an approach to environmental care which converges upon the biblical picture of a world entrusted to us as stewards. National and international agreements are identifying the need for an ethic of responsible stewardship (Chapters 7 and 8), to the extent that it may now be possible to recognise the skeleton of a global ethic (p. 194). The degree of convergence from independent quarters in the constituents of this ethic, together with the unforced marrying of secular and religious approaches suggest that we may be viewing the appearance of a truly natural theology. Put another way, the nature and properties of creation are such that certain features are appearing that determine (or better, prescribe) a proper treatment for it. These commonalties tell us virtually nothing about the nature of God as revealed in the scriptures, but they do point to the credibility of that God, and the coherence between his special and general revelations (or between his Book of Works and his Book of Words: p. 32).

A sign of God-revealed-in-nature is the widespread – perhaps even universal – feeling of awe experienced by religious believers and unbelievers alike when confronted with 'nature' (which can include anthropogenic marvels such as a building or engineering structure as well as 'natural' nature) (Chapter 10). It is difficult to express this emotion in scientific language: it is real but non-rational; but it is certainly not irrational. For the non-believer it is a bonus; for the believer it is an acknowledgement of God's handiwork. The psalmist had no doubts: 'When I look up at your heavens, the work of your fingers, at the moon, and the stars you have set in place, what is a frail mortal, that you should be mindful of him, a human being, that you should take notice of him?' (Psalm 8.3–4).

Chris Patten, former Governor of Hong Kong, crystallised this understanding:

> The relationships between man and his environment depend, and always will depend, on more than just sound science and sound economics. For individuals part of the relationship is metaphysical. Those of us with

religious conviction can, if we are lucky, experience the beauties, as well as the utilities of the world as direct manifestations of the love and creative power of God. (Patten, 1990)

Intriguingly, in view of the nature and practice of science (Chapter 2), Warren Brown (2000) describes biblical 'wisdom' as an 'emergent property' and cites Donald MacKay, the champion of God's action in complementarity in support of his argument.

Stewardship is a rational conclusion from a study of the natural world and its misuse; when awe is added to stewardship it provides a motive for action as well as an occasion for enjoyment. Awe can be regarded as an empowerment of stewardship. It is easy to misunderstand or misdirect awe as mere emotion. Ecotourism is often no more than a capitalisation on awe. But if we couple awe to stewardship, we have a powerful engine for creation care.

NOTES

1   These claims are still made by the 'creationists'. Their absurdity has been exposed by Pennock (1999).

2   'Hypotheses' about the fall and the relevance of the Adam and Eve story are legion, although most commentators regard them as mere 'myth'. One of the more considered recent approaches is by Dennis Edwards in Russell, Stoeger and Ayala (1998:377–92).

3   Genesis 3.20, naming Eve as 'mother of all the living'. The concern of the verse, however, is principally to reiterate, in the context of death, the promise of salvation through 'her seed' (Genesis 3.15).

4   The fall is a specifically Christian doctrine. Neither the rabbinic nor the Jewish apocalyptic tradition has any doctrine of the fall. The Genesis 3 story is never directly referred to elsewhere in the Old Testament. Whereas it may be possible to 'explain away' (or spiritualise) the fall story in Genesis in a way parallel to the origin of gender in Genesis 2.22 (i.e. Eve made from Adam's rib), most such demythologising fails to take seriously any New Testament references.

5   This is well documented in the Reports of the Royal Commission on Environmental Pollution, especially the Tenth (1984) and the Twenty-third (2000).

6   Interestingly, there is an important caveat to Paul's assertion ('Knowing God, they have refused to honour him as God, or to render him thanks. Hence all their thinking has ended in futility, and their misguided minds are plunged in darkness. They boast of their wisdom, but they have made fools of themselves ...' Romans 1.21–22) because it highlights the significance of decisions made on partial evidence. For Paul, those who refused to take into account all the facts were indulging in illegitimate reductionism, the attitude we have described as 'nothing–buttery' (p. 23).

7   Robinson's stated concern was 'in no way to change the Christian doctrine of God, but precisely to see that it does not disappear with the outmoded view [as being *only* 'out there' and denying his immanence]' (Robinson, 1963:44).

8   Although this is still a common understanding, a careful reading of the Bible shows the *continuity* of the present earth with the renewed earth which God promises. Even such texts as 2 Peter 3.3–15 which seem to indicate cataclysm can be better interpreted as prophesying a purging as distinct from an annihilating event (Finger, 1998).

12
Redemption – and Hope

For John Polkinghorne,

> it is clear that natural theology by itself could never lead us to the Christian God. It is a limited kind of investigation, based on certain general ideas about the pattern and structure of the world, and so it is only capable of affording limited insight. The critical question is whether that insight is such that it is capable of being reconciled with the Christian's belief in a personal and caring God, addressed in prayer and active in his providential government of the world. (Polkinghorne, 1989:4)

The answer to Polkinghorne's 'critical question' is an emphatic 'yes'. Indeed it would be very odd if there were any significant dissonance between God's Two Books. On occasions when conflict appears (as over questions of origins, cosmology or embryology), we need to look carefully at our understandings of both the natural world and the Scriptures and check whether our interpretations are the only ones. This was necessary following the discoveries of Galileo and Darwin; we are currently facing disagreements about human development and consciousness which need similar treatment (Jones, 1994; Jeeves, 1997).

However, Polkinghorne's 'critical question' is about academic discourse, not action. It is encouraging if we can remove dissension from our debates about religion and science, but does it *matter*? I believe there is a positive interaction – or feedback – between God's Two Books, between his special and general revelations, that overrides the niceties of debate and introduces an urgency into our interpretations and response.

Science can inform faith, because an understanding of the multiple nature of causation and the limits of science means that we can embrace a picture of God as both immanent and transcendent with no need for linguistic gymnastics or philosophical straining. God does not *intervene* in nature; he upholds his creation moment by moment. We do not have to shout across vast distances to be heard by God; he is here with us, in us, behind us. We are not puppets or robots dependent upon a careful designer, but individuals cared for, protected and guided by an indwelling Spirit, once we acknowledge his presence and authority. Commentators from David Hume to C. S. Lewis have wrestled with God's action in the world, but to no avail. They have been asking the wrong question: the problem is not where or how to fit God into a causal nexus, but how to relate to an ever-present and personal agent.

Interestingly, C. S. Lewis, despite his perspicacity and perhaps because of his great knowledge and roots in classical literature, persisted on the wrong track throughout his life. Nowhere is this clearer than in his book on *Miracles* (Lewis, 1947), where he defines a miracle as 'an interference with Nature by supernatural power' (p. 15); Nature is 'what happens of itself' or 'of its own accord' (p. 16). This implies that Nature (Lewis uses a capital 'N') is a cosmic power, an idea which Lewis gets from Greek philosophy, not from the Bible. Lewis calls on the Greeks (especially Plato) when he speaks of 'an eternal self-existent Reason' (capital 'R') which 'must exist and must be the source of my own imperfect and intermittent rationality' (p. 36). Lewis swallowed the common assumption that we cannot escape from a massive causal network, which in his case he attributed to an external 'Reason' in order to free himself from physical events in the brain. But this smacks of medieval astronomers flailing around to rescue Ptolemy's understanding of the universe. Ironically for such a great apologist, Lewis fell into the 'nothing-buttery' trap.

What about 'evil'? We have seen that the consequences (or 'curses') of the fall can be interpreted as failures of stewardship, that is, of disobedience to God's first command to our forebears, 'to have dominion'. But even worse, as Oliver O'Donovan (1986:19) argues, they lead to 'not only [our] persistent rejection of the created order, but also to an inescapable confusion in our perceptions of it'. Disobedience leads to compounding the effects of natural disasters (as when deforestation is followed by erosion and landslips), but it also introduces moral problems because of the failed relationship between God and creature (which is spiritual death in biblical terms). God controls the world he made ('the winds and waves obey him', Matthew 8.27), but moral evil stems from a moral problem – disobedience. This leads us to the ways that faith can inform science.

Creation can only be understood from the perspective of redemption. There is too much wastage, pain and untimely death to make this view possible apart from a particular conviction about the meaning of Christ's death and resurrection. Yet the resurrection takes place within the context of Jewish hopes about the general resurrection from the dead, the coming of the kingdom, and the establishment of God's right- eousness. In this way the understanding of the ways of God in creation already looks toward the end of all things. (Fergusson, 1998:87)

In Colossians Paul explicitly links *all things* to Christ's reconciling work on the cross:

> He [the Son] is the image of the invisible God ... In him everything was created, not only things visible but also the invisible orders of thrones, sovereignties, authorities and powers: the whole universe was created through him and for him ... [God chose] through him to reconcile *all things* to himself, making peace through the shedding of his blood on the cross – *all things*, whether on earth or in heaven. (Colossians 1.15–20)

If we accept that biological nature was not changed by the fall – and Augustine believed it was not: 'Man's sin did not so change the nature of animals' (*Summa Theologiae* 1.96.1, quoted by Rolston, 1994:208) – then why did 'all things' need reconciling? The answer can only be that their relationship to God had failed in some way. Somehow the invocation of the psalmist had got lost:

> Praise the Lord from the earth,
> you sea monsters and ocean depths;
> fire and hail, snow and ice,
> gales of wind that obey his voice;
> all mountains and hills;
> all fruit trees and cedars;
> wild animals and all cattle,
> creeping creatures and winged birds.
>
> (Psalm 148.7–10)

This casts us back on the exposition of Romans 8.20–22 by Charles Cranfield that 'the praises of the sub-human creation ... are prevented from being fully that which they were created to be so long as man's part is missing' (see p. 232), an interpretation echoed by Derek Kidner (1967) commenting on the curses in Genesis: 'Leaderless, the choir of creation can only grind in discord. It seems from Romans 8:19-23 and from what is known of the pre-human world, that there was a state of travail in nature from the first, which man was empowered to '"subdue" until he relapsed into disorder himself.' Gordon Wenham (1987) agrees: 'The sentences on the man and woman take the form of a disruption of their appointed roles.' Henri Blocher (1984:184) reinforces the same point: 'If man obeys God, he would be the means of blessing the earth; but in his insatiable greed ... and in his short-sighted selfishness he pollutes and destroys it. He turns the garden into a desert (cf. Revelation 11:18). That is the main thrust of the curse of Genesis 3.'

Theology – the Study of God Not Forgetting Man

So we come full circle. The earth declares the glory of God which means that we can learn something about God from it. A theology of nature cannot be separated from natural theology. Anthony O'Hear (1997:7) has written, 'Unless the natural world is regarded as God's handiwork, regarding it as "a source of wonder and inspiration" comes close to idolatry.' But the failure of the earth to declare the glory of God is firmly laid on us, and our disobedience. We are right back with Lynn White's (1967) 'Historical roots of our ecologic crisis': in White's words, we regard ourselves 'as superior to nature, contemptuous of it, willing to use it for our slightest whim ... What we do about ecology depends on our ideas of the man–nature relationship ... But since the roots of our trouble are so largely religious, the remedy must be essentially religious, whether we call it that or not' (see p. 44). Robin Grove-White (1994:24) makes exactly the same point from the point of view of a sociologist when he identifies orthodox analysis of the environmental crisis as depending on 'a seriously inadequate conception of human nature'.

The enormous advantage of this conclusion is that it provides hope – hope for the environment, hope for us as stewards of the world, hope for a sustainable future for life on earth. The source of this hope is the saving and unconditional love of God in sending his Son to reconcile us to himself, as the Colossians passage (p. 245) reminds us. God so loved the *kosmos* that he sent his only Son (John 3.16). The answer for creation's groaning and for our own bewilderment in the modern world is not the gnosis of scientism or the syncretism of the New Age, but the traditional one of salvation through Christ.

This is not a plea for Christian pietism or triumphalism. Donald Worster got it right:

> I cannot now recommend that we slip backwards in time and solve the crisis by reading the Bible or Koran again. It is not possible, or even desirable, to try to go back to a pre-modern religious world-view. We cannot so simply undo what we have become. For this reason I must disagree with Lynn White, who proposed that the world convert to the religious teachings of

St. Francis of Assisi, the famous thirteenth-century Italian monk who embraced the plants and animals as his equals and beloved kinfolk. The idea of making Franciscans of everyone in the world would be an ethnocentric and anachronistic solution to the modern dilemma.

So what can we do? What is the solution to the environmental crisis brought on by modernity and its materialism? The only deep solution open to us is to begin transcending our fundamental world-view – creating a post-materialist view of ourselves and the natural world, a view that summons back some of the lost wisdom of the past but does not depend on a return to old discarded creeds. I mean a view that acknowledges that all scientific description is only an imperfect representation of the cosmos, and acknowledgement that this is the foundation of respect. (Worster, 1993:218)

This is where God's initiative comes in. Although bitter experience shows we are incapable of fully reversing the causes (as distinct from the effects) of environmental degradation on our own initiative or in our own strength, God has provided the means of restoring our proper stewardly relationship through Christ's atoning death, and the strength to enable us by the power of the Holy Spirit. Northcott (1996:255) sees this as the 'ecological repristination of the natural law tradition'. I prefer to describe it as an emancipation from the consequences and condemnations of law. Blocher (1997:78) has shown that Paul's argument in the fifth chapter of Romans is properly interpreted to mean that we are condemned for our own sins, not that we are inequitably blamed for Adam's sin ['It was through one man that sin entered the world, and through sin death, and thus death pervaded the whole human race' (Romans 5.12)]; that the effect of Adam's originating disobedience was to make possible the judicial treatment of human sin. Because God sees us through Adam in the framework of the creation covenant, he is able to include us in his justifying reconciliation. The problem is not our innate weakness but our unwillingness to accept and appropriate God's immeasurable grace.[1]

Christianity is both a gospel faith and a reasoned faith. It is gospel because it gives hope, albeit a hope which requires response on our part; it is reasonable because it is not only compatible with faith, but reason is necessary for faith to mature and express itself in both individuals and communities. Jesus set out the 'first and greatest commandment' as 'Love the Lord your God with all your heart, with all your soul, and *with all your mind*' (Matthew 22.37). The original form in Deuteronomy 6.5 refers to heart, soul and *strength*. Perhaps true strength should be seen as stemming from intellectual understanding rather than physical capability. What is certain is that the Bible reiterates the importance of mind in many places: Paul exhorts us to *think* radically ('*Conform* no longer to the pattern of this world, but be transformed by the renewal of your minds', Romans 12.2); Peter castigates ignorance (2 Peter 3.16), as does the writer to the Hebrews (6.1, 2); guidance involves both faith (Psalm 32.8) and reason (Psalm 32.9). 'Alleluia psalms', such as Psalms 103 and 104, are sandwiches of understanding in a framework of praise. Lack of thought is a sign of immaturity (1 Corinthians 14.20). Paul persuaded (2 Corinthians 5.11), reasoned and held discussions with his contacts (Acts 18.4).

The biblical emphasis on reason and thought as necessary for the development of a 'Christian mind' is clear. Problems arise where faith and reason fail to interact and strengthen each other: too often Christians are coldly rational and spiritually inert; or excitable, and unable to defend faith or explore its implications. They do not have a mature 'Christian mind', a concept popularised by Harry Blamires in a book with that title. He condemned British Christians:

> Except over a very narrow field of thinking, chiefly touching questions of strictly personal conduct, we Christians in the modern world accept, for the purpose of mutual activity, a frame of reference constructed by the secular mind and a set of criteria reflecting secular evaluations. There is no Christian mind; there is no shared field of discourse in which we can move at ease as thinking Christians by trodden ways and past established landmarks. (Blamires, 1963:4)

Mark Noll (1994) has made even more trenchant criticisms of American Christians, especially evangelicals.

The wisdom writings of the Old Testament repeatedly warn that 'the fear of the Lord is the beginning of wisdom'. And that is where our ambition should be. We need a complete doctrine of creation, not the emasculated one of the 'creationists' who fail to read properly the book of nature; not the empty one of the liberals who censor the books of nature and Scripture so severely that it is difficult to find where God is; not the mutilated one of the deists, who push God so far away that he becomes irrelevant; not the sacramental one of the panentheists and their allies, who seek to fit God to their own perceptions; and not the God of the philosophers who has to be small enough to fit into the gaps of their understanding. Only when we are bold and brave enough to face up to the real world and to God's word, written and made flesh, will we begin to have a truly robust doctrine. Only then will we be able to develop a positive ethic of life and rightly discern the limits of humankind, and only then will we become good stewards of our own life and our environment.

It is fashionable to seek wisdom from primitive religion and native people. The danger is that we accept selectively and uncritically all we think they are telling us.[2] Notwithstanding, it is certainly worth peeling away the irrelevant shells in which we hide in our western postmodern culture (de Waal, 1991). We live in God's world; let us study and rejoice in this world: 'The heavens declare the glory of God; the skies proclaim the work of his hands' (Psalm 19:1).

Those of us who live in great cities and shield ourselves from the raw environment would do well to remember God's questions to Job:

> Who is this that darkens my counsel
> with words without knowledge?
> Brace yourself like a man;
> I will question you,
> and you shall answer me.
>
> Where were you when I laid the earth's foundation?
> Tell me, if you understand.
> Who marked off its dimensions? Surely you know!
> Who stretched a measuring line across it?
> On what were its footings set,
> or who laid its cornerstone -
> while the morning stars sang together
> and all the angels shouted for joy?
>
> (Job 38.2–7)

Hopefully this will lead us to a humility in which we can share the contentment of the Orkney crofter described by Robert Rendall:

> Scant are the few green acres I till,
> But arched above them spreads the boundless sky,
> Ripening their crops; and round them lie
> Long miles of moorland hill.
>
> Beyond the cliff-top glimmers in the sun
> The far horizon's bright infinity;
> And I can gaze across the sea
> When my day's work is done.
>
> The solitudes of land and sea assuage
> My quenchless thirst for freedom unconfined
> With independent heart and mind
> Hold I my heritage.
>
> (Rendall, 1946)

Our need is not a new religion, nor even great faith; it is faith in a great God. Is it not that to which Adam Gifford was calling us?

NOTES

1   There is a Screwtape type story of three young devils who were completing their training in hell. Immediately before their despatch to earth, they appeared before the chief devil for their concluding examination. Turning to the first of the three, he asked: 'What will you tell them when you go up to earth?' 'I shall tell them that there is no God', the first devil replied. 'That's not much use', said the examining devil, 'they've been told that many times before. The trouble is that too many of them know Him personally.' He turned to the second devil. 'And what will you tell them?' he enquired. 'I shall say that there is no hell,' the second responded. 'Ah,' said the old devil, 'that's more ingenious. But unfortunately it won't work. Too many of them are living in hell already.' Finally he asked the third, 'What will you say?' And the third answered, 'I shall tell them that there is no hurry.' 'Excellent!' exclaimed the chief demon. 'Go up immediately and set to work.'

2   'The Aztec culture was heavily anchored in human sacrifice and conquest; the woodland Iroquois tribes warred with each other continually until they were brought together into a confederacy, after which the alliance itself became highly predatory in relationship to many of its Algokian neighbours; the remote Yuqui Indians of South America practised hereditary slavery in the Amazon despite a deculturation that left them with little more of a technology than longbows and boar-tooth scrapers. Egalitarian as some presumably "Pleistocene," "Neolithic" or "Mesolithic" communities were *internally*, it is no exaggeration to say they often lived in chronic hostility to "outside" tribes and villages' (Bookchin, 1994:9).

References

Abramowitz, J. N. (1997). 'Valuing nature's services', in *The State of the World 1997*: 95–114. Brown, L. R. (ed.). London: Earthscan

Adams, D. (1979). *The Hitchhiker's Guide to the Galaxy*. London: Pan

Adams, J. (1970). 'Westminster: the fourth London Airport?' *Area*, 2: 1–9

Allee, W. C., Emerson, A. E., Park, O., Park, T. and Schmidt, K. P. (1949). *Principles of Animal Ecology*. Philadelphia: Saunders

Allen, D. E. (1976). *The Naturalist in Britain*. London: Allen Lane

Anderson, B. W. (ed.) (1984). *Creation in the Old Testament*. Philadelphia: Fortress

Anderson, E. N. (1996). *Ecologies of the Heart*. New York: Oxford University Press

Andrews, L. (1981). *Medicine Woman*. New York: Harper & Row

—— (1984). *Flight of the Seventh Moon*. New York: Harper & Row

—— (1985). *Jaguar Woman and the Wisdom of the Butterfly Tree*. New York: Harper & Row

Anglican Consultative Council (1999). *Lambeth 1998, Section I. Called to Full Humanity*. Harrisburg, PA: Morehouse

Arendt, H. (1963). *On Revolution*. New York: Viking

Armstrong, P. (2000). *The English Parson-Naturalist*. Leominster: Gracewing

Ashby, E. (1975). *A Second Look at Doom*. Twenty-first Fawley Foundation Lecture. Southampton: Southampton University Press

—— (1978). *Reconciling Man with the Environment*. London: Oxford University Press

—— (1980). *The Search for an Environmental Ethic*. The Tanner Lecture on Human Values, delivered at the University of Utah, 4 April 1979. New York: Oxford University Press

Ashby, E., and Anderson, M. (1981). *The Politics of Clean Air*. Oxford: Clarendon Press

Assisi Declarations (1986). Messages on man and nature. Gland, Switzerland: Worldwide Fund for Nature

Atkins, P. (1994). *Creation Revisited*. Harmondsworth: Penguin

Attfield, R. (1983). *The Ethics of Environmental Concern*. Oxford: Blackwell (Revised edition 1991; Athens, GA: University of Georgia Press)

Austin, R. C. (1987). *Baptized into Wilderness. A Christian Perspective on John Muir*. Atlanta, GA: John Knox

Ayala, F. J. (1974). 'Introduction', in *Studies in the Philosophy of Biology: Reductionism and Related Problems*: vii–xvi. Ayala, F. J. and Dobzhansky, Th. (eds). London: Macmillan

—— (1998). 'Human nature: one evolutionist's view', in *Portraits of Human Nature*: 31–48. Brown, W. S., Murphy, N., and Malony, H. N. (eds). Minneapolis, MN: Fortress

Bakken, P. W., Engel, J. G., and Engel, J. R. (1995). *Ecology, Justice and Christian Faith: A Critical Guide to the Literature*. Westport, CT: Greenwood.

Barber, L. (1980). *The Heyday of Natural History.* London: Jonathan Cape

Barbour, I. G. (1966). *Issues in Science and Religion.* London: SCM Press

—— (1974). *Myths, Models and Paradigms.* New York: Harper & Row

—— (1990). *Religion in an Age of Science.* London: SCM Press

—— (1998). *Religion and Science. History and Contemporary Issues.* London: SCM Press

—— (2000). *When Science Meets Religion.* London: SPCK

Baring, A., and Cashford, J. (1991). *The Myth of the Goddess: Evolution of an Image.* London: Viking

Barnett, S. A. (1988). *Biology and Freedom.* Cambridge: Cambridge University Press

Barr, J. (1993). *Biblical Faith and Natural Theology.* Oxford: Oxford University Press

Bate, J. (2000). *The Song of the Earth.* London: Picador

Bauckham, R. (1995). *The Theology of Jürgen Moltmann.* Edinburgh: T&T Clark

—— (2000). 'Stewardship and relationship', in *The Care of Creation*: 99–106. Berry, R. J. (ed.). Leicester: IVP

Beach Thomas, W. (1946). *A Countryman's Creed.* London: Michael Joseph

Beckerman, W. (1995). *Small is Stupid.* London: Duckworth

Beckmann, D., Agarwala, R., Burmester, S., and Serageldin, A. (1991). *Friday Morning Reflections at the World Bank.* Washington, DC: Seven Locks Press

Bennett, G. (1992). *Dilemmas.* London: Earthscan

Beringer, J. (1726). *Lithographiae Wirceburgeinsis*

Berry, R. J. (1972). *Ecology and Ethics.* London: IVP

—— (1981). 'Mimicry 1981'. *Biological Journal of the Linnean Society,* 16: 1–3

—— (1982). *Neo-Darwinism.* London: Edward Arnold

—— (1983). 'Polymorphic shell banding in the dog-whelk, *Nucella lapillus* (Mollusca)'. *Journal of Zoology, London,* 200:455–70

—— (1989). 'Ecology: when genes and geography meet'. *Journal of Animal Ecology,* 58: 733–59

—— (1990). 'Industrial melanism and peppered moths (*Biston betularia* [L.])'. *Biological Journal of the Linnean Society,* 39: 301–22

—— (1993a). 'Green religion and green science'. *RSA Journal,* 141: 305–18

—— (ed.). (1993b). *Environmental Dilemmas.* London: Chapman & Hall

—— (1996a). *God and the Biologist.* Leicester: Apollos

—— (1996b). 'The virgin birth of Christ'. *Science and Christian Belief,* 8: 101–110

—— (1999a). 'A worldwide ethic for sustainable living'. *Ethics, Place and Environment,* 2: 97–107

—— (1999b). 'This Cursed Earth: is "the Fall" credible?'. *Science and Christian Belief,* 11: 29–49

—— (ed.) (2000a). *The Care of Creation.* Leicester: IVP

—— (2000b). 'Science and religion: friends or foes?'. *Science Progress,* 83: 3–22

—— (2001). 'John Ray, father of natural historians'. *Science and Christian Belief,* 13: 25–38.

Berry, R. J., and Bradshaw, A. D. (1992). 'Genes in the real world', in Berry, Crawford and Hewitt (1992): 431–49

Berry, R. J., and Crothers, J. H. (1968). 'Stabilizing selection in the Dog whelk (*Nucella lapillus*)'. *Journal of Zoology, London,* 155: 5–17

Berry, R. J., Crawford, T. J. S., and Hewitt, G. M. (eds) (1992). *Genes in Ecology*. Oxford: Blackwell Scientific

Berry, T. (1988). *The Dream of the Earth*. San Francisco. CA: Sierra Club Books

Birch, B. C., and Rassmussen, L. L. (1978). *The Predicament of the Prosperous*. Philadelphia: Westminster

Black, J. N. (1970). *The Dominion of Man*. Edinburgh: Edinburgh University Press

Blamires, H. (1963). *The Christian Mind*. London: SPCK

Blocher, H. (1984). *In the Beginning*. Leicester: IVP

—— (1997). *Original Sin*. Leicester: IVP

Blumenberg, H. (1983). *The Legitimacy of the Modern Age*. Cambridge, MA: MIT Press

Bohm, D. (1952). 'A suggested interpretation of the quantum theory in terms of "hidden variable"'. *Physics Review*, 85: 166–93

Bohr, N. (1958). *Atomic Physics and Human Knowledge*. New York: John Wiley

Bolen, J. S. (1984). *Goddesses in Everywoman*. San Francisco, CA: Harper & Row

Bonhoeffer, D. (1971). *Letters and Papers from Prison*. London: SCM Press

Bookchin, M. (1994). *Which Way for the Ecology Movement?* Edinburgh: AK Press

Bouma-Prediger, S. (1998). 'Creation care and character: the nature and necessity of the ecological virtues'. *Perspectives on Science and Christian Faith*, 50: 6–21

Bouma-Prediger, S., and Bakken, P. (eds) (2000). *Evocation of Grace: The Writings of Joseph Sittler on Ecology, Theology and Ethics*. Grand Rapids, MI: Eerdmans

Bourdeau, Ph., Fasella, P. M., and Teller, A. (eds) (1990). *Environmental Ethics: Man's Relationship with Nature, Interaction with Science*. Luxembourg: Commission of the European Communities

Bowker, J. (1995). *Is God a Virus?* London: SPCK

Boyd, J. M. (1993). 'Nature conservation – a Scottish memoir', in Berry (1993*b*): 150–63

Bradley, I. (1993). *The Celtic Way*. London: Darton, Longman & Todd

Bratton, S. P. (1993). *Christianity, Wilderness and Wildlife*. Toronto: Associated University Press

—— (1994). 'Ecofeminism and the problem of divine immanence/transcendence in Christian environmental ethics'. *Science and Christian Belief*, 6: 21–40

Brennan, A. (1988). *Thinking About Nature*. London: Routledge

Brenton, T. (1994). *The Greening of Machiavelli*. London: Earthscan

Brimblecombe, P. (1987). *The Big Smoke*. London: Methuen

Brooke, J. H. (1991). *Science and Religion: Some Historical Perspectives*. Cambridge: Cambridge University Press

Brooke, J. H., and Cantor, G. (1998). *Reconstructing Nature: The Engagement of Science and Religion*. Edinburgh: T&T Clark

Brown, W. S. (2000). 'A scientific study of wisdom', in *Understanding Wisdom*: 307–15. Brown, W. S. (ed.). Philadelphia: Templeton Foundation Press

Brueggemann, W. (1977). *The Land*. Philadelphia: Fortress

Bryant, A. (1940). *English Saga (1840–1940)*. London: Collins

Callewaert, J. (1994). 'International documents and the movement towards a global environmental ethic'. Paper circulated at the International Union for the Conservation of Nature General Assembly, Buenos Aires

Capra, F. (1975). *The Tao of Physics*. London: Wildwood House
—— (1982). *The Turning Point*. New York: Simon & Schuster
Caring for the Earth (1991). The revision of the World Conservation Strategy. Gland, Switzerland: IUCN, WWF, UNEP
Caring for the Future (1996). Report of the Independent Commission on Population and Quality of Life. Oxford: Oxford University Press
Carroll, P. N. (1969). *Puritanism and the Wilderness: The Intellectual Significance of the New England Frontier, 1629–1700*. New York: Columbia University Press
Carson, R. (1962). *Silent Spring*. Boston: Houghton Mifflin
Cela-Conde, C. J., and Marty, G. (1998). 'Beyond biological evolution: mind, morals and culture', in *Evolutionary and Molecular Biology*: 463–89. Russell, R. J., Stoeger, W. R., and Ayala, F. J. (eds). Vatican City: Vatican Observatory Publications
Chadwick, O. (1970). *The Victorian Church*. New York: Oxford University Press
Chambers, R. (1844). *Vestiges of the Natural History of Creation*. London: John Churchill
Chappell, T. D. J. (ed.) (1997). *The Philosophy of the Environment*. Edinburgh: Edinburgh University Press
Christians and the Environment (1991). A Report by the Board for Social Responsibility. GS Misc. 367. London: General Synod Board for Social Responsibility
Christianson, G. E. (1999). *Greenhouse: The 200-Year Story of Global Warming*. London: Constable
Clapham, A. R. (ed.). (1978). *Upper Teesdale*. London: Collins
Clark, S. R. L. (1993). *How to Think About the Earth*. London: Mowbray
Clements, F. E. (1936). 'Nature and structure of the climax'. *Journal of Ecology*, 24: 252–84
Clifton, R. K., and Regehr, M. G. (1990). 'Towards a sound perspective on modern physics: Capra's popularization of mysticism and theological approaches re-examined'. *Zygon*, 25: 73–104
Cobb, J. B. (1972). *Is It Too Late?* Beverly Hill: Bruce
Cobb, J. B., and Birch, L. C. (1981). *The Liberation of Life*. Cambridge: Cambridge University Press
Cohen, J. E. (1995). *How Many People Can the Earth Support?* New York: W. W. Norton
—— (1996). 'Ecologists ask economists: is the price right?' *The Scientist*, 10(6): 11
Connell, J. H. (1978). 'Diversity in tropical rain forests and coral reefs'. *Science N. Y.* 199: 1302–10
—— (1979). 'Tropical rain forests and coral reefs as open non-equilibrium systems'. In *Population Dynamics*: 141–63. Anderson, R. M., Taylor L. R., and Turner, B. D. (eds). Oxford: Blackwell Scientific
The Conservation and Development Programme for the UK (1983). A Response to the World Conservation Strategy. London: Kogan Page
Cornell, H. V., and Lawton, J. H. (1992). 'Species interactions, local and regional processes, and limits to the richness of ecological communities: a theoretical perspective'. *Journal of Animal Ecology*, 61: 1–12
Costanza, R., d'Arge, R., deGroot, R., Farber, S., Grasso, M., Hannon, B.,

Limburg, K., Naeem, S., O'Neill, R. V., Paruelo, J., Raskin, R. G., Sutton, P. and van den Belt, M. (1997). 'The value of the world's ecosystem services and natural capital'. *Nature*, 387: 254–60.

Coulson, C. A. (1955). *Science and Christian Belief.* Oxford: Oxford University Press

Cranfield, C. E. B. (1974). 'Some observation on Romans 8:19–21', in *Reconciliation and Hope: New Testament Essays on Atonement and Eschatology presented to L. L. Morris on his 60th birthday*: 224–30. Banks, R. (ed.). Grand Rapids, MI: Eerdmans

Crumley, J. (2000). *A High and Lonely Place.* 2nd ed. Latheronwheel, Caithness: Whittles

Cupitt, D. (1984). *The Sea of Faith.* London: BBC

Daly, G. C. (1997). *Nature's Services. Societal Dependence on Natural Ecosystems.* Washington, DC: Island Press

Darwin, C. R. (1858). 'On the variation of organic beings in a state of nature; on the natural means of selection; on the comparison of domestic races and true species'. *Journal of the Linnean Society (Zoology)*, 3: 45–62

—— (1859). *The Origin of Species by Means of Natural Selection.* London: John Murray

—— (1871). *The Descent of Man.* London: John Murray

—— (1887). *Autobiography.* London: John Murray

Davies, P. (1983). *God and the New Physics.* Harmondsworth: Pelican

—— (1992). *The Mind of God.* New York: Simon & Schuster

Davies, P. Maxwell (2001). *Notes from a Cold Climate.* London: Browns

Dawkins, R. (1982). *The Extended Phenotype.* Oxford: Oxford University Press

—— (1983). 'Universal Darwinism', in *Evolution from Molecules to Men*: 403–25. Bendall, D. S. (ed.). Cambridge: Cambridge University Press

—— (1986). *The Blind Watchmaker.* London: Longman

—— (1992). 'A scientist's case'. *Independent*, 20 April 1992

—— (1993). 'Is Religion Just a Disease?' *The Daily Telegraph*, 15 December 1993

—— (1996). *Climbing Mount Improbable.* London: Viking

De Beer, G. R. (1958). *Evolution by Natural Selection.* Cambridge: Cambridge University Press

Deane-Drummond, C. (1993). *Gaia and Green Ethics.* Grove Ethical Studies, 88. Bramcote, Notts: Grove

—— (1996). *A Handbook in Theology and Ecology.* London: SCM Press

—— (2000). *Creation through Wisdom.* Edinburgh: T&T Clark

Delors, J. (1990). 'Opening Address', in Bourdeau, Fasella, and Teller (1990): 19–28

Derr, T. S. (1973). *Ecology and Human Liberation.* Geneva: WCC

Desmond, A. (1989). *The Politics of Evolution.* Chicago: University of Chicago Press

Desmond, A., and Moore, J. R. (1991). *Darwin.* London: Michael Joseph

Devine, T. M. (1994). *Clanship to Crofters' War: The Social Transformation of the Scottish Highlands.* Manchester: Manchester University Press

Diamond, J. (1991). *The Rise and Fall of the Third Chimpanzee.* London: Radius

Doye, J., Goldy, J., Line, C., Lloyd, S., Shellard, P., and Tricker, D. (1995). 'Contemporary perspectives on chance, providence and free will'. *Science and Christian Belief*, 7: 117–39

Draper, W. (1875). *History of the Conflict between Religion and Science.* London: International Scientific Series

Drees, W. B. (1998). 'Evolutionary naturalism and religion', in *Evolutionary and Molecular Biology*: 303–28. Russell, R. J., Stoeger, W. R. and Ayala, F. J. (eds). Vatican City: Vatican Observatory Publications

Drummond, H. (1894). *The Ascent of Man.* New York: James Pott

Dubos, R. (1973). *A God Within.* London: Angus & Robertson

Duke of Edinburgh (1986). 'A credible philosophy'. *The New Road (Bulletin of the WWF Network on Conservation and Religion)*, 1: 2

Durant, J. (1985). 'Darwinism and Divinity: a century of debate', in *Darwinism and Divinity*: 9–39. Durant, J. (ed.). Oxford: Blackwell

Dyke, F. G. van (1985). 'Beyond *Sand County*: a biblical perspective on environmental ethics'. *Journal of the American Scientific Affiliation*, 37: 40–8

Edwards, D. (1998). 'Original sin and saving grace in evolutionary context', in *Evolutionary and Molecular Biology*: 377–92. Russell, R. J., Stoeger, W. R. and Ayala, F. J. (eds). Vatican City: Vatican Observatory Publications

Egerton, F. N. (1973). 'Changing concepts in the balance of nature'. *Quarterly Review of Biology*, 48: 322–50

Elliott, R., and Gare, A. (eds) (1983). *Environmental Philosophy.* Milton Keynes: Open University Press

Elton, C. (1930). *Animal Ecology and Evolution.* Oxford: Oxford University Press
—— (1949). 'Population interspersion: an essay on animal community patterns'. *Journal of Ecology*, 37: 1–23

Ettlinger, G. (1984). 'Humans, apes and monkeys: the changing neuropsychological viewpoint. *Neuropsychologia*, 22: 685–96

Evelyn, J. (1661). *Fumifugium* or *The Inconvenience of the Aer and the Smoke of London Dissipated.* London

Fagan, B. (2000). *The Little Ice Age.* New York: Basic Books

Faith, Science and the Future (1978). Preparatory readings for the 1979 Conference of the World Council of Churches Conference, Cambridge, MA. Geneva: WCC

Farrer, A. (1966). *A Science of God?* London: Geoffrey Bles

Fergusson, D. A. S. (1998). *The Cosmos and the Creator.* London: SPCK

Fiddes, P. (1988). *The Creative Suffering of God.* Oxford: Clarendon Press

Finger, T. (1998). *Evangelicals, Eschatology and the Environment.* Wynnewood, PA: Evangelical Environmental Network

Forsythe, D. (1982). *Urban–Rural Migration, Change and Conflict in an Orkney Island Community.* North Sea Oil Panel Occasional Paper, 14. London: Social Science Research Council

Forward, M., and Alam, M. (1994). 'Islam', in *Attitudes to Nature*: 79–100. Holm, J., and Bowker, J. (eds). London: Pinter

Fox, M. (1983). *Original Blessing: A Primer in Creation Spirituality.* Sante Fe, CA: Bear and Co.

Fox, M. V. (1989). *Qohelet and his Contradictions.* Sheffield: Almond

Fox, W. (1996). 'A critical overview of environmental ethics'. *World Futures*, 46: 1–21

Fraser Darling, F. (1951). 'The ecological approach to the social sciences'. *American Scientist*, 39: 248

—— (1970). *Wilderness and Plenty.* The Reith Lectures for 1989. London: BBC

French, H. (2000). 'Coping with ecological globalization', in *The State of the World 2000*: 184–202. Brown, L. R. (ed.). London: Earthscan

Galton, F. (1869). *Hereditary Genius.* London: Macmillan

German, C. R., and Angel, M. V. (1995). 'Hydrothermal fluxes of metals to the oceans: a comparison with anthropogenic discharge'. *Geological Society Spec. Publn*, 87: 365–72

Gillispie, C. C. (1951). *Genesis and Geology.* Cambridge, MA: Harvard University Press

Glacken, C. J. (1967). *Traces on the Rhodian Shore: Nature and Culture in Western Thought from Ancient Times to the End of the Eighteenth Century.* Berkeley, CA: University of California Press

Glover, J. (1984). *What Sort of People Should There Be?* Harmondsworth: Penguin

Goldsmith, E., Allen, R., Allaby, N., Davoll, J., and Lawrence, S. (1972). 'A blueprint for survival'. *The Ecologist*, 2(1) (Reprinted by Penguin, 139pp. 1972)

Golley, F. B. (1987). 'Deep ecology from the perspective of environmental science'. *Environmental Ethics*, 9: 45–55

—— (1993*a*). *A History of the Ecosystem Concept in Ecology.* New Haven: Yale University Press

—— (1993*b*). 'Environmental attitudes in North America', in Berry (1993*b*): 20–32

Gorssen, L. (1970). 'La coherence de la conception de Dieu dans l'Ecclesiaste'. *Ephemerides Theologicae Lovanienses*, 46: 282–324

Gosling, D. L. (1992). *A New Earth: Covenanting for Justice, Peace and the Integrity of Creation.* London: Council of Churches of Britain and Ireland

Gould, S. J. (1981). *The Mis-Measure of Man.* New York: W. W. Norton

—— (1993). 'The Golden Rule: A Proper Scale for our Environmental Crisis', in *Eight Little Piggies*: 41–51. London: Jonathan Cape

—— (1996). *Full House: The Spread of Excellence from Plato to Darwin.* New York: Harmony Books

—— (1999). *Rocks of Ages.* New York: Ballantine

Goulet, D. (1990). 'Development ethics and ecological wisdom', in *Ethics of Environment and Development*: 36–49. Engel, J. R., and Engel, J. G. (eds). London: Belhaven

—— (1995). *Development Ethics.* London: Zed Books

Grant, P. R. (ed.) (1998). *Evolution on Islands.* Oxford: Oxford University Press

Grimble, J. (1962). *The Trial of Patrick Sellar.* London: Routledge & Kegan Paul

Groothius, D. (1986). *Unmasking the New Age.* Downer's Grove, IL: IVP

Grove-White, R. (1992). 'Human identity and the environmental crisis', in *The Earth Beneath*: 13–34. Ball, J., Goodall, M., Palmer, C., and Reader, J. (eds). London: SPCK

Gunton, C. (1993). *The One, the Three and the Many: God, Creation and the Culture of Modernity.* Cambridge: Cambridge University Press

Habgood, J. (1993). 'Is there reliable knowledge about God?', in *Humanity, Environment and God*: 214–25. Spurway, N. (ed.). Oxford: Blackwell

Haeckel, E. (1866). *Generelle Morphologie der Organismen.* Berlin: Reimer

Haldane, J. (1990). *Environmental Philosophy: An Introductory Survey.* University of St Andrews: Centre for Philosophy and Public Affairs

Haldane, J. B. S. (1927). *Possible Worlds.* London: Chatto & Windus

—— (1932). *The Causes of Evolution.* London: Longmans Green

Hale, M. (1677). *The Primitive Origination of Mankind.* London

Hall, D. J. (1986). *Imaging God: Dominion as Stewardship.* Grand Rapids, MI: Eerdmans

Hallman, D. (ed.) (1994). *Ecotheology: Voices from North and South.* Maryknoll, NY: Orbis Books

Hamilton, W. D. (1964). 'The genetical evolution of social behaviour'. *Journal of Theoretical Biology*, 7: 1–52

Hardin, G. (1968). 'The tragedy of the commons'. *Science, N. Y.*, 162: 1243–8

Hardy, A. C. (1965). *The Living Stream.* London: Collins

—— (1966). *The Divine Flame.* London: Collins

—— (1975). *The Biology of God.* London: Collins

—— (1984). *Darwin and the Spirit of Man.* London: Collins

Harris, M. (1968). *The Rise of Anthropological Theory.* New York: Crowell

Harrison, P. (1998). *The Bible, Protestantism and the Rise of Natural Science.* Cambridge: Cambridge University Press

—— (1999). 'Subduing the Earth: Genesis 1, early modern science, and the exploitation of nature'. *Journal of Religion*, 79: 86–109

Havel, V. (1994). Speech given on Independence Day in Philadelphia, 4 July 1994

Hay, D. (1982). *Exploring Inner Space: Is God Still Possible in the Twentieth Century?* Harmondsworth: Pelican

Hobhouse, L. T. (1913). *Development and Purpose: An Essay towards a Philosophy of Evolution.* London: Macmillan

Holdgate, M. W. (1996). *From Care to Action: Making a Sustainable World.* London: Earthscan

Holland, A. (1995). 'The assumptions of cost-benefit analysis: a philosopher's view', in *Environmental Valuation: Some New Perspectives*: 21–38. Willis, K., and Corkindale, J. (eds). Reading: Commonwealth Agricultural Bureaux International

Holmes, A. F. (1977). *Fact, Value and God.* Grand Rapids, MI: Eerdmans

Hookyaas, R. (1971). *Religion and the Rise of Science.* Edinburgh: Scottish Academic Press

—— (1999). *Fact, Faith and Fiction in the Development of Science.* Dordrecht: Kluwer Academic

Hughes, Ted (1994). *Winter Pollen: Occasional Prose.* Scammell, W. (ed.). London: Faber & Faber

Hunter, J. (1976). *The Making of a Crofting Community.* Edinburgh: John Donald

—— (1995). *On the Other Side of Sorrow.* Edinburgh: Mainstream

Huxley, A. (1932). *Brave New World.* London: Chatto & Windus

Huxley, E. (1993). *Peter Scott.* London: Faber & Faber

Huxley, J. S. (1942). *Evolution: The Modern Synthesis.* London: Allen & Unwin

—— (1953). *Evolution in Action.* London: Chatto & Windus

—— (1957). *Religion without Revelation.* Revised ed. London: Allen & Unwin

—— (ed.) (1961). *The Humanist Frame.* London: Allen & Unwin

—— (1970). *Memories.* London: Allen & Unwin

Huxley, T. H. (1893). *Collected Essays,* II. London: Macmillan

International Covenant on Environment and Development (1995). Document presented to the United Nations, New York, 1995

Jacobs, P., and Munro, D. A. (eds) (1987). *Conservation with Equity. Strategies for Sustainable Development.* Gland, Switzerland: International Union for the Conservation of Nature

Jacoby, A. (1968). *Señor Kon-Tiki.* London: Allen & Unwin

Jaki, S. L. (1995). *Lord Gifford and His Lectures.* Revised ed. Edinburgh: Scottish Academic Press

Jantzen, G. (1984). *God's World, God's Body.* Philadelphia: Westminster

Jeeves, M. A. (1968). *The Scientific Enterprise and Christian Faith.* London: Tyndale

—— (1994). *Mind Fields.* Leicester: Apollos

—— (1997). *Human Nature at the Millennium.* Grand Rapids, MI: Baker Book House

Jeeves, M. A., and Berry, R. J. (1998). *Science, Life and Christian Belief.* Leicester: Apollos

Jegen, M. E. (1987). 'The church's role in healing the earth', in *Tending the Garden*: 93–113. Granberg-Michaelson, W. (ed.). Grand Rapids, MI: Eerdmans

Johnson, P. E. (1995). *Defeating Darwinism.* Downer's Grove, IL: IVP

Johnson, P. E., Lamoureux, D.O. *et al.* (eds) (1999). *Darwinism Defeated?* Vancouver: Regent College

Johnston, P., and Walker, P. (eds) (2000). *The Land of Promise: Biblical, Theological and Contemporary Perspectives.* Leicester: Apollos

Jones, D. G. (1994). *Coping with Controversy.* Dunedin: Visjon

Jones, J. S. (1993). *The Language of the Genes.* London: HarperCollins

Jones, R. (1986). *Science and Mysticism.* London: Associated University Presses

Joseph, L. E. (1990). *Gaia: The Growth of an Idea.* Harmondsworth: Penguin

Jowett, B. *et al.* (1860). *Essays and Reviews.* London: Longman, Green, Longman & Roberts

Kellogg, V. (1907). *Darwinism Today.* London: Bell

Kevles, D. J. (1985). *In the Name of Eugenics.* New York: Knopf

Kidner, D. (1967). *Genesis.* London: Tyndale

Kilmer, A. D. (1972). 'The Mesopotamian concept of overpopulation and its solution as reflected in the mythology'. *Orientalia,* 41: 160–76

Knox, R. (1928). 'The New Sin', in *Essays in Satire*: 77–97. London: Sheed & Ward

Kottler, M. J. (1985). 'Charles Darwin and Alfred Russel Wallace', in *The Darwin Heritage*: 367–432. Kohn. D. (ed.). Princeton, NJ: Princeton University Press

Küng, H. (1990). *Global Responsibility: In Search of a New World Earth Ethic.* English ed., 1991. London: SCM Press

—— (ed.) (1995). *Yes to a Global Ethic.* English ed., 1996. London: SCM Press

Küng, H. and Kuschel, K.-J. (eds) (1993). *A Global Ethic.* The Declaration of the Parliament of the World's Religions. London: SCM Press

Lamarck, J. B. (1809). *Philosophie zoologique.* Paris

Larson, E. J. (1997). *Summer for the Gods.* Cambridge, MA: Harvard University Press

Larson, E. J., and Whitham, L. (1997). 'Scientists are still keeping the faith'. *Nature, London*, 386: 437–8

Law, R., and Watkinson, A. (1989). 'Competition', in *Ecological Concepts*: 243–84. Cherrett, J. M. (ed.). Oxford: Blackwell Scientific

Lawton, J. H. (1989). 'Food webs', in *Ecological Concepts*: 43–78. Cherett, J. M. (ed.). Oxford: Blackwell Scientific

Lawton, J. H., and Jones, C. G. (1995). 'Linking species and ecosystems: organisms as ecosystem engineers', in *Linking Species and Ecosystems*: 141–50. Jones, C. G., and Lawton, J. H. (eds). New York: Chapman & Hall

Lees, D. R. (1981). 'Industrial melanism: genetic adaptation of animals to air pollution', in *Genetic Consequences of Man Made Change*: 129–76. Bishop, J. A., and Cook, L. M. (eds). London: Academic

Lenton, T. M. (1998). 'Gaia and natural selection'. *Nature*, 394: 439–47

Leopold, A. (1949). *A Sand County Almanac.* New York: Oxford University Press

Levine, S. A. (1999). *Fragile Dominion.* Reading, MA: Perseus

Lewis, C. S. (1947). *Miracles.* London: Geoffrey Bles

Lewontin, R. C. (1981). 'Evolution/creation debate: a time for truth'. *Bioscience*, 31: 559

Light, A., and Katz, E. (eds) (1996). *Environmental Pragmatism.* New York: Routledge

Lillard, R. G. (1947). *The Great Forest.* New York: Knopf

Linnaeus, C. (1749). *Amoenitates Academicae. XIX. Oeconomia naturae.* Uppsala

Linzey, A. (1990). 'Human and animal slavery: a theological critique of genetic engineering', in *The Bio-Revolution: Cornucopia or Pandora's Box*: 175–88. Wheale, P., and McNally, R. (eds). London: Pluto

Livingstone, D. N. (1987). *Darwin's Forgotten Defenders: The Encounter between Evangelical Theology and Evolutionary Thought.* Grand Rapids, MI: Eerdmans

Locke, J. (1690). *Two Treatises on Government.* London

Lomborg, B. (2001). *The Skeptical Environmentalist.* (English translation by Matthews, H.). Cambridge: Cambridge University Press

Lovejoy, A. O. (1936). *The Great Chain of Being.* Cambridge, MA: Harvard University Press

Lovelock, J. E. (1979). *Gaia: A New Look at Life on Earth.* Oxford: Oxford University Press

—— (1989). 'Gaia'. *Journal of the Marine Biological Association, U.K.*, 69: 746–58

—— (1990). 'Hands up for the Gaia hypothesis'. *Nature, London*, 344: 100–102

Lucas, E. (1996). *Science and the New Age Challenge.* Leicester: Apollos

Lyell, C. (1863). *Antiquity of Man.* London: John Murray

Mabey, R. (1980). *The Common Ground.* London: Hutchinson

McDaniel, J. (1988). *Of God and Pelicans: A Theology of Reverence for Life.* Louisville, KY: Westminster/John Knox

McDonald, H. D. (1981). *The Christian View of Man.* London: Marshall, Morgan & Scott

McFague, S. (1993). *The Body of God: An Ecological Theology.* Minneapolis, MN: Augsburg/Fortress.

—— (1997). *Super, Natural Christians*. London: SCM Press

McHarg, I. L. (1969). *Design with Nature*. New York: Doubleday

McIntosh, R. P. (1995). 'Gleason's "individualistic" concept and theory of animal communities: a continuing controversy'. *Biological Reviews*, 70: 317–57

MacIntyre, A. (1981). *After Virtue*. London: Duckworth

MacKay, D. M. (1960). *Science and Christian Faith Today*. London: Falcon

—— (1991). *Behind the Eye*. Oxford: Blackwell

—— (1998). *The Open Mind and Other Essays*. Tinker, M. (ed.). Leicester: IVP

McLean, M. (1991). *The People of Glengarry*. Montreal: McGill-Queen's University Press

McMullin, E. (1993). 'Evolution and special creation'. *Zygon*, 28: 299–335

McNeish, C. (2001). *The Wilderness World of Cameron McNeish*. Glasgow: In Pinn

McVean, D. N., and Lockie, J. D. (1969). *Ecology and Land Use in Upland Scotland*. Edinburgh: Edinburgh University Press

Man in His Living Environment. (1969). London: Church House

Manes, C. (1990). *Green Rage: Radical Environmentalism and the Unmaking of Civilization*. Boston: Little, Brown

Manning, R. (1981). 'Environmental ethics and John Rawls' Theory of Justice'. *Environmental Ethics*, 3: 155–65

Margulis, L. (1995). 'A pox called man', in *Science for the Earth*: 19–37. Wakeford, T., and Walters, M. (eds). Chichester: John Wiley

May, G. (1994). *Creation Ex Nihilo*. (English translation by Worrall, G. S.) Edinburgh: T&T Clark

May, R. M., and Anderson, R. M. (1983). 'Epidemiology and genetics in the coevolution of parasites and hosts'. *Proceeding of the Royal Society of London B*, 219: 281–313

Mayr, E. (1982). *The Growth of Biological Thought*. Cambridge, MA: Harvard University Press

Meadows, D. H., Meadows, D. L., and Randers, J. (1972). *The Limits to Growth*. New York: Universe Books

Meadows, D. H., Meadows, D. L., Randers, J., and Behrens, W. W. (1992). *Beyond the Limits*. London: Earthscan

Medawar, J. (1990). *A Very Decided Preference*. Oxford: Oxford University Press

Medawar, P. (1984). *The Limits of Science*. New York: Harper & Row

Midgley, M. (1992). *Science as Salvation*. London: Routledge

—— (1997). 'Sustainability and moral pluralism', in *The Philosophy of the Environment*: 89–101. Chappell, T. D. J. (ed.). Edinburgh: Edinburgh University Press

Miller, K. R. (1999). *Finding Darwin's God*. New York: HarperCollins

Milne, A. J. M. (1986). 'Human rights and the diversity of morals', in *Rights and Obligations in North–South Relations*: 8–33. Wright, M. (ed.). New York: St Martin's Press

Moltmann, J. (1985). *God in Creation*. London: SCM Press

—— (1992). *The Spirit of Life*. London: SCM Press

Monod, J. (1972). *Chance and Necessity*. London: Collins

Montefiore, H. (1969). *The Question Mark: The End of Homo Sapiens*. London: Collins

—— (1985). *The Probability of God.* London: SCM Press

—— (1997). *Time to Change.* Oxford: Bible Reading Fellowship

Moore, A. (1889). 'The Christian doctrine of God', in *Lux Mundi*: 57–109. Gore, C. (ed.). London: John Murray

Moore, J. R. (1979). *The Post-Darwinian Controversies.* Cambridge: Cambridge University Press

—— (1985). 'Herbert Spencer's henchmen: the evolution of Protestant Liberals in late Nineteenth Century America', in *Darwinism and Divinity*: 76–100. Durant, J. (ed.). Oxford: Blackwell

Moore, N. W. (1987). *The Bird of Time: The Science and Politics of Nature Conservatism.* Cambridge: Cambridge University Press

Moss, R. (1982). *The Earth in Our Hands.* Leicester: IVP

Moule, C. F. D. (1964). *Man and Nature in the New Testament.* London: Athlone Press

Murphy, N. (1998). 'Supervenience and the nonreducibility of ethics to biology', in *Evolutionary and Molecular Biology*: 445–62. Russell, R. J., Stoeger, W. R. and Ayala, F. J. (eds). Vatican City: Vatican Observatory Publications

Murphy, R. E. (1992). *Ecclesiastes.* Word Bible Commentary, 23A. Dallas, TX: Word Books

—— (1996). *The Tree of Life: An Exploration of Biblical Wisdom Literature.* 2nd ed. Grand Rapids, MI: Eerdmans

Naess, A. (1973). 'The shallow and the deep, long-range ecology movement'. *Inquiry*, 16: 95–100

—— (1984). 'Identification as a source of Deep Ecological attitudes', in *Deep Ecology.* Tobias, M. (ed.). San Diego, CA: Avant Books

—— (1989). *Ecology, Community and Lifestyle.* Cambridge: Cambridge University Press

Nash, R. F. (1982). *Wilderness and the American Mind.* 3rd ed. New Haven, CT: Yale University Press

—— (1989). *The Rights of Nature: A History of Environmental Ethics.* Madison, WI: University of Wisconsin Press

Nature Conservancy Council. (1984). *Nature Conservation in Great Britain.* NCC's contribution to the World Conservation Strategy. Shrewsbury: NCC

Newbigin, L. (1986). *Foolishness to the Greeks.* London: SPCK

Nicholson, E. M. (1966). 'The "Countryside in 1970" Conferences'. *Quarterly Review*, April 1966: 121–30

—— (1970). *The Environmental Revolution.* London: Hodder & Stoughton

—— (1987). *The New Environmental Age.* Cambridge: Cambridge University Press

Niles, E. P. (ed.) (1992). *Between the Flood and the Rainbow.* Geneva: WCC

Noll, M. A. (1994). *The Scandal of the Evangelical Mind.* Grand Rapids, MI: Eerdmans

Noll, M. A., and Livingstone, D. N. (eds) (2000). *B. B. Warfield: Evolution, Science and Scripture.* Grand Rapids, MI: Baker Book House

Nordenskïold, E. (1928). *The History of Biology.* New York: Knopf

Nordhaus, W. D. (1996). Review of *How Many People Can the Earth Support?, New York Times*, 14 January 1996

Northcott, M. S. (1996). *The Environment and Christian Ethics.* Cambridge: Cambridge University Press

Norton, B. G. (1987). *Why Preserve Natural Variety?* Princeton, NJ: Princeton University Press

—— (1991). *Towards Unity Among Environmentalists.* New York: Oxford University Press

Numbers, R. L. (1992). *The Creationists: The Evolution of Scientific Creationism.* New York: Knopf

O'Donovan, O. M. T. (1986). *Resurrection and Moral Order.* Leicester: IVP

Odum, E. P. (1953). *Fundamentals of Ecology.* Philadelphia: Saunders

Oeschlaeger, M. (1991). *The Idea of Wilderness. From Prehistory to the Age of Ecology.* New Haven: Yale University Press

—— (1994). *Caring for Creation: An Ecumenical Approach to the Environmental Crisis.* New Haven, CT: Yale University Press

O'Hear, A. (1997). *NonSense About Nature.* London: The Social Affairs Unit, no. 72

Olding, A. (1991). *Modern Biology and Natural Theology.* London: Routledge

Osborn, L. (1990). *Stewards of Creation.* Latimer Study, 34. Oxford: Latimer House

Ospovat, D. (1979). *The Development of Darwin's Theory.* Cambridge: Cambridge University Press

Our Responsibility for the Living Environment (1986). A Report of the General Synod Board for Social Responsibility. London: Church House Publishing

Oxford Companion to the Mind (1987). Gregory, R. L. (ed.). Oxford: Oxford University Press

Paden, R. (1994). 'Against Grand Theory in environmental ethics'. *Environmental Values*, 3: 61–70

Paine, R. T. (1980). 'Food webs: linkage, interaction strength and community infrastructure'. *Journal of Animal Ecology*, 49: 667–85

Paley, W. (1802). *Natural Theology.* London

Palmer, C. (1992). Stewardship: a case study in environmental ethics', in *The Earth Beneath*: 67–86. Ball, I., Goodall, M., Palmer, C., and Reader, J. (eds). London: SPCK

Passingham, R. (1982). *The Human Primate.* Oxford: Oxford University Press

Passmore, J. (1974, revised 1980). *Man's Responsibility for Nature.* London: Duckworth

Patten, C. (1990). Unpublished lecture given at Godolphin & Latymer School, London

Patten, C., Lovejoy, T., Browne, J., Brundtland, G., Shiva, V., and the Prince of Wales (2000). *Respect for the Earth: Sustainable Development.* London: Profile

Peacocke, A. R. (1993). *Theology for a Scientific Age.* London: SCM Press

Pearce, D., Markandya, A., and Barbier, E. B. (1989). *A Blueprint for a Green Economy.* London: Earthscan

Pearce, E. V. K. (1969). *Who Was Adam?* Exeter: Paternoster

Pelikan, J. (1993). *Christianity and Classical Culture: The Metamorphosis of Natural Theology in the Christian Encounter with Hellenism.* New Haven CT: Yale University Press

Pennock, R. T. (1996). 'Naturalism, creationism and the meaning of life: the case of Phillip Johnson revisited. *Creation/Evolution*, 16: 10–30

—— (1999). *Tower of Babel.* Cambridge, MA: MIT Press

Perrin, J. (1997). *Spirits of Place.* Llandysul: Gomer

Personal Origins (1985). The Report of a Working Party on Human Fertilization and Embryology of the Board for Social Responsibility. London: Church Information Office

Perutz, M. (1992). Letter to *The Independent*, 23 March 1992

Phillips, T. F. V. (1934–35). 'Succession, development, the climax and the complex organism'. *Journal of Ecology*, 22: 554–71; 23: 210–43, 488–508

Pimm, S. L. (1982). *Food Webs.* London: Chapman & Hall

—— (2001). *The World According to Pimm.* New York: McGraw–Hill

Plantinga, A. (1991). 'When faith and reason clash: evolution and the Bible'. *Christian Scholar's Review*, 21: 8–32

Plimer, I. (1994). *Telling Lies for God.* Sydney: Random House

Polanyi, M. (1969). *Knowing and Being.* London: Routledge & Kegan Paul

Polkinghorne, J. C. (1986). *One World.* London. SPCK

—— (1988). *Science and Creation.* London: SPCK

—— (1989). *Science and Providence.* London: SPCK

—— (1994). *Science and Christian Belief.* London: SPCK

Pollution: Nuisance or Nemesis? (1972). A report to the Secretary of State for the Environment in connection with the UN Conference on the Human Environment, Stockholm. London: HMSO

Ponting, C. (1991). *A Green History of the World.* London: Sinclair-Stevenson

Popper, K. (1978). 'Natural selection and the emergence of mind'. *Dialectica*, 32: 339–55

Porritt, J., and Winner, D. (1988). *The Coming of the Greens.* London: Fontana

Porter, R. (2000). *Enlightenment: Britain and the Creation of the Modern World.* London: Allen Lane

Prebble, J. (1963). *The Highland Clearances.* London: Secker & Warburg

Price, G. McC. (1902). *Outlines of Modern Christianity and Modern Science.* Oakland, CA: Pacific Press

—— (1923). *The New Geology.* Mountain View, CA: Pacific Press

Primavesi, A. (1991). *From Apocalypse to Genesis.* Minneapolis, MN: Fortress

—— (2000). *Sacred Gaia.* London: Routledge

Radl, E. (1930). *The History of Biological Theories.* London: Oxford University Press

Raven, C. E. (1953). *Natural Religion and Christian Theology: Science and Religion.* Cambridge: Cambridge University Press

—— (1954). *Organic Design.* London: Oxford University Press

Rawls, J. (1971). *A Theory of Justice.* Cambridge, MA: Harvard University Press

Ray, J. (1691). *The Wisdom of God Manifested in the Works of Creation.* London

Reichenbach, B. R., and Anderson, V. E. (1995). *On Behalf of God.* Grand Rapids, MI: Eerdmans

Reiss, M. J., and Straughan, R. (1996). *Improving Nature? The Science and Ethics of Genetic Engineering.* Cambridge: Cambridge University Press

Rendall, R. (1946). *Country Sonnets.* Kirkwall: Orcadian

Richards, E. (2000). *The Highland Clearances.* Edinburgh: Birlinn

Riencourt, A. de (1980). *The Eye of Shiva.* London: Souvenir

Robinson, J. A. T. (1963). *Honest to God.* London: SCM Press

Rolston, H. (1986). *Philosophy Gone Wild.* Buffalo, NY: Prometheus

—— (1988). *Environmental Ethics.* Philadelphia: Temple University Press

—— (1994). 'Does nature need to be redeemed?' *Zygon,* 29: 205–29

—— (1999). *Genes, Genesis and God.* New York: Cambridge University Press

Ross, H. (1994). *Creation and Time: A Biblical and Scientific Perspective on the Creation-Date Controversy.* Colorado Springs, CO: NavPress

Roszak, T. (1977). *Unfinished Animal.* New York: Harper & Row

Rothschild, M., and Clay, T. (1952). *Fleas, Flukes and Cuckoos.* London: Collins New Naturalist

Royal Commission on Environmental Pollution (1971). First Report. London: HMSO, Cmnd 4585

Royal Commission on Environmental Pollution (1984). Tenth Report. *Tackling Pollution – Experience and Prospects.* London: HMSO, Cmnd 9149

Royal Commission on Environmental Pollution (1989). Thirteenth Report. *Release of Genetically Engineered Organisms to the Environment.* London: HMSO, Cm 720

Royal Commission on Environmental Pollution (2000). Twenty-second Report. *Energy – the Changing Climate.* London: HMSO, Cm 4749

Rudman, S. (1997). *Concepts of Person and Christian Ethics.* Cambridge: Cambridge University Press

Ruether, R. (1992). *Gaia and God: An Ecofeminist Theology of Earth Healing.* San Francisco, CA: Harper

Russell, C. A. (1985). *Cross-Currents: Interactions between Science and Faith.* Leicester: IVP

—— (1989). 'The conflict metaphor and its social origins'. *Science and Christian Belief,* 1: 3–26

—— (1994). *The Earth, Humanity and God.* London: UCL Press

Russell, P. (1982). *The Awakening Earth.* London: Routledge & Kegan Paul

Russell, R. J., Stoeger, W. R., and Ayala, F. J. (eds) (1998). *Evolutionary and Molecular Biology: Scientific Perspectives on Divine Action.* Vatican City: Vatican Observatory Publications

Sagoff, M. (1974). 'On preserving the natural environment'. *Yale Law Journal,* 84: 205–67

—— (1988). *The Economy of the Earth.* Cambridge: Cambridge University Press

Santmire, P. (1985). *The Travail of Nature.* Philadelphia: Fortress

—— (2000). *Nature Reborn: The Ecological and Cosmic Promise of Christian Theology.* Minneapolis, MN: Fortress

Schama, S. (1995). *Landscape and Memory.* London: HarperCollins

Schoener, T. W. (1989). 'The ecological niche', in *Ecological Concepts*: 79–113. Cherett, J. M. (ed.). Oxford: Blackwell Scientific

Schumacher, E. F. (1973). *Small is Beautiful.* London: Blond & Briggs

—— (1977). *A Guide for the Perplexed.* New York: Harper & Row

Scott, E. C., and Padian, K. (1997). 'The new antievolution – and what to do about it'. *Trends in Ecology and Evolution,* 12: 84

Secord, J. A. (2000). *Victorian Sensation.* Chicago: University of Chicago Press

Seddon, P. (1990). *The New Age – an Assessment.* Grove Spirituality Series, 34. Bramcote, Notts.: Grove.

Sedgwick, A. (1845). 'Vestiges of the natural history of creation'. *Edinburgh Review*, 82: 1–85

Serageldin, I. (1991). 'A justly balanced society: one Muslim's view', in Beckmann, Agarwala, Burmester, and Serageldin (1991): 55–73.

Shackleton, E. (1919). *South.* London: Heinemann

Shaw, D. W. D. (1975). 'Process thought and creation'. *Theology*, 78: 346–55

Sheldon, J. K. (1989). 'Twenty-one years after "the historical roots of our ecologic crisis": how has the church responded?'. *Perspectives on Science and Christian Faith*, 41: 152–8

Sheldrake, R. (1981). *A New Science of Life.* London: Blond & Briggs.

Singer, C. (1931). *A Short History of Biology.* Oxford: Clarendon Press

Singer, P. (1981). *The Expanding Circle: Ethics and Sociobiology.* Oxford: Clarendon Press

—— (ed.). (1994). *Ethics.* Oxford: Oxford University Press

Sittler, J. (1954). 'A theology for Earth'. *The Christian Scholar*, 37: 367–74

—— (1970). 'Ecological commitment as theological responsibility'. *Zygon*, 5: 172–81

Skolimowski, H. (1993). *A Sacred Place to Dwell.* Rockport, MA: Element

Smout, T. C. (1991). 'The Highlands and roots of green consciousness'. *Proceedings of the British Academy*, 76: 237–63

Smythe, F. S. (1937). *Camp Six. An Account of the 1933 Mount Everest Expedition.* London: Hodder & Stoughton

Southwood, T. R. E. (1978). 'Habitat, the templet for ecological strategies?' *Journal of Animal Ecology*, 46: 337–65

—— (1988). 'Tactics, strategies and templets'. *Oikos*, 52: 3–18

Spencer, H. (1893). *The Principles of Ethics.* London: Williams & Northgate

Sperry, R. W. (1990). 'Forebrain commissurotomy and conscious awareness', in *Brain Circuits and Functions of the Mind: Essays in Honor of Roger W. Sperry*: 371–88. Trevathen, C. (ed.). Cambridge: Cambridge University Press

Spurway, N. (ed.) (1993). *Humanity, Environment and God.* Oxford: Blackwell

Starhawk (Miriam Simos) (1989). *Spiral Dance.* San Francisco, CA: Harper

Stone, C. (1972). 'Should trees have standing?' *Southern California Law Review*, 45: 450–1

—— (1987). *Earth and Other Ethics: The Case for Moral Pluralism.* New York: Harper & Row

Storm, R. (1991). *In Search of Heaven on Earth.* London: Bloomsbury

Stott, J. R. W. (1992). *The Contemporary Christian.* Leicester: IVP

—— (1994). *The Message of Romans.* Leicester: IVP

Sulloway, F. (1982). 'Darwin's conversion: the *Beagle* voyage and its aftermath'. *Journal of the History of Biology*, 15: 325–96

Suzuki, D. (1995). 'Blinded by our minds', in *Science for the Earth*: 3–17. Wakeford. T., and Walters, M. (eds). Chichester: John Wiley

Tansley, A. G. (1935). 'The use and abuse of vegetational concepts and terms'. *Ecology*, 16: 284–307

Tawney, R. H. (1938). *Religion and the Rise of Capitalism.* Harmondsworth: Pelican

Teilhard de Chardin, P. (1959). *The Phenomenon of Man.* London: Collins

Temple, F. (1885). *The Relations Between Religion and Science.* London: Macmillan

Thatcher, M. (1989). Speech at the Royal Society Annual Dinner, 27 September 1988. *Science and Public Affairs*, 4: 3–6

Theissen, G. (1987). *Psychological Aspects of Pauline Theology*. Edinburgh: T&T Clark

This Common Inheritance (1990). White Paper on the environment. London: HMSO, Cm 1200

Thomas, J. M. (ed.). (1993). 'Evangelicals and the environment'. *Evangelical Review of Theology*, 12 (2)

Thomas, K. (1971). *Religion and the Decline of Magic*. London: Weidenfeld & Nicolson

—— (1983). *Man and the Natural World*. London: Allen Lane

Thomson, K. (1993). 'The Rio Declaration on Environment and Development', in *The Earth Summit Agreements*: 85–95. Grubb, M., Koch, M., Munson, A., Sullivan, F., and Thomson, K. (eds). London: Earthscan

Thoreau, H. D. (1906). *The Writings of Henry Thoreau*. Torrey, B. (ed.). Boston: Houghton Mifflin

Thorpe, W. H. (1961). *Biology, Psychology and Belief*. Cambridge: Cambridge University Press

—— (1974). *Animal Nature and Human Nature*. London: Methuen

Timm, R. E. (1994). 'The ecological fallout of Islamic creation theology', in *Worldviews and Ecology*: 83–95. Tucker, M. E., and Grimm, J. A. (eds). Maryknoll, NY: Orbis

Torrance, T. F. (1985). *Reality and Scientific Theology*. Edinburgh: Scottish Academic Press

Toulmin, S., and Goodfield, T. (1965). *The Discovery of Time*. London: Hutchinson

Tribe, L. H. (1974). 'Ways not to think about plastic trees: new foundations for environmental law'. *Yale Law Journal*, 83: 1315–48

Turner, F. J. (1893). *The Frontier in American History*. New York

VanDeVeer, D., and Pierce, C. (eds) (1986). *People, Penguins and Plastic Trees*. Belmont, CA: Wadsworth

Veitch, J. (1887). *The Feeling for Nature in Scottish Poetry*. 2 vols. London: William Blackwood

Waal, E. de (1991). *A World Made Whole: Rediscovering the Celtic Tradition*. London: HarperCollins

Wackernagel, M. and Rees, W. (1996). *Our Ecological Footprint*. Gabriola Island, BC: New Society Publishers

Waddington, C. H. (1960). *The Ethical Animal*. London: Allen & Unwin

Wallace, B. (1975). 'Hard and soft selection revisited'. *Evolution*, 29: 465–73

Ward, B., and Dubos, R. (1972). *Only One Earth: The Care and Maintenance of a Small Planet*. London: André Deutsch

Ward, J. F. K. (1996). *God, Chance and Necessity*. Oxford: Oneworld

—— (1998). *God, Faith and the New Millennium*. Oxford: Oneworld

Washington, P. (1993). *Madame Blavatsky's Baboon*. London: Secker & Warburg

Watson, A. J., and Lovelock, J. E. (1983). 'Biological homeostasis of the global environment: the parable of daisyworld'. *Tellus*, 35B: 284–9

Watt, K. E. F. (1971). 'Dynamics of populations: a synthesis', in *Dynamics of*

Populations: 568–80. Den Boer, P. J., and Gradwell, G. R. (eds). Waageningen: Centre for Agricultural Publication and Documentation

—— (1973). *Principles of Environmental Science*. New York: McGraw–Hill

WCS (1980). *World Conservation Strategy*. Gland, Switzerland: IUCN, WWF, UNEP

Weil, A. (1983). *Health and Healing*. Boston: Houghton Mifflin

Wenham, G. (1987). *Genesis, 1–15*. Word Bible Commentary, vol. 1. Waco, TX: Word

Westermann, C. (1971). *Creation*. (English translation by Scullion, J. J.). London: SPCK

Whitcomb, J. C., and Morris, H. M. (1961). *The Genesis Flood*. Grand Rapids, MI: Baker Book House

White, A. D. (1886). *A History of the Warfare of Science with Theology*. New York: Appleton

White, L. (1967). 'The historical roots of our ecologic crisis'. *Science, NY*, 155: 1203–7

—— (1973). 'Continuing the conversation', in *Western Man and Environmental Ethics*. Barbour, I. (ed.). Reading, MA: Addison–Wesly

Wilkinson, D. (1993). *God, the Big Bang and Stephen Hawking*. Crowborough: Monarch

Williamson, M. (1981). *Island Populations*. Oxford: Oxford University Press

Wilson, E. O. (1975). *Sociobiology: The New Synthesis*. Cambridge, MA: Harvard University Press

—— (1978). *On Human Nature*. Cambridge, MA: Harvard University Press

—— (1994). *Naturalist*. Washington, DC: Island Press

—— (1998). *Consilience: The Unity of Knowledge*. New York: Knopf

Winchester, S. (2001). *The Map that Changed the World*. London: Viking

Wolpert, L. (1992). *The Unnatural Nature of Science*. London: Faber & Faber

World Charter for Nature (1992). Legislative history and commentary by Burhenne, W. E., and Irwin, W. A. Berlin: Eric Schmidt

World Commission on Environment and Development (1987). *Our Common Future*. The Brundtland Commission Report. Oxford: Oxford University Press

Worster, D. (1985). *Nature's Economy*. Cambridge: Cambridge University Press (first published by Sierra Books in 1977)

—— (1993). *The Wealth of Nature*. New York: Oxford University Press

Young, D. A. (1982). *Christianity and the Age of the Earth*. Grand Rapids, MI: Zondervan

Zukav, G. (1979). *The Dancing Wu Li Masters*. London: Hutchinson

Index of Names

Index of Scriptural References

Index of Subjects